ALSO BY BILL MCKIBBEN

Wandering Home

Enough:
Staying Human in an Engineered Age

Long Distance:
Testing the Limits of Body and Spirit in
a Year of Living Strenuously

Hundred Dollar Holiday:
The Case for a More Joyful Christmas

Maybe One:
A Case for Smaller Families

The Comforting Whirlwind:
God, Job, and the Scale of Creation

Hope, Human and Wild:
True Stories of Living Lightly on the Earth

The Age of Missing Information

The End of Nature

DEEP ECONOMY

THE WEALTH OF COMMUNITIES AND THE DURABLE FUTURE

BILL MCKIBBEN

for ANDREA —
with so many,
thanks for stopping
it up!

Bill M

TIMES BOOKS
HENRY HOLT AND COMPANY
NEW YORK

DEEP ECONOMY

Times Books
Henry Holt and Company, LLC
Publishers since 1866
175 Fifth Avenue
New York, New York 10010
www.henryholt.com

Henry Holt® is a registered trademark of
Henry Holt and Company, LLC.

Library of Congress Cataloging-in-Publication Data

McKibben, Bill.
    Deep economy : the wealth of communities and the durable future / Bill
McKibben.—First ed.
        p.   cm.
    Includes index.
    Contents: After growth—The year of eating locally—All for one or one for all—
The wealth of communities—The durable future.
    ISBN-13: 978-0-8050-7626-4
    ISBN-10: 0-8050-7626-3
    1. Economic development—Social aspects.   2. Community development.
I. Title.

HD75.M353   2007
306.3—dc22   2006051100

Henry Holt books are available for special promotions and
premiums. For details contact: Director, Special Markets.

First Edition 2007

Designed by Kelly Too

Printed in the United States of America
10 9 8 7 6 5 4 3 2 1

FOR WENDELL BERRY

CONTENTS

INTRODUCTION

For most of human history, the two birds More and Better roosted on the same branch. You could toss one stone and hope to hit them both. That's why the centuries since Adam Smith have been devoted to the dogged pursuit of maximum economic production. The idea that individuals, pursuing their own individual interests in a market society, make one another richer and the idea that increasing efficiency, usually by increasing scale, is the key to increasing wealth has indisputably produced More. It has built the unprecedented prosperity and ease that distinguish the lives of most of the people reading this book. It is no wonder and no accident that they dominate our politics, our outlook, even our personalities.

But the distinguishing feature of our moment is this: Better has flown a few trees over to make her nest. That changes everything. Now, if you've got the stone of your own life, or your own society, gripped in your hand, you have to choose between them. It's More *or* Better.

Some of the argument I'll make in these pages will seem familiar: growth is no longer making most people wealthier, but instead generating inequality and insecurity. And growth is bumping against physical limits so profound—like climate change and peak oil—that continuing to expand the economy may be impossible; the very attempt may be dangerous. But there's something else too, a wild card we're just now beginning to understand: *new research from many quarters has started to show that even when growth does make us wealthier, the greater wealth no longer makes us happier.*

Taken together, these facts show that we need to make a basic shift. Given all that we now know about topics ranging from the molecular structure of carbon dioxide to the psychology of human satisfaction, we need to move decisively to rebuild our local economies. These may well yield less stuff, but they produce richer relationships; they may grow less quickly, if at all, but they make up for it in durability.

Shifting our focus to local economies will not mean abandoning Adam Smith or doing away with markets. Markets, obviously, work. Building a local economy will mean, however, ceasing to worship markets as infallible and consciously setting limits on their scope. We will need to downplay efficiency and pay attention to other goals. We will have to make the biggest changes to our daily habits in generations—and the biggest change, as well, to our worldview, our sense of what constitutes progress.

Such a shift is neither "liberal" nor "conservative." It borrows some elements from our reigning political philosophies, and is in some ways repugnant to each. Mostly, it's *different*. The key questions will change from whether the economy produces an ever larger pile of stuff to whether it builds or undermines community—for community, it turns out, is the key to physical survival in our environmental predicament and also to human satisfaction. Our exaltation of the individual, which was the key to More, has passed the point of diminishing returns. It now masks a deeper economy that we should no longer ignore.

In choosing the phrase "deep economy," I have sought to echo the insistence, a generation ago, of some environmentalists that instead of simply one more set of smokestack filters or one more set of smokestack laws, we needed a "deep ecology" that asked more profound questions about the choices people make in their daily lives. Their point seems more valid by the month in our overheating world. We need a similar shift in our thinking about economics—we need it to take human satisfaction and societal durability more seriously; we need economics to mature as a discipline.

This shift will not come easily, of course. Focusing on economic growth, and assuming it would produce a better world, was extremely convenient; it let us stop thinking about ends and concentrate on means. It made economics as we know it now—a science of means—extraordinarily powerful. We could always choose our path by fixing our compass on More; we could rely on economists, skilled at removing the obstacles to growth, to act as guides through the wilderness. Alan Greenspan was the wisest of wise men.

But even as that idea of the world reigns supreme, with the rubble of the Iron Curtain at its feet as deserved proof of its power, change is bubbling up from underneath. You have to look, but it's definitely there. A single farmers' market, for instance, may not seem very important compared to a Wal-Mart, but farmers' markets are the fastest-growing part of our food economy. They've doubled in number and in sales and then doubled again in the last decade, suggesting new possibilities for everything from land use patterns to community identity. Similar experiments are cropping up in many other parts of the economy and in many other places around the world, driven not by government fiat but by local desire and necessity. That desire and necessity form the scaffolding on which this new, deeper economy will be built, in pieces and from below. It's a quiet revolution begun by ordinary people with the stuff of our daily lives. Eventually it will take form as legislation, but for now its most important work is simply to crack the consensus that what we need is More.

A word of caution, however. It's easy for those of us who already have a lot to get carried away with this kind of thinking.

Recently I was on a reporting trip to China, where I met a twelve-year-old girl named Zhao Lin Tao, who was the same age as my daughter and who lived in a poor rural village in Sichuan province—that is, she's about the most statistically average person on earth. Zhao was the one person in her crowded village I could talk to without an interpreter: she was proudly speaking the pretty good English she'd learned in the overcrowded village school. When I asked her about her life, though, she was soon in tears: her mother had gone to the city to work in a factory and never returned, abandoning her and her sister to their father, who beat them regularly because they were not boys. Because Zhao's mother was away, the authorities were taking care of her school fees until ninth grade, but after that there would be no money to pay. Her sister had already given up and dropped out. In Zhao's world, in other words, it's perfectly plausible that More and Better still share a nest. Any solution we consider has to contain some answer for her tears. Her story hovers over this whole enterprise. She's a potent reality check.

And in the end it's reality I want to deal with—the reality of what our world can provide, the reality of what we actually want. The old realism—an endless More—is morphing into a dangerous fantasy. (Consider: if the Chinese owned cars in the same numbers as Americans, the world would have more than twice as many vehicles as it now does.) In the face of energy shortage, of global warming, and of the vague but growing sense that we are not as alive and connected as we want to be, I think we've started to grope for what might come next. And just in time.

1 | AFTER GROWTH

For almost all of human history, said the great economist John Maynard Keynes, from "say, two thousand years before Christ down to the beginning of the eighteenth century, there was really no great change in the standard of living of the average man in the civilized centers of the earth. Ups and downs, certainly visitations of plague, famine and war, golden intervals, but no progressive violent change." At the utmost, Keynes calculated, the standard of living had increased 100 percent over those four thousand years. The reason was, basically, that we didn't learn how to do anything new. Before history began we'd learned about fire, language, cattle, the wheel, the plow, the sail, the pot. We had banks and governments and mathematics and religion.[1]

And then, in 1712, something new finally happened. A British inventor named Thomas Newcomen developed the first practical steam engine. He burned coal, and used the steam pressure built up in his boiler to drive a pump that, in turn, drained water from coal mines, allowing them to operate far more cheaply and efficiently. How much more efficiently? His engine replaced a team of five hundred horses walking in a circle.[2] And from there—well, things accelerated. In the words of the economist Jeffrey Sachs, "The steam engine marked the decisive turning point of human history." Suddenly, instead of turning handles and cranks with their own muscles or with the muscles of their animals (which had in turn to be fed by grain that required hard labor in the fields), men and women could exploit the earth's storehouse of fossilized energy to do the turning for them. First coal, then oil, then natural gas allowed for *everything* we consider normal and obvious about the modern world, from making fertilizer to making steel to making electricity. These in turn fed all the subsidiary revolutions in transportation and chemistry and communications, right down to the electron-based information age we now inhabit. Suddenly, one-hundred-percent growth in the standard of living could be accomplished in a few decades, not a few millennia.

In some ways, the invention of the *idea* of economic growth was almost as significant as the invention of fossil fuel power. It also took a little longer. It's true that by 1776 Adam Smith was noting in *The Wealth of Nations* that "it is not the actual greatness of national wealth, but its continued increase" which raises wages. But, as the economist Benjamin Friedman points out in *The Moral Consequences of Economic Growth*, his recent and compelling argument for economic expansion, it's "unclear whether the thinkers of the mid-18th century even understood the concept of economic growth in the modern sense of sustained increase over time," or whether they thought the transition to modern commerce was a one-time event—that they'd soon hit a new plateau.[3] The theorists didn't control affairs, though; and the dynamic entrepreneurial actors unleashed by the new economic revolution soon showed that businesses could keep improving their operations, apparently indefinitely. By the early twentieth century, increasing efficiency had become very nearly a religion, especially in the United States, where stopwatch-wielding experts like Frederick Taylor broke every task into its smallest parts, wiping out inefficiencies with all the zeal of a pastor hunting sins, and with far more success. (Indeed, as many historians have noted, religious belief and economic expansion were soon firmly intertwined: "*economic* effort, and the material progress that it brought, were central to the vision of *moral* progress," notes Friedman.)[4] Soon, as Jeremy Rifkin observes, the efficiency revolution encompassed everything, not just factory work but homemaking, schoolteaching, and all the other tasks of modern life: "efficiency became the ultimate tool for exploiting both the earth's resources in order to advance material wealth and human progress." As the nation's school superintendents were warned at a meeting in 1912, "the call for efficiency is felt everywhere throughout the length and breadth of the land, and the demand is becoming more insistent every day." As a result, "the schools as well as other business institutions, *must submit* to the test of efficiency."[5] It was a god from whom there was no appeal.

Even so, policy makers and economists didn't really become fixated on growing the total size of the economy until after World War II. An economic historian named Robert Collins recently described the rise of what he called "growthmanship" in the United States. During the Great Depression, he pointed out, mainstream economists thought the American economy was "mature." In the words of President Franklin D. Roosevelt, "our industrial plant is built. . . . Our last frontier has long since been reached. . . . Our task now is not discovery or exploitation of natural resources, or necessarily producing more goods. It is the soberer, less dramatic business of administering resources and plants already in hand . . . of adapting economic organizations to the service of the people." It was left to former president Herbert Hoover to protest that "we are yet but on the frontiers of development," that there were "a thousand inventions in the lockers of science . . . which have not yet come to light." And Hoover, of course, did not carry the day. Even a decade later, as the country began to emerge from hardship with the boom that followed Pearl Harbor, many businessmen—the steelmakers, the utility executives, the oilmen—were reluctant to build new plants, fearing that over-production might bring on another depression.

But they were wrong. Mobilization for war proved just how fast the economy could grow; by 1943, even in the midst of battle, the National Resources Planning Board sent this report to Roosevelt: "Our expanding economy is likely to surpass the wildest estimates of a few years back and is capable of bringing to all of our people freedom, security and adventure in richer measure than ever before in history." From that point on, growth became America's mantra, and then the world's. Hoover had been right—there *were* all kinds of technological advances to come. Plastics. Cars that kept dropping in price. Television. Cheap air-conditioning that opened whole regions of the country to masses of people.

Per capita gross national product grew 24 percent between 1947 and 1960, and during that year's presidential election John F. Kennedy insisted he could speed it up if the voters would only reject "those who have held back the growth of the U.S." Indeed, he proved correct: between 1961 and 1965, GNP grew more than 5 percent a year while the percentage of Americans living in poverty dropped by nearly half. Economists scrambled to catch up, and in doing so they built the base for modern growth theory. The general mood was captured by Lyndon Johnson, who, not long after moving into the White House, told an aide: "I'm sick of all the people who talk about the things we can't do. Hell, we're the richest country in the world, the most powerful. We can do it all. . . . We can do it if we believe it." And he wasn't the only one. From Moscow Nikita Khrushchev thundered, "Growth of industrial and agricultural production is the battering ram with which we shall smash the capitalist system."

There were hiccups along the way, as Robert Collins points out in his account. LBJ's belief that we could do anything led us deep into Vietnam, which in turn led us into inflation and recession. The oil shocks of the 1970s and the spectacles of burning rivers and smoggy cities led some, even outside what was then called the counterculture, to question the idea of endless expansion. In 1972, a trio of MIT researchers published a series of computer forecasts they called *Limits to Growth*, and a year later the German-British economist E. F. Schumacher wrote the best-selling *Small Is Beautiful*, with its commitment to what he called "Buddhist economics" and its exhortation to people to "work to put our own inner house in order." (Four years later, when Schumacher came to the United States on a speaking tour, Jimmy Carter even received him at the White House.) By the end of the 1970s, their message resonated: the sociologist Amitai Etzioni reported to President Carter that 30 percent of Americans were "pro-growth," 31 percent were "anti-growth," and 39 percent were "highly uncertain."

That kind of ambivalence, Etzioni predicted, "is too stressful for societies to endure," and in 1980 Ronald Reagan's election proved his point. Reagan convinced us it was "Morning in America" again, and under various banners—supply-side economics, globalization—it has stayed morning ever since. Out with limits, in with Trump. The collapse of communism drove the point home, and now mainstream liberals and conservatives compete mainly on the question of what can flog the economy faster.[6] The British prime minister Margaret Thatcher used to use the acronym TINA to underscore her contention that There Is No Alternative to a world fixated on growth.[7] But conservatives weren't the only ones enamored of growth. Lawrence Summers, who served as Bill Clinton's secretary of the Treasury, put it like this: the Democratic administration "cannot and will not accept any 'speed limit' on American economic growth. *It is the task of economic policy to grow the economy as rapidly, sustainably, and inclusively as possible.*"[8] (Emphasis added.) Even that was not enough—in the vice presidential debates during the 1996 campaign, Republican Jack Kemp shouted, "We should *double* the rate of growth."[9]

People kept seeing new opportunities for faster growth:

microtechnology, nanotechnology. (Sometimes the speeding up is literal: "microediting," for instance, now allows call centers and radio stations to edit out pauses and speed up speech with no discernible changes. "We call it the 66-second minute," the president of one firm said recently. "In normal conversation only a small part of the brain is taxed."[10]) The evangelism for efficiency and growth grew louder, too. It was not just, as Benjamin Friedman insists, that a growing economy gets us more stuff—"better food, bigger houses, more travel"—but that it makes us better people: more open, more tolerant, more confident.[11] The "quality of our democracy—more fundamentally, the moral character of American society—is at risk," he said, unless we grow the economy more vigorously.[12] As the new millennium began, growth had become the organizing ideology for corporations and individuals, for American capitalists and Chinese communists, for Democrats and Republicans. For everyone. "Harnessing the 'base' motive of material self-interest to promote the common good is perhaps the most important social invention mankind has achieved," said Charles Schultze, a former chair of the president's Council of Economic Advisers.[13] George Gilder, the fervent apostle of tech-driven high-growth economics, went further: entrepreneurs, he said, "embody and fulfill the sweet and mysterious consolations of the Sermon on the Mount."[14] The so-called Washington consensus dominated far more of the world than the Union Jack ever had; it was an empire of the mind.

And it is easy to understand why. For one thing, under present arrangements any faltering of growth leads quickly to misery: to recession and all its hardships. For another, endless growth allows us to avoid hard choices, to reconcile, in Collins's words, the American "love of liberty with its egalitarian pretensions."[15] The administration of George W. Bush assures us that we can have tax cuts and still protect Social Security because the tax cuts will stimulate economic growth so much that we'll have more than enough cash on hand to take care of our old. No need to choose. Having found what has been truly a magic wand, the strong temptation is to keep waving it.

But, as readers of fairy tales know, magic can run out. Three fundamental challenges to the fixation on growth have emerged. One is political: growth, at least as we now create it, is producing more inequality than prosperity, more insecurity than progress. This is both the most common and least fundamental objection to our present economy, and I will spend relatively little time on it. By contrast, the second argument draws on physics and chemistry as much as on economics; it is the basic objection that we do not have the energy needed to keep the magic going, and can we deal with the pollution it creates? The third argument is both less obvious and even more basic: *growth is no longer making us happy.* These three objections mesh with each other in important ways; taken together, they suggest that we'll no longer be able to act wisely, either in our individual lives or in public life, simply by asking which choice will produce More.

LET'S BEGIN WITH THE SIMPLEST OBJECTION, THE ONE THAT FITS most easily into our current political debates. *Though our economy has been growing, most of us have relatively little to show for it.* The median wage in the United States is the same as it was thirty years ago.[16] The real income of the bottom 90 percent of American taxpayers has declined steadily: they earned $27,060 in real dollars in 1979, $25,646 in 2005.[17] Even for those with four-year college degrees, and even though productivity was growing faster than it has for decades, earnings fell 5.2 percent between 2000 and 2004 when adjusted for inflation, according to the most recent data from White House economists.[18] Much the same thing has happened across most of the globe; in Latin America, for instance, despite a slavish devotion to growth economics, real per capita income is the same as a quarter century ago. More than eighty countries, in fact, have seen per capita incomes fall in the last decade.[19]

The mathematics that makes possible this seeming contradiction between rapid growth and individual stagnation is the mathematics of inequality. Basically, almost all the growing wealth accumulates in a very few (silk-lined) pockets. The statistics are such that even an arch-conservative commentator like Dinesh D'Souza calls them "staggering."[20] Between 1997 and 2001, according to a pair of Northwestern University economists, the top 1 percent of wage earners "captured far more of the real national gain in income than did the bottom 50 percent."[21] Economists calculate a "Gini coefficient" to measure income inequality across a society; the U.S. coefficient has risen steadily since the late 1960s, to the point where many economists believe wealth is more stratified today than any time since the Gilded Age. And that gap will continue to grow: the 2006 round of tax cuts delivers 70 percent of its benefits to the richest 5 percent of Americans, and 6.5 percent to the bottom 80 percent.[22]

Economists can't explain all the underlying reasons for this spreading gap. The decline of unions had something to do with it, and so did the advent of computerization. Clearly, in a globalized economy, workers in the rich world now find themselves competing with far more people than they used to—and since per capita income is $1,700 in China, it will be a long time before that playing field levels. With the spread of the Internet, the number of jobs that can be transferred across continents has grown exponentially. Beyond all that, though, there's the simple ideology of growth. Bill Clinton signed us up for the North American Free Trade Agreement (NAFTA), the General Agreement on Tariffs and Trade (GATT), and all the rest with the promise that international trade would spur efficiency and thereby increase growth. George W. Bush sold his massive tax cut with the argument that it would "get the economy moving." Every argument for raising minimum wages or corporate

taxes, on the other hand, meets the response that such measures would stifle our economic growth. Growth is always the
final answer, the untrumpable hand, and its logic keeps inequality growing, too.

Any debate on these issues has been muffled in the last few
decades; the growth consensus usually carried the day without
much trouble, in part because elite journalists and pundits
found themselves on the happy side of the economic chasm.
The extremes have become so enormous, though, that debate
can't help but emerge, even if only by accident. Take, for example, the juxtaposition of two stories on a recent front page of the
New York Times. One concerned the record-setting Christmas
bonuses Wall Street executives had received. It quoted a real
estate broker who said clients were suddenly shopping for
apartments in "the $6 million range" instead of contenting
themselves with $4 million digs. "One senior trader is building
a sports complex for triathlon training at his house in upstate
New York," the article reports. "It will include a swim-in-place
lap pool, a climbing wall, and a fitness center." Another investment banker seemed flummoxed by his windfall: " 'I have a
sailboat, a motor boat, an apartment, an SUV. What could I possibly need?' After brief reflection, however, he continued:
'Maybe a little Porsche for the Hamptons house.' "[23] Meanwhile, a few columns away, there was a picture of a Mexican
farmer in a field of sickly tomatoes. His small cooperative,
post-NAFTA, had tried to sell its produce to the global supermarket giants like Ahold, Wal-Mart, and Carrefour, which had
moved into the country with their vast capital and their vast
commitment to efficiency. Lacking the money to invest in
greenhouses and pesticides, however, he and his neighbors
couldn't produce the perfectly round fruit the chains' executives demanded. "The stark danger," the reporter Celia Dugger
notes, "is that millions of struggling small farmers . . . will go
bust and join streams of desperate migrants to America and to
the urban slums of their own countries." She closes her story

by interviewing José Luis Pérez Escobar, who after twenty years as a Mexican potato farmer, went under and then left for the United States, without his wife and five children. He now earns $6 an hour, working the graveyard shift tending grass at a golf course.[24] Alongside the exhilaration of the flattening earth celebrated by Thomas Friedman, the planet (and our country) in fact contains increasing numbers of flattened people, flattened by the very forces that are making a few others wildly rich.

Even when the question of inequality has been engaged, though, the standard liberal line is to question not expansion but only the way that the new money is spread around. Left-wing "social critics continue to focus on income," says the sociologist Juliet Schor. "Their goals are redistribution and growth."[25] In fact, critics in the Democratic party and the union movement typically demand even faster growth. They're as intellectually invested in the current system as the average CEO.

I agree with the argument for fairness, that we should distribute wealth more equitably both here and around the globe. (In fact, there's persuasive evidence that if all you cared about was growth, the best way to speed it up would be to redistribute income more fairly.) And it's extremely important to bear in mind that we're *not*, despite the insistence of our leaders, growing wealthier; that is one of several stubborn and counterintuitive facts about the world that will stud this book, undergirding its argument. *Growth simply isn't enriching most of us.*

But I'm not going to tarry long here, because I also think that a program of redistribution, however wise or moral, will do relatively little to deal with the even more fundamental, and much less discussed, problems that a growth-centered, efficiency-obsessed economy faces. It's to those problems, and to the physical world, that we now turn.

IT'S USEFUL TO REMEMBER WHAT THOMAS NEWCOMEN WAS UP to when he launched the Industrial Revolution. He was using coal to pump water out of a coal mine. The birth of the Industrial Revolution was all about fossil fuel, and so, in many ways, was everything that followed. We've learned an enormous amount in the last two centuries—our body of scientific knowledge has doubled so many times no one can count—but coal and oil and natural gas are still at the bottom of it all.

And no wonder. They are miracles. A solid and a liquid and a gas that emerge from the ground pretty much ready to use, with their energy highly concentrated. Of the three, oil may be the most miraculous. In many spots on the face of the earth, all you have to do is stick a pipe in the ground and oil comes spurting to the surface. It's compact, it's easily transportable, and it packs an immense amount of energy into a small volume. Fill the tank of my hybrid Honda Civic with ten gallons—sixty pounds—of gasoline and you can move four people and their possessions from New York to Washington, D.C., and back. Coal and gas are almost as easy to use, and coal in particular is often even cheaper to recover—in many places it's buried just a few feet beneath the surface of the earth, just waiting to be taken.

That simple, cheap, concentrated power lies at the heart of our modern economies. Every action of a modern life burns fossil fuel; viewed in one way, modern Western human beings are flesh-colored devices for combusting coal and gas and oil. "Before coal," writes Jeffrey Sachs, "economic production was limited by energy inputs, almost all of which depended on the production of biomass: food for humans and farm animals, and fuel wood for heating and certain industrial processes."[26] That is, energy depended on how much you could *grow*. But *fossil* energy depended on how much had grown eons before, on all those millions of years of ancient biology squashed by the weight of time till they'd turned into strata and pools and seams of hydrocarbons, waiting for us to discover them.

To understand how valuable, and how irreplaceable, that lake of fuel was, consider a few figures. Ethanol is one modern scientific version of using old-fashioned "biomass" (that is, stuff that grows anew each year) for creating energy. It's quite high-tech, backed with billions of dollars of government subsidy. But if you're using corn, as most American ethanol production does, then by the time you've driven your tractor to plant and till and harvest the corn, and your truck to carry it to the refinery, and then powered your refinery to turn the corn into ethanol, the best-case "energy output-to-input ratio" is something like 1.34 to 1. That is, you've spent 100 BTU of fossil energy to get 134 BTU of ethanol. Perhaps that's worth doing, but as Kamyar Enshayan of the University of Northern Iowa points out, "It's not impressive. The ratio for oil (from well to the gas station) is anywhere between 30 and 200," depending on where you drill.[27] To go from our fossil fuel world to that biomass world would be a little like going from the Garden of Eden to the land outside its walls, where bread must be earned by "the sweat of your brow."

And east of Eden is precisely where we may be headed. As everyone knows, the last three years have seen a spate of reports and books and documentaries insisting that humanity may have neared or passed the oil peak—that is, the point where those pools of primeval plankton are half used up, where each new year brings us closer to the bottom of the bucket. The major oil companies report that they can't find enough new wells most years to offset the depletion of their old ones; worrisome rumors circulate that the giant Saudi fields are dwindling faster than expected; and, of course, all this is reflected in the rising cost of oil. The most credible predict not a sharp peak but a bumpy ride for the next decade along an unstable plateau, followed by an inexorable decline in supply. So far that seems to be spot-on—highly variable prices, trading higher over time.

One effect of those changes, of course, can be predicted by everyone who's ever sat through Introductory Economics. We should, theory insists, use less oil, both by changing our habits and by changing to new energy sources. To some extent that's what has happened: SUV sales slowed once it appeared high gas prices were here to stay, and the waiting lists for Toyota Priuses were suddenly six months long. Buses and subways drew more riders. People turned down their thermostats a touch, and sales of solar panels started to boom. This is a classic economic response. But it's hard for us to simply park our cars, precisely because cheap oil coaxed us to build sprawling suburbs. And Americans can switch to hybrids, but if the Chinese and the Indians continue to build auto fleets themselves, even if they drive extremely small cars, then the pressure on oil supplies will keep building. Meanwhile, solar power and the other renewables, wondrous as they are, don't exactly replace coal and oil and gas. The roof of my home is covered with photovoltaic panels, and on a sunny day it's a great pleasure to watch the electric meter spin backward, but the very point of solar power is that it's widely diffused, not compacted and concentrated by millennia like coal and gas and oil.

It's *different*: if fossil fuel is a slave at our beck and call, renewable power is more like a partner. As we shall eventually see, that partnership could be immensely rewarding for people and communities, but can it power economic growth of the kind we're used to? The doctrinaire economist's answer, of course, is that no particular commodity matters all that much, because if we run short someone will have the incentive to develop a substitute. In general, this has proved true in the past—run short of nice big sawlogs and someone invents plywood—but it's far from clear that it applies to fossil fuel, which in its ubiquity and its cheapness is almost certainly a special case. Wars are fought over oil, not over milk, not over semiconductors, not over timber. It's plausible—indeed, it's likely—that if we begin to run short, the nature of our lives may fundamentally change as the scarcity wreaks havoc on our economies. "The essence of the first Industrial Revolution was not the coal; it was how to use the coal," insists Jeffrey

Sachs.[28] Maybe he's right, but it seems more likely that fossil fuel was an exception to the rule, a onetime gift that underwrote a onetime binge of growth. In any event, we seem to be on track to find out.

THE DIMINISHED AVAILABILITY OF FOSSIL FUEL IS NOT THE ONLY limit we face. In fact, it's not even the most important. Even before we run out of oil, we're running out of planet.

One consequence of nearly three hundred years of rapid economic growth has been stress on the natural world: we've dug it up, eroded it away, cut it down. You could point to a thousand different types of environmental damage, and taken together the toll has been enormous. In the spring of 2005, a panel of 1,300 scientists assembled by the United Nations issued a "Millennium Ecosystem Assessment" report. They found that "human actions are depleting Earth's natural capital, putting such strain on the environment that the ability of the planet's ecosystems to sustain future generations can no longer be taken for granted."[29] And you could list a dozen such warnings. A majority of the living Nobel laureates in the sciences recently warned that, "if not checked, many of our current practices . . . may so alter the living world that it will be unable to sustain life in the manner we know."[30] This is the planetary equivalent of the doctor clearing his throat and asking you to sit down.

Furthermore, there's every reason to think the situation will deteriorate further as the rest of the world begins to develop. If you want to argue that an economy structured like ours makes sense for the whole world, here are the kind of numbers you need to contend with: given current rates of growth in the Chinese economy, the 1.3 billion residents of that nation alone will, by 2031, be about as rich as we are. If they then eat meat, milk, and eggs in the same quantities as we do, calculates the eco-statistician Lester Brown, they'll consume 1,352 million tons of grain, or two-thirds of the world's entire 2004 grain harvest. They'd use 99 million barrels of oil a day, 20 million more barrels than the entire world consumes at present. If China's coal burning were to reach the current U.S. level of nearly two tons per person, says Brown, the country would use 2.8 billion tons annually—more than the current world production of 2.5 billion tons. They'd use more steel than all the West combined. Paper? At the American rate, they'd consume 303 million tons, roughly double the current world production. Cars? They'd have 1.1 billion on the road, half again as many as the current world total.[31] And that's just China. By then, India will have a higher population, and its economy is growing almost as fast. And then there's the rest of the world.

Trying to meet that kind of demand would stress the earth past its breaking point in an almost endless number of ways. Instead of examining every crisis, however—nitrogen runoff, mercury contamination, rainforest destruction, species extinction, water shortage—let me take the overarching one: climate change.

You can imagine global warming this way: all those pools of oil and beds of coal beneath our feet are being drilled and dug. Emptied. For a brief moment, the resulting energy burns and does something useful: moves your car, heats your shower. But after that instant of combustion, most of the carbon in the coal or oil mixes with oxygen in the air to form the gas carbon dioxide, which drifts into the atmosphere. (A gallon of gasoline weighs about six pounds, and when you burn it you release about five pounds of carbon into the atmosphere.) It accumulates in the atmosphere, creating almost a mirror image of the reservoir you drilled it from in the first place. Which is a problem, because the molecular structure of carbon dioxide traps heat from the sun that would otherwise radiate back out to space. That's all global warming is—the gaseous remains of oil fields and coal beds acting like an insulating blanket.

When Thomas Newcomen fired up his pump that day in 1712, the atmosphere was 275 parts per million carbon dioxide. All our burning since has increased that number to 380 parts per million, higher than it's been for many millions of years. And we're starting to see the results—in fact, we're starting to see that the results are much more dire than scientists predicted even a few years ago. The year 2005 was the warmest on record, and nine of the ten hottest years were in the decade that preceded it; as a result of that heat, about an extra degree Fahrenheit globally averaged, all kinds of odd things have begun to happen. For instance, everything frozen on earth is melting, and melting fast. In the fall of 2005, polar researchers reported that Arctic ice had apparently passed a "tipping point": so much sun-reflecting white ice had been turned to heat-absorbing blue water that the process was now irreversible. Meanwhile, other scientists showed that because of longer growing seasons, temperate soils and forests like the ones across America were now seeing more decay, and hence giving off more of their stored carbon, accelerating the warming trend. So far, this young millennium has already seen a killer heat wave that killed fifty-two thousand people across Europe in the course of a couple of weeks, and an Atlantic hurricane season so bizarrely intense that we ran out of letters in the alphabet for naming storms. The point is, climate change is not some future specter; it's already emerging as the biggest problem the world faces.

And it's only just begun. The *median* predictions of the world's climatologists—*by no means* the worst-case scenarios—show that unless we take truly enormous steps to rein in our use of fossil fuels we can expect that the globally averaged temperature will rise another four or five degrees before the century is out. If that happens, the world will be warmer than it's been for millions of years, long before primates appeared on the planet. We don't know exactly what that world would feel like, but almost every guess is hideous. Since warm air holds more water vapor than cold air, for instance, we can expect more drought in the middles of our continents where grain growing is concentrated, and more floods on the coasts where many people live. The World Health Organization expects vast increases in mosquito-borne disease. Researchers warned in 2006 that climate change could kill 184 million people in Africa alone before this century is out, destruction on a scale so staggering it has no precedent.[32] We might as well have a contest to pick a new name for Earth, because it will be a different planet. Humans have never done anything bigger, not even the invention of nuclear weapons.

How does this tie in with economic growth? The link between environmental destruction and wealth is deep and long-standing. Clearly, getting rich means getting dirty; that's why the air over England turned from fresh to foul in the decades after Newcomen's new engine, and it's why, when I was in Beijing recently, you could stare straight at the sun (if you could even figure out where in the sky it was). But eventually, those riches translate into a desire for the new "luxury" of clean air and the technological means to achieve it: England's air is relatively fresh now, and even in Beijing planners are busy figuring out how they'll move enough industry and install enough smokestack scrubbers and catalytic converters to have sparkling skies for the 2008 Olympics. "Many forms of pollution begin to abate when incomes on average rise above some level," says Benjamin Friedman, and he is clearly right. Sulfur levels in the American air, for example, have fallen 54 percent in the last two decades, and lead levels are down 94 percent.[33] You can see the mountains around Los Angeles again; more of our rivers are swimmable every year. And economists have found clever ways to speed this cleaning—creating markets for tradable pollution permits, for instance, helped cut those sulfur and nitrogen clouds more rapidly and cheaply than almost anyone had imagined.

Unfortunately—and this is the key point—there are *two* kinds of environmental destruction. The kind I've been describing—dirty air, dirty water—result from something going wrong. You haven't bothered to attach the necessary filter to your pipes, and so the crud washes into the stream; a little regulation, and a little money, and the problem disappears. But the second, deeper form of environmental degradation comes from things operating more or less as they're supposed to, just at much too high a level. We've started to run short of water, for instance, because there are 6 billion of us who want to drink it and wash in it and use it for irrigating crops in places where they wouldn't otherwise grow (and where we need them to grow, precisely because there are 6 billion of us). The richer we get, and the more meat we want to eat as a result, the worse the pinch gets.

Global warming belongs in this second category, of pollution that's caused by doing too much of something, not by doing it badly. In fact, it's the prime example. Carbon dioxide isn't even really a pollutant—it's not brown or smelly, and breathing it in the concentrations we're producing doesn't make you sick. What's more, carbon dioxide is an *inevitable* by-product of burning coal or gas or oil, not a result of something going wrong. Researchers are struggling to figure out costly and complicated methods to trap some of the carbon dioxide as it pours from power plant smokestacks and then inject it into underground mines so it never enters the atmosphere; but, for all practical purposes, the vast majority of the world's cars and factories and furnaces will keep belching carbon dioxide into the atmosphere as long as we burn fossil fuels.

It therefore doesn't follow that getting richer automatically leads to producing less carbon dioxide in the same way that it does to less smog; in fact, so far the case is mostly the reverse. Carbon dioxide, says Benjamin Friedman with commendable frankness, "is the one major environmental contaminant for which no study has ever found any indication of improvement as living standards rise."[34] As companies and countries get richer, they can afford more efficient machinery that makes better use of fossil fuel: my hybrid car, for one. But so far these improvements have not matched the rate of growth in the amount we burn. American industry uses less energy per dollar's worth of stuff it produces, but it produces so much more stuff each year that our carbon emission totals keep rising. The Bush administration asserted briefly that its purely voluntary controls had actually cut carbon emissions in the first two years of the presidency. It soon became clear, though, that the reduction had taken place only because a mild recession had slowed the economy; as soon as growth resumed, so did the rise in energy use and carbon emissions.

And what's true here is even more true in the rest of the world. In China, the amount of carbon dioxide produced has actually been rising faster than economic output. Partly that's because energy-intensive manufacturing jobs are moving to Asia and taking their energy demand with them. But the emergence of a consumer class that likes the same stuff we do is also pushing demand—demand that has a long way to go before it catches up with our levels. (The percentage of Chinese who own cars matches that of Americans in 1912.)[35] To understand this growth conundrum at its most basic, consider the average American home. The appliances have gotten more efficient, but there are far more of them; the furnace is better than it used to be, but the average size of the house it heats has doubled since 1970. The enormous flat-screen TV? The always-on cable modem? No need for you to do the math: the electric company does it for you, every month. Between 1990 and 2003, precisely the years in which we learned about the peril presented by global warming, annual American carbon dioxide emissions increased by 16 percent.

There may be ways around this conundrum. When nations negotiated the Kyoto treaty on global warming in the 1990s, they based their work on the premise that with

enough investment and new technology we could keep growing our economies and simultaneously wean ourselves from
fossil fuel. But the United States has refused to sign on because we worry it would interfere with . . . economic growth.
Anyway, there's no breakthrough technology in sight. The
Chinese, for instance, have embarked on the world's most ambitious nuclear energy program, but even if they manage the
financial and engineering challenges and get all the reactors
built that they have planned, by 2020 those reactors will be
producing just 4 percent of the nation's power.[36] Several European nations have announced plans to cut their carbon dioxide
emissions by 50 percent by midcentury, but so far they're having trouble meeting much less ambitious interim standards.
And since the United Nations has estimated that the economies of developing countries will need to grow five to ten
times larger in coming decades if those countries are to end
poverty, it's hard to see how, precisely, it's all going to work
out—especially since the apparent speed and severity of climate change, according to scientists, are growing steadily, too.

Still, as with peak oil, the men and women at the center of
our economic and political lives have not treated climate
change as anything more than another problem to be dealt with
as we've dealt with problems in the past; certainly they don't
perceive it as something that would call into question the doc-
trine of endless economic expansion. Alert to every sniffle of
our constantly monitored economy, they seem entirely oblivi-
ous to the scale of the physical challenge—to the idea that civi-
lization may be at stake. Here again is Larry Summers, former
chief economist of the World Bank, former secretary of the Treasury, former president of Harvard University: "There are no . . .
limits to the carrying capacity of the earth that are likely to bind
any time in the foreseeable future. There isn't a risk of an apocalypse due to global warming or anything else. The idea that we
should put limits on growth because of some natural limit is a
profound error."[37] Well, he sounds confident. But the facts just

keep getting in the way. In late October 2006, a large-scale British economic analysis predicted the effect of unabated climate change would be to make us 20 percent poorer by century's end—an economic hit larger than the combined impact of World War I, World War II, and the Great Depression.[38]

THE NEW ENVIRONMENTAL PREDICAMENTS HAVE LONG TESTED mainstream economics. In 1990, not long after scientists unveiled the computer models showing just how dire global warming really was, Yale economist William Nordhaus calculated how much America should be willing to spend in order to deal with the problem. Not much, in his widely publicized estimation, because "climate has little economic impact upon advanced industrial societies. Humans thrive in a wide variety of climatic zones. Cities are increasingly climate-proofed by technological changes like air-conditioning and shopping malls." True, he mused, "snow skiing will be hurt—but water skiing will benefit." In general, "most economic activity in industrialized countries depends very little on the climate. Intensive care units of hospitals, underground mining, science laboratories, communications, heavy manufacturing, and microelectronics are among the sectors likely to be unaffected by climatic change." In fact, he said, the damage from global warming *will be confined to farming and forestry,* which represent only 3 percent of the country's GNP. Therefore, he said, it's not worth spending anything more than 2 percent of our national income to reduce greenhouse gas emissions. This testimony went a long ways toward convincing many political leaders to ignore the problem as either too small or too expensive to address.[39]

Well, it's true that not many of us make our livings as farmers anymore (maybe not enough of us do, as we shall see). But it's also true that, first thing in the morning, before we go to work in the software design cubicle (or the economics department), most of us prefer to eat breakfast. It's nice to have microelectronics; it's necessary to have lunch. If global warming "only" damages agriculture, the rest may not matter much. It's as if the doctor said, "True, your heart is shot—but look at those six-pack abs!"

The creeping recognition that economics, even in its ever-growing mathematical sophistication, had become abstracted from the actual planet we inhabit has spurred the steady development of an increasingly impressive new school of ecological economics. As far back as the 1960s, economists like Kenneth Boulding were at work on what he termed "the economics of the coming spaceship earth. . . . The closed earth of the future requires economic principles that are entirely different from the open 'cowboy' economy of the past."[40] (He managed to summarize the basic problem in a short chunk of doggerel: "One principle that is an ecological upsetter / Is that if anything is good, then more of it is better, / And this misunderstanding sets us very, very wrong / For no relation in the world is linear for long.") In the 1970s, a World Bank economist named Herman Daly published a collection titled *Toward a Steady State Economy* that actually began to nose around the question whether perpetual growth was possible. And by the 1980s, Daly, with the help of a young professor named Bob Costanza, had formed the Society of Ecological Economics.

Costanza is, in certain ways, the opposite of someone like Larry Summers. From his office at the University of Vermont, where he runs the Gund Institute for Ecological Economics, he's become the loudest voice of an unconventional economic wisdom. He's had to shout to make himself heard, but it's getting easier—ecological economics seems to be on the verge of breaking through into the mainstream.

Costanza began his education as an engineer, and then an architect; by the time he earned his Ph.D. at the University of Florida, he'd switched to systems ecology. "But I'd also recognized that everything that was happening was being driven by economics," he recalled, "so I took economics courses—in fact, I talked them into letting me take economics as my foreign language." He specialized in energy flows across systems; and his first important paper, published in *Science*, established that the embedded energy in a final product (the amount of power it took, say, to mine the ore for the car, and grow the food for the automakers, and so on) correlated pretty closely with its final value. Which, if you think about it, raises some difficult questions for the theory of eternal expansion. Or, as he put it, "the universally appealing notion of unlimited economic growth with reduced energy consumption must be put firmly to rest beside the equally appealing but impossible idea of perpetual motion."[41]

Since then, Costanza has been at least on the periphery of most of the important advances in ecological economics. In 1997, for instance, he joined with twelve coauthors to publish a paper in *Nature* that for the first time tried to set an economic value on "ecosystem services," such as pollination and decomposition, that had always been counted as free. (Their estimate of the worth of these services was $33 trillion annually, far larger than the human economy taken all together.) He and many others have also developed the theoretical tools to explain how important it is to "get prices right"—for instance, to make the cost of a gallon of gasoline reflect the actual damage its production and use do to the environment. (By some estimates, gasoline would cost $7 or $8 a gallon, and the SUV would never have been invented.) Such strategies have led to clever new markets—there is now a trade in permits to emit sulfur and nitrogen, for instance, and as a result utilities have managed to reduce those pollutants quite dramatically and inexpensively. Few economists speak as easily of clean air or clean water as "externalities" as they once did: the essential logic of accounting for costs is slowly spreading.

Indeed, the last decade has seen one effort after another to replace, or at least supplement, gross national product as the measure of our success. Under the current system, as many have pointed out, all we do is add together expenditures, so that the most "economically productive" citizen is a cancer patient who totals his car on his way to meet with his divorce lawyer. Instead, many have proposed a "green national product" or "an index of sustainable economic welfare" or some such new measure that would more accurately reflect progress (or regress) by subtracting for pollution or disease. What is needed is some signal "that would tell us whether economic activity was making us better off or worse off," writes John Cobb, the coauthor (with Herman Daly) of *For the Common Good*, a 1994 account of ecological economics.[42] It's not simple to calculate—do you count money spent on advertising as providing useful information, or do you not count it because it's an annoying distraction?—but more and more nations are trying. The British, for instance, announced plans in 2005 to develop an "index of well-being," and the director of Canada's statistics bureau, Statistics Canada, is trying to measure education, environmental quality, and "community vitality," while the Australians have an "inclusive wealth framework."[43] Costanza's team at the University of Vermont is at work on the ambitious "Earth Shareholders Report," which begins with the radical premise that the planet actually belongs to each of us; it is full of graphs about timber harvests and fish stocks to detail just how much our investment depreciates annually.

Such measures haven't yet worked their way up to the level of policy makers like the Federal Reserve Board: "community vitality" wasn't really Alan Greenspan's thing, nor is it likely to be his successor's. As Costanza concedes, "It's relatively easy for the academic economist to follow the new research, whereas the politician, who's running for office on economic growth, will have a harder time breaking out of that paradigm." But the logic of the new measures is compelling enough that eventually some such scheme will emerge. As the economist Eban Goodstein says in his best-selling textbook, *Economics and the Environment*, "Ecological economists argue that natural and created capital are fundamentally complements"—that is, that you actually need to think about the planet. You can't get richer, at least for long, by impoverishing the world around you. This insight is so clear that, sooner rather than later, all economists will almost certainly embrace it in their work.

In fact, what in retrospect will probably seem like an intellectual turning point came in the summer of 2004, when the Nobel Prize–winning Stanford economist Kenneth Arrow joined with a number of other researchers, including several ecologists, to publish a paper in the *Journal of Economic Perspectives* titled "Are We Consuming Too Much?" Looking at all kinds of capital, including the services performed by nature, the authors asked, "Is our use of the earth's resources endangering the economic possibilities open to our descendants?" After a few dense pages of equations, the answers started to emerge. By the authors' calculations, the poorer nations are eating their seed corn—or, rather, the rich world is eating much of it for them. Taking the planet as a whole, they concluded, "We find reason to be concerned that consumption is excessive."[44] That's about as basic as it gets: we're taking too much, not replacing enough.

Even when we start to absorb that fundamental lesson, however, it alone may not be enough to cause real change. Our momentum is enormous. So enormous, in fact, that to most of us the health of the economy seems far more palpable, far more real, than the health of the planet. Think of the terms we use—the economy, whose temperature we take at every newscast via the Dow Jones average, is "ailing" or "on the mend." It's "slumping" or "in recovery." We cosset and succor it with enormous devotion, even as we more or less ignore the increasingly urgent fever that the globe is now running. The ecological economists have an enormous task ahead of them.

Thankfully, however, they have unexpected allies, who are

raising an even deeper question, an even more powerful challenge to the reigning orthodoxy. They ask, What does richer mean? Even if I am getting richer, am I getting happier? Those are the *really* radical questions, and the ones to which we now turn.

TRADITIONALLY, IDEAS LIKE HAPPINESS AND SATISFACTION ARE the sorts of notions that economists wave aside as poetic irrelevancies, questions that occupy people with no head for numbers who have to major in something else at college. An orthodox economist can tell what makes someone happy by what they do. If they buy a Ford Expedition, then ipso facto a Ford Expedition is what makes them happy. That's all you need to know.

The economist calls this behavior "utility maximization"; in the words of the economic historian Gordon Bigelow, "The theory holds that every time a person buys something, sells something, quits a job, or invests, he is making a rational decision about what will . . . provide him 'maximum utility.' 'Utility' can be pleasure (as in, 'Which of these Disney cruises will make me happiest?' or security (as in 'Which 401(k) will let me retire before age 85?') or self-satisfaction (as in, 'how much will I put in the offering plate at church?'). If you bought a Ginsu knife at 3 A.M., a neoclassical economist will tell you that, at that that time, you calculated that this purchase would optimize your resources."[45] The beauty of this notion lies in its simplicity: it reassures the economist that all the complex math he builds on top of the assumption adds up to something real. It reassures the politician that all his efforts to increase GNP are sensible and rational even when they may seem otherwise. It is perhaps the central assumption of the world we live in: you can tell who I really am by how I spend.

But is the idea of utility maximization simple, or simple-minded? Economists have long known that people's brains don't work quite as rationally as the model might imply. When Bob Costanza was first edging into economics in the early 1980s, for instance, he had a fellowship to study "social traps," for example, a nuclear arms race, "where short-term behavior can get out of kilter with longer broad-term goals." It didn't take long to demonstrate, as others had before him, that, if you set up an auction in a certain way, people will end up bidding $1.50 to take home a dollar. Other economists have shown that people give too much weight to "sunk costs"—that they're too willing to throw good money after bad, or that they value items more highly if they already own them than if they are thinking of acquiring them. Building on such insights, a school of "behavioral economics," pioneered by researchers like Princeton's Daniel Kahneman, Stanford's Amos Tversky, and Harvard's Andrei Shleifer, has emerged as a "robust, burgeoning sector" of mainstream economics, "opening the way for a richer and more realistic model of the human being in the marketplace."[46]

The real wonder, in a sense, is that it took so long. Each of us knows how irrational much of our behavior is, and how unconnected to any real sense of what makes us happy. I mean, there you are at three A.M. thinking about the Ginsu knife. You're only thinking about it in the first place because someone is advertising it, devoting half an hour of infomercial time to imagining every possible way to make you think that your life will be more complete with this marvel of the cutler's trade—that you will be hosting dinner parties full of witty conversation and impressing potential mates with your suave carving ability, your paper-thin tomato slices. There you are at the car lot thinking about the Ford Expedition. If you are like 95 percent of other buyers, you will never drive it off a paved road. By any objective and rational assessment, the Expedition is a very poor decision, given that it will harm the earth in irreparable ways, and given the fact that it's more dangerous than a car, not only to everyone else on the road but even to yourself—not to mention what its thirst for fuel will cost you. But you are wondering, in some back part of your cortex, if the manliness inherent in such a very large conveyance will perhaps win you new and robust friends, as has been suggested by a number of recent commercials you have had the pleasure of observing. Or maybe you were completely freaked out by 9/11 and there's something mysteriously comforting about the yards of unnecessary sheet metal surrounding you. Such thoughts are not rational; in fact, they set us up for as much unhappiness as pleasure.

So the orthodox economist's premise that we can figure out what constitutes a good economy by summing the *rational individual* actions of consumers is suspect. "Rational" is a stretch; and, as we shall see, "individual" may cause even more trouble. But until fairly recently, that orthodox economist had a pretty good comeback to these kinds of objections, namely "Well, what other way is there?" I mean, it seems unlikely that you'd get any closer by appointing someone (me, say) to decide that everyone had to have a Juiceman in the kitchen and that if they did, happiness would reign. The misery of centrally planned economies testifies to that.

In recent years, however, something new has happened. Researchers from a wide variety of disciplines have begun to figure out how to assess satisfaction more directly, and economists have begun to sense the implications that ability holds for their way of looking at the world. In 2002, Daniel Kahneman won the Nobel Prize in economics even though he was trained as a psychologist. To get a sense of some of his preoccupations you can pick up a book called *Well-being* in which, with a pair of coauthors, he announces the existence of a new field called hedonics, defined as "the study of what makes experience and life pleasant and unpleasant. It is concerned with feelings of pleasure and pain, of interest and boredom, of joy and sorrow, and of satisfaction and dissatisfaction. It is also concerned with the whole range of circumstances, from the biological to the societal, that occasion suffering and enjoyment."[47] If you are worried that there might be something altogether too airy about this, be reassured that Kahneman thinks like an economist. Indeed, in the book's very first chapter, "Objective Happiness," as he attempts to figure out how accurately people can determine their own mental states, Kahneman describes an experiment that compares "records of two patients undergoing colonoscopy." Every sixty seconds, he insists they rate their pain on a scale of 1 to 10, and eventually he forces them to "make a hypothetical choice between a repeat colonoscopy and a barium enema."[48] Dismal science, indeed.

As more and more scientists turned their attention to the field, researchers have studied everything from "biases in recall of menstrual symptoms" to "fearlessness and courage in novice paratroopers undergoing training." On occasion, the findings have a distinctly academic ring: there is one paper entitled "The Importance of Taking Part in Daily Life," and in another a researcher "note[s] that there is no context in which cutting oneself shaving will be a pleasant experience." But the sheer variety of experiments is intriguing: subjects have had to choose between getting an "attractive candy bar" and learning the answers to geography questions; they've been made to wear devices that measured their blood pressure at regular intervals; their brains have been scanned. And by now most observers are convinced that saying "I'm happy" is more than just a subjective statement. In the words of the economist Richard Layard, "We now know that what people say about how they feel corresponds closely to the actual levels of activity in different parts of the brain, which can be measured in standard scientific ways."[49] Indeed, people who call themselves happy, or who have relatively high levels of electrical activity in the left prefrontal region of the brain, are also "more likely to be rated as happy by friends," "more likely to respond to requests for help," "less likely to be involved in disputes at work," and even "less likely to die prematurely." In other words, conceded one economist, "It seems that what the psychologists call subjective well-being is a real phenomenon. The various empirical measures of it have high consistency, reliability, and validity."[50]

The idea that there is a state called happiness, and that we can dependably figure out what it feels like and how to measure it, is extremely subversive. It would allow economists to start thinking about life in far richer terms, allow them to stop asking "What did you buy?" and to start asking "Is your life good?"

It won't happen overnight, but it will happen eventually. Because if you can ask someone "Is your life good?" and count on the answer to mean something, then you'll be able to move to the real heart of the matter, the question haunting our moment on earth: *Is more better?*

IN SOME SENSE, YOU COULD SAY THAT THE YEARS SINCE WORLD War II in America have been a loosely controlled experiment designed to answer this very question. The environmentalist Alan Durning found that in 1991 the average American family owned twice as many cars, drove two and a half times as far, used twenty-one times as much plastic, and traveled twenty-five times farther by air than did the average family in 1951.[51] Gross domestic product per capita has tripled since 1950.[52] We are, to use the very literal vernacular, living three times as large. Our homes are bigger: the size of new houses has doubled since 1970, even as the average number of people living in each one has shrunk. Despite all that extra space, they are stuffed to the rafters with belongings, enough so that an entire new industry—the storage locker—has sprung up and indeed has reached huge size itself. We have all sorts of other new delights and powers: we can communicate online, watch a hundred cable stations, find food from every corner of the world. Some people have clearly taken more than their share of all this new stuff, but still, on average, all of us in the West are living lives materially more abundant than most people did a generation ago. As the conservative writer Dinesh D'Souza noted recently, we have created not just the first middle class but "the first mass affluent class in world history."[53]

What's odd is, none of this stuff appears to have made us happier. All that material progress—and all the billions of barrels of oil and millions of acres of trees that it took to create it—seems not to have moved the satisfaction meter an inch. In 1946, the United States was the happiest country among four advanced economies; thirty years later, it was eighth among eleven advanced countries; a decade after that it ranked tenth among twenty-three nations, many of them from the third world.[54] There have been steady *decreases* in the percentage of Americans who say that their marriages are happy, that they are satisfied with their jobs, that they find a great deal of pleasure in the place they live. Ever since World War II, the National Opinion Research Council has once a year polled Americans with the fundamental question: "Taken all together, how would you say things are these days—would you say that you are very happy, pretty happy, or not too happy?" (It must be somewhat unsettling to receive this phone call.) The proportion of respondents saying they were very happy peaked sometime in the 1950s and has slid slowly but steadily in the years since. Between 1970 and 1994, for instance, it dropped five full percentage points, dipping below the mark where one-third of Americans were able to count themselves as very happy. As Richard Layard points out, this trend is even more remarkable than it seems. "People must seek anchors or standards for such evaluations, and it is natural for them to compare their current situation with their situation in the recent past: if last year was bad, than an average current year would appear to be good. Such annual corrections would tend to wipe out any trend."[55] Yet there the trend is, as plain as can be and continuing to the present. In the winter of 2006, the National Opinion Research Center published data about "negative life events" covering the years 1991 to 2004, a period dominated by the rapid economic expansion of the Clinton boom. "The anticipation would have been that problems would have been down," the study's author said. Instead the data showed a rise in problems—the percentage of respondents who reported breaking up with a steady partner doubled, for instance. As one reporter summarized the findings, "There's more misery in people's lives today."[56]

The phenomenon isn't confined to the United States; as other nations have followed us into mass affluence, their experiences have begun to yield similar, though less dramatic, results. In the United Kingdom, for instance, per capita gross domestic product grew 66 percent between 1973 and 2001, yet people's satisfaction with their lives changed not at all.[57] Japan saw a fivefold increase in per capita income between 1958 and 1986 without any reported increase in satisfaction.[58] In one place after another, in fact, rates of alcoholism, suicide, and depression have gone up dramatically even as the amount of stuff also accumulated. The science writer Daniel Goleman noted in the *New York Times* that people born in the advanced countries after 1955 are three times as likely as their grandparents to have had a serious bout of depression.[59] Indeed, one report in 2000 found that the *average* American child reported now higher levels of anxiety than the average child *under psychiatric care* in the 1950s: our new normal is the old disturbed.[60] The British researcher Richard Douthwaite noted that between 1955 and 1988, the doubling of the UK's national income had coincided with increases in everything from crime to divorce.[61] That's not to say that getting richer caused these problems, only that it didn't alleviate them. All in all, we have more stuff and less happiness. *The experiment we've undertaken has yielded a significant, robust, and largely unexpected result.*

The reasons for the failure of stuff to make us happier are much less clear, and will be one of the chief subjects of this book. You could argue, for instance, that we've simply begun to run out of useful or fun new things—that despite vast numbers of patents, there's not much we can buy that really runs much chance of making us happier. Those who fly frequently (a good slice of the most affluent) will be familiar, for example, with the ubiquitous SkyMall catalogue, thoughtfully placed in the seat-back pocket in front of you in order to tease your acquisitive impulse during long flights. The catalogue is a testimony to satiation: there's nothing in it a normal person would ever need, or even really want. For instance, should anyone who requires a "revolutionary new laser technology system" in order to figure out if they're parking in the right spot inside their own garage really be allowed behind the wheel in the first place? Compared with the other tasks of a driver—making right-hand turns, making left-hand turns, deciphering the red-amber-green code of a stoplight—safely positioning your auto within the confines of your own garage seems like a fairly straightforward task, the kind of thing that might not require a laser.

If satiation isn't what has cast a pall over our satisfaction, then perhaps the pall is the *effect* of all that economic buildup: if growth has filled the field behind your house with megamansions and you can't see the horizon anymore, maybe that loss cancels out the effect of the flat-screen TV. Or maybe the pall is cast by the fact that more of us have had to work more hours to afford all that new stuff. Or perhaps we're worried about keeping thieves from taking our stuff—or, more likely, wondering how we'll be able to hold on to it as an increasingly insecure old age looms. Most of all, perhaps the very act of acquiring so much stuff has turned us ever more into individuals and ever less into members of a community, isolating us in a way that runs contrary to our most basic instincts.

For the moment, however, the why is less important than the simple fact. We're richer, but we're not happier. We have more music, more education, more communication, and certainly more entertainment than any people who have ever lived—we can be entertained literally around the clock, and we can carry our entertainment with us wherever we go as long as we remember the Nano and the earbuds. But if satisfaction was our goal, then the unbelievable expenditures of effort and resources since 1950 to accomplish all this (and by most measures humans have used more raw materials since the end of World War II than in all of prior human history) have been largely a waste. "Estimates suggest," said one team of economists, "that 20 percent of the American population are flourishing and over 25 percent are languishing, with the rest somewhere in between."[62]

In fact, the more we study the question, the less important affluence seems to be to human happiness. In one open-ended British questionnaire, people were asked about the factors that make up "quality of life." They named everything from "family and home life" to "equality and justice," and when the results were totted up, 71 percent of the answers were nonmaterialistic.[63] The best predictor of happiness was health, followed by factors like being married. Income seemed not to matter at all in France, Holland, or England, and it was only the seventh or eighth most important predictor in Italy, Ireland, and Denmark.[64] In one classic study of how various "domains" contributed to life satisfaction, "goods and services you can buy" came in twelfth among thirty areas, behind even "political attitudes" and swamped by "feelings about recreation and family."[65]

HOW IS IT, THEN, THAT WE BECAME SO TOTALLY, AND APPARENTLY wrongly, fixated on the idea that our main goal, as individuals and as nations, should be the accumulation of more wealth?

The answer is interesting for what it says about human nature. *Up to a certain point*, none of what I've just been saying holds true. *Up to a certain point*, more really does equal better.

Consider the life of a very poor person in a very poor society. Not, perhaps, a hunter-gatherer—it may not make much sense to think of hunter-gatherers as poor. But, say, a peasant farmer in China, trying to survive on too little land. (China has one-third of the world's farmers, but one-fifteenth of its arable land; in many places the average holding is less than a sixth of an acre, an area smaller than the footprint of the average new American home.) You lack very basic things, including any modicum of security for when your back finally gives out; your diet is unvaried and nutritionally lacking; you're almost always cold in the winter.

To compensate you for your struggles, it's true that you also likely have the benefits of a close and connected family, and a village environment where your place is clear. Your world makes sense. Still, in a world like that, a boost in income delivers tangible benefits. I remember one reporting trip when I visited a shower-curtain factory in rural China, staffed by people who had grown up on such farms. I wandered through the workrooms, watching kids—almost everyone was between eighteen and twenty-two, as if the factory was some kind of shower-curtain college—smooth out long bolts of polyester on huge cutting-room tables, and sew hems and grommets, and fold them up in plastic bags, and pack them into cartons. It's hard to imagine a much simpler product than a shower curtain, basically, a big square of fabric with a row of holes along the top.

The workday here was eight hours; because of the summer heat everyone was working from seven-thirty to eleven-thirty in the morning and then again from three to seven in the afternoon. I'd been there a few minutes when all labor ceased and everyone poured down the stairs into the cafeteria for lunch. Rice, green beans, eggplant stew, some kind of stuffed dumpling, and a big bowl of soup: 1.7 yuan, or about 20 cents. While the workers ate, I wandered into the dormitory rooms. Each one had four sets of bunkbeds, one set of which stored suitcases and clothes. The other beds were for sleeping, six to a room. MP3 players sat on most pillows; in the girls' rooms, big stuffed animals graced most beds. There were posters of boy bands, and stacks of comic books, and lots of little bottles of cosmetics. One desk to share, one ceiling fan. Next to the dormitory, a lounge housed a big-screen TV and twenty or thirty battered chairs; the room next door had a Ping-Pong table.

Virtually all the workers came from Junan county in Shandong province, a few hundred kilometers to the south, where the factory owner had grown up. He let me select at random and interview as many workers as I liked. He was especially pleased with my first pick, Du Pei-Tang, who was twenty years old—a goofy grin, nervous, but with very bright and shining eyes. His father had died and his mother had remarried and moved away, so he'd grown up with his grandparents. His first job had been as a guard at an oil company in Shandong province, but it only paid a few hundred yuan a month and there was no food or dormitory. One of his relatives had introduced him to the shower-curtain factory owner, who had the reputation of being nice to his workers, so he'd come to work, earning about 1,000 yuan a month. From that, he'd been able to save 12,000 yuan in a little less than two years. And here's the thing you need to understand: 12,000 yuan—call it $1,200—is actually a pretty big sum of money, enough to be life changing. In a year or two more, he said, he'd have enough to build a small house back in his hometown and to get married. For fun, Du played table tennis and watched videos on the factory TV—which was good because, as the owner pointed out, buying a single Coke every night would come near to halving his savings. I asked him if he'd seen any movie that showed him a life he might aim for. He got very quiet, and said yes, he'd recently seen a film "about a young man successful in both business and family life. That's important to me because I grew up lacking the family atmosphere. I hope I would have that kind of life—not be that person, but have a good wife, a good family, a good business."

My next pick was Liu-Xia, eighteen years old, a lovely young woman nervous as hell about talking to a strange American who inexplicably and impertinently wanted to know about her life. "There are four people in my home—my parents, my elder brother, and me," she said. "My parents aren't healthy. They do farm work, but my father has a bad knee so my mother carries most of the load. I really wanted to help her. And my brother could go to college, but it is a very big cost. He is in the Shandong School of Science and Technology, studying mechanical engineering." In fact, it turned out, he had graduated the week before, thanks to her earnings at the curtain factory. Making small talk, I asked her if she had a stuffed animal on her bed like everyone else. Her eyes filled ominously. She liked them very much, she said, but she had to save all her earnings for her future.

It may well be that moving away to the factory for a few years will disrupt the lives of these young people in unforeseen ways and leave them rootless and unhappy; it may well be that the world can't afford the ecological implications of everyone in China making lots of plastic stuff, or lots of money. The only point I'm trying to make is that China's relentless economic growth—9 percent a year for the last couple of decades, the fastest in the history of the planet—was indeed lifting lots of people out of poverty and in the process making their lives somewhat happier.

And it wasn't, as it turns out, just my anecdotal impression. In general, researchers report that *money consistently buys happiness right up to about $10,000 per capita income, and that after that point the correlation disappears.*[66] That's a useful number to keep in the back of your head—it's like the freezing point of water, one of those random numbers that just happens to define a crucial phenomenon on our planet. "As poor countries like India, Mexico, the Philippines, Brazil, and South Korea have experienced economic growth, there is some evidence that their average happiness has risen," Richard Layard reports. But *past the $10,000 point,* there's a complete scattering: when the Irish were making a third as much as

Americans they were reporting higher levels of satisfaction, as were the Swedes, the Danes, the Dutch.[67] Costa Ricans score higher than Japanese; French people are about as satisfied with their lives as Venezuelans.[68] In fact, past the point of basic needs being met, the "satisfaction" data scramble in mind-bending ways. A sampling of Forbes magazine's "richest Americans" has happiness scores identical with those of the Pennsylvania Amish and only a whisker above those of Swedes, not to mention Masai tribesmen. The "life satisfaction" of pavement dwellers—that is, homeless people—in Calcutta was among the lowest recorded, but it almost doubled when they moved into a slum, at which point they were basically as satisfied with their lives as a sample of college students drawn from forty-seven nations.[69] And so on.

ON THE LIST OF IMPORTANT MISTAKES WE'VE MADE AS A species, this one seems pretty high up. A single-minded focus on increasing wealth has driven the planet's ecological systems to the brink of failure, without making us happier. How did we screw up?

The answer's pretty obvious: we kept doing something past the point where it worked. Since happiness had increased with income in the past, we assumed it would do so in the future. We make these kinds of mistakes regularly: two beers made me feel good, so ten beers will make me feel five times better. But this case was particularly extreme and easy to understand, because human beings have spent so much of their history trying to satisfy basic needs. As the psychologists Ed Diener and Martin Seligman observe, "At the time of Adam Smith, a concern with economic issues was understandably primary. Meeting simple human needs for food, shelter and clothing was not assured, and satisfying these needs moved in lockstep with better economics."[70] Consider, say, America in 1820, two generations after Adam Smith. The average American earned, in current dollars, less than $1,500, which is somewhere near the current African average. As the economist Deirdre McCloskey explains, "Your great-great-great grandmother had one dress for church and one for the week, if she were not in rags. Her children did not attend school, and probably could not read. She and her husband worked eighty hours a week for a diet of bread and milk—they were four inches shorter than you."[71] Even in 1900, the average American lived in a house the size of today's typical garage.[72] Is it any wonder, then, that we built up a considerable velocity trying to escape the gravitational pull of that kind of poverty? Richard Layard calls it a "cultural lag": "Market democracies, by the logic of their own success, continue to emphasize the themes that have brought them to their current position."[73] An object in motion stays in motion; our economy—and the individual expectations that make it up—is a mighty object indeed.

You could call it, I think, the Laura Ingalls Wilder effect. I grew up reading her books—*Little House on the Prairie, Little House in the Big Woods*—and my daughter grew up listening to me read them to her, and I have no doubt she will read them to her children. They tell the ur-American story. A life rich in family, rich in connection to the natural world, rich in adventure—but materially deprived. That one dress, that same bland dinner. At Christmastime, a penny—a *penny*! And a stick of candy, and the awful deliberation about whether to stretch it out with tiny licks or devour it in an orgy of happy greed. A rag doll was the zenith of aspiration—it was like the Chinese girl I met at the shower-curtain factory who teared up when she thought about how nice it might be to own a stuffed animal. In that world, possessions still deliver. When I returned to the factory with the largest stuffed dog available in that corner of northern China, the girl was as pleased as I've ever seen a person. Not only that, but the other kids living in the factory seemed enormously happy for her as well.

My daughter would have appreciated the same stuffed animal, but not with anything approaching the same intensity. Her bedroom boasts a density of Beanie Babies (made, doubtless, in some other Asian factory) that mimics the manic biodiversity of the deep rainforest. Another stuffed animal? Really? So what? Its marginal utility, as an economist might say, is low. And so with all of us. Which is why, for instance, our current approach to Christmas doesn't work very well. Pollsters find that at least two-thirds of Americans dread the onset of the holiday season, because it simply adds more stuff to our lives. A few years ago a group of us in the Methodist churches in my part of the Northeast started a campaign called Hundred Dollar Holidays to persuade people to celebrate the Nativity a little differently—with homemade gifts, gifts of service and time, and so forth. When we started it, we were thinking as pious environmentalists: we could rid the world of all those batteries! But the reason the campaign worked so well was because so many people were desperate for permission to celebrate Christmas in a new way that fit better what we actually need out of the holidays. We need time with family, we need silence for reflection, we need connection with nature—all the stuff that the Ingalls family had in abundance. We don't need candy; we have candy every day of our lives. We just haven't figured that out, because the momentum of the past is still with us: we still imagine we're in that Little House on the Big Prairie, when most of us inhabit the Oversized House on the Little Cul de Sac.

In the immortal words of Mr. Jagger and Mr. Richards, "I can't get no satisfaction." Bling won't do it anymore; that's why all those sterile mansions on *Cribs* look so amazingly empty. But we can't figure out where else to look. We've run out of ideas. When Americans in one survey were asked what single factor would most improve the quality of their lives, the most frequent answer was more money.[74] This isn't the fault of economists: economists built us a wonderful set of tools for getting More. And those tools work. We can steer our way around recessions, smooth out bumps in our upward climb. It's easy to understand why they, and the political leaders they advise, would be pleased to try and keep using those tools—pleased to keep us becoming ever more efficient, achieving ever greater economies of scale. But there's something profoundly unrealistic and sentimental about that approach, given what we've discovered about the limits on growth's ability to produce human happiness. As Richard Layard says in the conclusion to his book *Happiness*, "Utilitarianism is the guiding philosophy of our time, but theories of what produces happiness have changed since Bentham. Both utilitarian philosophers and their critics speak in the language of the past."

We need, in short, a new utilitarianism. When More and Better shared a branch, we could kill two birds with one stone. Since they've moved apart, we can't. We in the rich countries no longer inhabit a planet where straight-ahead Newtonian economics, useful as it has been, can help us. We need an Einsteinian economics, a more complicated and relativistic science that asks deeper questions, questions that will fill the rest of this book.

But first, we need something to eat.

2 | THE YEAR OF EATING LOCALLY

September. The farmers' market in Middlebury, Vermont, is in absolute fever bloom: sweet sweet corn, big ripe tomatoes; bunches of basil; melons. This is the bounty of our short but intense summer, when the heat of the long days combines with the moisture of these eastern uplands to produce almost anything you could want. It's the great eating moment of the year.

But I'm wandering the market trying to keep the image of midwinter in mind—the short, bitter days of January, when the snow is drifted high against the house and the woodstove is cranking. I'm used to getting the winter's wood in, but not to putting the winter's food by. In our globalized world, it's always summer somewhere, and so we count on the same fever bloom of produce the year round.

For one winter, though, I wanted to try an experiment. I wanted to see if I could make it through the cold months living entirely on the food that comes from where I live, from the valley around Lake Champlain. In summer, it's easy to eat locally; you'd be crazy not to. But this is one of the northernmost valleys in the Lower Forty-eight, and far removed from the vast fields of the Midwest and the irrigated valleys of California where most of our calories come from. I designed my modest experiment to see how much was left of the agricultural infrastructure that once fed people here, and everywhere else, on local food. My experiment was designed, more grandly, to give me some slight hint of what a truly local economy might feel like. Because if the larger society is running up against the realization that More is not necessarily Better, then one of the alternatives is to think on a different scale.

And food may be the place to begin. After all, for almost all people throughout history (and for most people still today), "the economy" is just a fancy way of saying "What's for dinner?" and "Am I having any?" Even today, in a world economy that churns out jet airplanes and iPods and laser guidance systems for parking your car, a Harvard Business School professor recently reported that "fifty percent of the world's assets and consumer expenditure belong to the food system."[1] Half the jobs, too.[2] The "food system" has been made over in the name of efficiency and growth as much as any other: the average bite of food an American eats has traveled fifteen hundred miles before it reaches her lips. I have no illusions about undoing all that; the point of this experiment is not to encourage others to eat an exclusively local diet. (As soon as the winter was over, I returned to a modest banana intake.) It was a small, highly artificial attempt to persuade myself that some other view of "the economy" was even remotely plausible, that in the absence of the industrial food system I wouldn't starve.

All of which explains why I'm here at the market bargaining for canning tomatoes, the Roma plums with perhaps a few blemishes. Though mostly I want to spend the winter buying what's available, I'll put up a certain amount. My friend Amy Trubek volunteers to help. A food anthropologist, she's the head of the Vermont Fresh Network, which partners farmers with chefs; she and her husband, Brad Koehler, one of the heads of Middlebury College's renowned dining halls, also own a small orchard and a big vegetable garden, not to mention a capacious freezer. "A lot of people associate canning with their grandmother, hostage in the kitchen for six weeks," she says.

"But hey, this is the twenty-first century. We can freeze, we can brine, we can Cryovac—we can do all this a hundred different ways." An afternoon's work, with the Red Sox beginning their stretch drive on the radio, and I've got enough tomato sauce frozen in Ziplocs to last me through the winter.

October. Fall lingers on (and the Red Sox, too). Our local food co-op still has the makings of a "normal," which is to say summery, salad; already, though, I'm regarding leaf lettuce with a kind of nostalgia, knowing it's about to disappear from my life.

And I'm regarding two small bins at the bottom of the co-op's bulk section as my lifeline. They're filled with local flour, 59 cents a pound. Once upon a time, the Champlain Valley was the nation's granary—but that was a long time ago indeed, back before the Erie Canal opened the way west and vast rivers of grain began flowing back from the deep topsoil of the Plains. Grain farming all but disappeared from the region; the most basic component of the American diet had to be imported from Nebraska.

But there's always an oddball, and this one's name is Ben Gleason. He is a short and modest man who came to Vermont, like many others, as a part of the back-to-the-land movement of the 1970s. He found an old farm in the Addison County town of Bridport, and he began to plant it in a rotation of hard red organic winter wheat. Last year, for instance, he grew thirty-two tons on thirty-two acres, a perfectly respectable number even by midwestern standards, and he ground all of it with a small, noisy machine in the shed next to his house. It makes economic sense: without any middlemen, he gets all the value from his crop, and so, even on a small farm, he and his wife are able to support their family. I pay 10 cents more a pound for flour than I would at the supermarket, but that's a pretty negligible cost over the course of a year. (If you're using Ben Gleason's flour to make your own bread instead of buying loaves from the store, you'll come out way ahead.) True, he has some idiosyncrasies. He only sells whole wheat flour; grinding white would require another machine, and anyway, as he points out, it's not nearly as good for you. Fortunately, Gleason's wheat is delicious—perfect for pancakes flavorful enough to stand up to the Grade B maple syrup that's the only kind we use. (Grade A, Fancy—that's for tourists. The closer to tar maple syrup is, the better.)

November. The traditional Thanksgiving dinner is also the traditional local foods dinner, at least for this part of the world. Which makes sense, since the Pilgrims weren't in any position to import much food; they just hunkered down with the beige cuisine that begins to predominate as the summer turns to memory. (On Cape Cod, they had cranberries for a flash of deep color; here we have beets, which make a ruby, tangy slaw.)

The self-sufficient all-around farms with which the colonists covered the continent have largely disappeared, at least outside Amish country. Even the tiny local growers in this valley often specialize in order to stay afloat—I can show you a potato farmer in the hills above Rutland with fifty varieties in his three acres, and a bison wrangler on the lakeshore, and an emu rancher. But there is an exception to this trend: the quick spread in the last decade of the "community-supported agriculture" or CSA farm. Consumers pay farmers a few hundred dollars apiece in midwinter and then are supplied with a weekly bin of incredibly diverse vegetables throughout the growing season and deep into the fall. Almost every corner of America now has a CSA nearby, but some of the original operations are in this area, and none produces vegetables more glorious than Golden Russet Farm in Shoreham, where Will and Judy Stevens are busy threshing dried beans when I stop by one afternoon to pick up some squash. But even Will and Judy aren't quite like the farmers of old: they go to the store for their milk.

Not so Mark Gunther and Kristin Kimball, the young proprietors of Essex Farm, on the New York side of the lake. If you want to join their CSA, you pay more like a few thousand dollars. But when you stop by on Friday afternoons for your pickup, you don't get just vegetables: they have a few milking cows, so they supply milk and cheese and butter; they have a small herd of grass-fed cattle, so there are steaks and burgers; the snorting tribe of pigs behind the barn provides bacon and lard; there are chickens and turkeys and even bees. Except for paper towels and dental floss, you'd never have to set foot in a store again. Think Currier and Ives, complete with a team of big Belgians instead of a tractor. "I don't think my intent is to create an historical farm, though," Mark insists. "There's nothing inherent about modern ways that I don't support. I'm trying to find out ways to increase the quality of my life." You can't leave the farm without Mark loading your trunk full of food—"Do you have room for another chicken there?"—and all of it tastes of the place. As you bump out of the driveway, a look in the rearview mirror reveals Mark juggling carrots and grinning. "Occasionally I feel like I'm doing some work," he says. "But usually it feels more like entertainment for myself."

Is this realistic? Could you feed Manhattan in this fashion? You could not; every place is different. (And Manhattan is lucky to have New Jersey, the Garden State, right next door, with some of the best truck-farming soil and weather anywhere on earth. In fact, as we shall see, urban areas around the world are rediscovering the cropland on their outskirts, with impressive results.) But you could feed the village of Essex, New York, this way: Mark figures the fifty acres he and Kristin are farming can support ten or twelve families at least, a reminder of just how fertile the earth can be in the right hands. He's making lunch as he calculates, whistling over a skillet of cheeseburgers. "The lard is from the pig we called Moose, who was the runt of the litter last year. And the bull, Charlie, we finished him on grass and ate most of him at our wedding. And there's some Delia and Melissa in the cheese." It's not just realistic, it's real. And delicious.

December. Here's what I'm missing—not grapefruit, not

chocolate: oats. And their absence helps illustrate what's happened to American agriculture, and what would be required to change it a little bit.

Once upon a time, oats were everywhere; people grew them for their horses, and for themselves. But oats aren't easy to deal with. Wheat you simply grind up, but oats have a hull that needs removing, and they need to be steamed, and dried, and rolled. You can do that more efficiently on a vast scale in places like Saskatoon, Saskatchewan, where a single mill turns out a million pounds of oat products a day. Such scale quickly undercut local markets, and soon no one was milling oats in the Champlain Valley—just as no one was raising pork, or canning tomatoes, or doing any of the other things that a local food economy would require. For the moment, large-scale, centralized farming works. But that may change if the price of oil (the lifeblood of industrial agriculture) continues to climb, or if the climate keeps changing rapidly, or if global politics deteriorates. Even now, stubborn people keep trying to rebuild smaller-scale food networks, but it's hard to swim against the tide of cheap good that keeps flowing in.

A few years ago a Vermonter named Andrew Leinoff decided to go into oats. He and a friend found some old equipment and started experimenting. They worked out a good rotation for their fields—soybeans, then buckwheat, then the oats—and they eventually managed to make their ancient machinery work at least sporadically. ("One time my friend turned on the huller and it blew apart," Leinoff recalled. "Missed him by inches and made a big hole in the roof of the barn.") After several seasons of struggling to overcome all the problems of a startup, they gave up, and a little bitterly. The state's department of agriculture talks a good game—the governor has a public service ad on the radio urging Vermonters to buy 10 percent of their food from within the state—but it spends most of its time and money propping up the state's slowly withering dairy industry, not supporting the pioneers trying to build what comes next. The only thing the oat farmers got from the state was "these bizarre tax notices fining us $250 because we hadn't filed something that said we had no income."

As a result, no oats for me, not until I cheated and found a tiny farm just across the Canadian border. Which makes this an appropriate place to interrupt my winter's tale, finely balanced between delight and frustration. It's the same balance that almost everyone eventually reaches when they start trying to change our food economy—indeed, any facet of our economy. I'm able to taste a different future, but the weight of the present is strong indeed. And that weight comes precisely from the remarkable success of our current food system, at least when measured in the ways we're used to measuring.

MODERN AGRICULTURE PRODUCES A LOT OF FOOD, AND PRO-duces it cheaply, two feats that people have spent all of human history trying to achieve.

The engine of this achievement has been, for a century, relentless consolidation and concentration, a process that is by now very nearly complete in the United States and is still accelerating elsewhere. Four companies slaughter 81 percent of American beef.[3] Cargill, Inc., controls 45 percent of the globe's grain trade, while its competitor Archer Daniels Midland controls another 30 percent.[4] Name your commodity: as the *New York Times* reported recently, the number of potato farmers in Idaho has fallen by half in the last fifteen years, to no more than eight hundred. (A typical farmer there may have eight tractors worth $130,000 apiece; he's likely to use global posititoning satellites to make sure his rows are straight. "With all that, you need 1,500 to 2,500 acres to make a decent living," one explained.)[5] Eighty-nine percent of American chickens are produced under contract to big companies, usually in broiler houses up to five hundred feet long holding thirty thousand or more birds. Four multinational companies control over 70 percent of fluid milk sales in the United States, and one Ohio "farm" produces 3 billion eggs per year.[6] Four firms control 85 percent of global coffee roasting, and a small group of multinationals handles 80 percent of the world trade in cocoa, pineapples, tea, and bananas. The merger of Philip Morris and Nabisco in 2000 created a food conglomerate that collects nearly 10 cents of every dollar an American consumer spends on food. Meanwhile, five companies control 75 percent of the global vegetable seed market, and their grip on the market is tightening as the seed companies patent more and more genetically modified varieties and prevent seed saving.[7] As a former Monsanto executive boasted not long ago, "What you are seeing is not just a consolidation of seed companies, it's really a consolidation of the entire food chain."[8]

The same forces that have created giant farms and processing plants have also worked to consolidate the retail end of the food business. As one Wal-Mart "meat procurement officer" said, "We've tried to apply our value proposition to all the meat products that we sell. The same principles of value, price, and quality that apply to things like television sets also apply to food."[9] Indeed—and Wal-Mart is now the largest seller of food in this country (and on this planet). It's not just in the United States that such forces play out. In Britain, the four biggest supermarket chains now control 80 percent of the food consumed there, and as a result the number of produce suppliers to the average supermarket chains has fallen from 800 in 1987 to fewer than 80 today. The consolidation continues—80 percent of the British potato crop comes from 250 growers, down from 5,000 in 2001, in part because the requirements for what constitutes an "acceptable" vegetable keep getting tighter.[10] Want to sell tomatoes? The store will take them only if they're between 53 and 63 millimeters in diameter. That 10-millimeter band (about the size of a pencil eraser) disqualified lots of tomatoes; more were tossed out because they were at "different color stages" or had "slightly chewy skin."[11]

This system of consolidation, which is working its way quickly into the developing world, is the epitome of a certain kind of efficiency, Adam Smith raised to the *n*th degree. People who specialize in 56-millimeter tomatoes get very good at growing them, especially when they're being constantly reminded to lower their price lest the buyer go elsewhere. Partly as a result of all this, the world produces 322 kilograms per person per year of grain in 2004, the biggest harvest ever, and we can walk into a supermarket and find a bounty of lovely food from all around the world at any season. The price of all that food has never been lower: Americans spend 11 percent of their paychecks on food, less than half what their grandparents spent before World War II.[12] As the dean of the College of Agriculture at the University of Maryland noted recently, "Large farms simply produce commodities at lower cost."[13] We've got what everyone who ever lived always wanted—plenty. End of story.

OR NOT. TO CREATE ALL THOSE EFFICIENCIES, AN AWFUL LOT OF inefficiencies had to be eliminated, and that process has not been free of pain. Cheap and plentiful food may well have been worth it, but let's at least itemize the various costs, especially since the process, though nearly complete in this country, is still in earlier stages in various spots around the globe. The first and most obvious of these costs has been damage to communities—to the people who were no longer necessary, and to the communities that they had built. It's hard to calculate this damage; in fact, many have questioned whether it is damage at all, or just change. Still, the numbers are stark. Since the end of World War II, America has lost a farm about every half hour, mostly because farming has grown more efficient.[14] Output went up, prices went down, and on the typical Iowa farm "the farmer's profit margin dropped from 35 percent in 1950 to nine percent today," according to the Worldwatch

Institute researcher Brian Halweil. To generate the same income as it did in 1950, a farm today would need to be roughly four times as large. And that's exactly what has happened: a few farmers, more skilled at financing or with better access to capital, bought out their neighbors. Before long, most of the real money was in the value-added phase: turning corn into corn syrup and then into Coca-Cola. "Tractor makers, agrochemical firms, seed companies, food processors, and supermarkets take most of what is spent on food, leaving the farmer less than ten cents of the typical food dollar," says Halweil.[15] Ezra Taft Benson, Dwight D. Eisenhower's secretary of agriculture, exhorted farmers to "get big or get out." They complied, but in the 1970s Nixon's agriculture secretary, Earl Butz, told them to "get bigger, get better, or get out." Everyone took his advice, too, and by 1980 there were so few farmers left in the country that the Census Bureau no longer bothered to list farming as one of the occupations you could check off on its form. American farmers over the age of sixty-five outnumber those under thirty-five by nearly six to one.[16]

The "farmers" who survive in this process are often living truly miserable lives. Imagine, for instance, what it's like to rear chickens for a huge grower like Perdue. The company doesn't own farms; instead, it contracts with farmers, telling them precisely how to build their sheds, what to feed the hens, how often to supplement with antibiotics. The farmer owns the land and the equipment, but Perdue can inspect them at any time. Most of the farmers, according to an investigative series in the *Baltimore Sun*, were lured into the business by "sophisticated company sales pitches promising independence and a middle-class income," but soon find themselves "landowning serfs in an agricultural feudal system." In return for a $250,000 start-up investment of his savings, the average contract chicken farmer takes in an annual net income of $8,160. No benefits—the farmer is an independent contractor—just the right to assume "round-the-clock responsibility, daily collecting dead birds by hand during strolls through dust and ankle-deep manure. A farmer battles heat waves, power outages, and outbreaks of avian disease, and his every move is controlled by the vagaries of a contract that can be canceled virtually anytime, cutting income to zero."[17]

I get to watch this process close up. I live in Vermont, long a dairy state—but the number of farms drops every year. In 2004, we lost 81 dairies, bringing the total below 1,300. But those remaining were bigger, more efficient. The state's agriculture secretary, Steve Kerr, seemed unruffled: "There is always a sadness in town when something changes, when the barn that had cows in it doesn't have cows anymore," he said. "But agriculture, like every business, changes over time. The year that will really worry me is the year our milk production takes a real dive. That hasn't happened."[18] Indeed, the most efficient production scheme would be a single giant cow with an udder the size of a volcano, squirting milk directly into a central processing plant. That's more or less where the current system is headed: Thomas Dorr, the current U.S. undersecretary of agriculture for rural development, believes "that the right scale for farms in the future will be about 200,000 acres of cropland under a single manager."[19] (In such a world, Vermont would have about five farms.) The same phenomenon is at work in other countries. In Britain, a thousand farmers and farmworkers leave the land each week; one expert recommends that British farmers join together in "Soviet-style collectives" of up to twenty thousand acres in order to produce commodity crops at world prices.[20] France lost half its farmers between 1982 and 1999, and in Germany the number of farmers declined by a quarter in the 1990s.[21] In Poland, 70 percent of farms may disappear as the country is absorbed into the European Union; in the Philippines, 1.2 million farmworkers, 10 percent of the total, lost their jobs in the single year between July 1999 and July 2000.[22]

To many economists, these numbers represent the "creative destruction" inherent in a market economy. Steven Blank of the University of California at Davis predicts that America may soon "get out of the food business" because it "will become unprofitable to tie up resources in farming and ranching" that could be better invested elsewhere. Our country is merely "moving up the Economic Food Chain," Blank says. "America doing agriculture is like a Ph.D. doing child's work— we can do it, but it is a waste. Much of our labor, capital, and management resources that remain in agriculture are there by choice but could be better invested elsewhere." Soon, he predicts, only those forms of agriculture "compatible with urban life" will still matter in America; "the main entries on that list include golf courses, nurseries, and turf farms." A golfer, he notes, pays $275 to "wander around on the turf at Pebble Beach for about four hours, and there is a waiting list to do it. How often do people pay farmers for the opportunity to wander around in their fields?"[23] Blank is an extreme example, but standard economic thinking basically agrees: the country is better off because people have been freed from working in the fields to do something "more productive." And surely some of those freed people agree; there have always been lots of farm kids seeking any way into some other, easier life. The 60 percent of Americans who were farming a hundred years ago and aren't now have built most of our modern way of life.

But, the costs have been real. As farms declined, so, too, did the communities around them. Even in the prosperous 1990s, farm consolidation was changing rural America: 676 of the nation's 3,141 counties lost population, and the drain was so strong in the northern Great Plains that "an area the size of the original Louisiana Purchase again qualifies for the 'frontier' designation that the Census Bureau gave remote regions before the great waves of settlement in the 19th century." Poverty rates, the journalist John Nichols adds, are now higher in vast stretches of the "heartland" than in inner cities. Nine of the ten counties in America with the lowest per capita income are in farm states west of the Mississippi.[24]

The specialization and consolidation are so intense that sociologists now designate many parts of rural America "food
deserts," dependent on convenience stores and without access
to fresh produce. The director of the nation's largest food relief
charity, Second Harvest, describes Midwesterners "going to a
food bank for a box of cornflakes to feed their children in a
community where thousands of acres are devoted to growing
corn."[25] Everything in town dries up and disappears: 20 percent
of the prairie churches in the Dakotas now stand vacant.[26] It
may be simply sentimental to mourn this loss, for America is
rich and productive enough that many of those forced from the
countryside find other things to do, most of them easier than
farming. But since the same efficiencies are quickly spreading
worldwide, and since half the world's people currently work as
farmers, it's worth at least wondering what the result will be
elsewhere, where the first stop (and often the permanent stop)
for displaced peasants is a cardboard box on the edge of the capital city.

IF THE DAMAGE TO COMMUNITY IS ARGUABLE, AN INDUSTRIAL-
ized food system has other costs that are both more prosaic
and more obvious. Part of the reason for that low, low price for
food is that we pay many fewer farmers a smaller percentage
of our food dollars. And food is cheap partly thanks to efficiencies like speeding up the processing lines where animals are
slaughtered. According to Human Rights Watch, as the Bush
administration has turned a blind eye to safety standards and
as the power of the meatpacking unions to set conditions has
eroded, "Workers in the industry now face a one-in-five chance
of severe disability or death on the job."[27] When Tyson opened a
plant in Missouri in 1995, it couldn't find enough immigrant labor, so the state began sending welfare recipients to work there
as a way to get them off the rolls. "The first job they get is the

'puller' job—pulling the internal organs out," one state bureaucrat explained. "A lot of these workers will lose their fingernails in two to three weeks from the bacteria in the chicken fat."[28]

Did you ever wonder how lobster could be so wondrously cheap at those chain restaurants next to the mall? Despite the old-fashioned lobster traps hanging on the wall, what you're eating isn't actually Maine lobster; it's spiny or rock lobster from the waters off Central America. Close to 100 percent of the divers who harvest those lobsters off the sea bottom show signs of neurological damage, according to a 1999 World Bank report, because they use ancient scuba equipment, without depth gauges or even an indicator to tell them how much air they have left, and because, as the lobsters have gotten scarcer thanks to the endless all-you-can-eat lobster buffets back home, the divers have fished out the 40-foot depths. They're down at 120 feet, 130 feet.[29]

In some places, the abuse of workers gets even more basic. On Brazil's frontier, there's a problem with slavery: as many as fifty thousand people engaged in clearing the Amazon jungle are effectively enslaved. ConAgra, one of the biggest food processors on earth, bought beef from that land once it was cleared and sold it in cans with the Mary Kitchen label. A spokeswoman, Kay Carpenter, said the company was "several steps removed" from the slaveholders. Another large agribusiness firm, Cargill, was accused in 2004 of buying soybeans from Brazilian slave farms; its spokeswoman said in response, "I think it is unfair of folks to point at Cargill and say Cargill is solely responsible for actions other people take."[30]

Of course, it's unfair. The logic of our current way of looking at the world is what points companies in this direction. It is more efficient to pay farmers the least we can get away with, to get the most possible work out of chicken pluckers, to not worry overmuch about exactly where that lobster came from. We are delivering huge quantities of food, cheaply. If people were paid more along the way, that efficiency would be compromised.

It also makes a certain kind of sense to abuse the environment along the way, again because doing so is efficient. For instance, the cheapest way to raise hogs is all in the same place, where one worker can "take care" of tens of thousands of animals. But this concentrates their waste in one place, where instead of being useful fertilizer to spread on crop fields it becomes a toxic threat. Hogs produce a lot of waste, much more than people do. One farm in Utah, with 1.5 million porkers, has a sewage problem larger than that of the city of Los Angeles.[31] In North Carolina, one of the centers of what boosters call Big Pig, hogs outnumber citizens, and they produce more fecal waste than California, New York, and Washington combined.[32] As one official for the American Farm Bureau puts it, "It's not like farmers and ranchers wake up one morning and say 'I want 10,000 pigs in one spot.' But we're in a world market. And if we're going to compete internationally, we have to be low-cost producers, and we have to do so for products that consumers demand." Attempts to alleviate the symptoms often only ends up adding to the consolidation; new rules about the smell from sewage lagoons, for instance, end up favoring "the largest farms that will be able to afford new technology to mask odors."[33]

But there's also another potential cost to our food system, one we've just begun to understand in the wake of 9/11: any enterprise so centralized is exquisitely vulnerable to sabotage. Lawrence Wein, a professor of management science at Stanford University's business school, offered a small example in the spring of 2005: say a terrorist, using instruction manuals that can be found on the Internet, fills a one-gallon jug with a sludgy substance containing a few grams of botulinum toxin. He sneaks onto a dairy farm and pours his jug into an unlocked milk tank, which is then picked up a by a milk truck and taken to a giant dairy-processing factory. About 100,000 gallons of milk go through an average plant's raw-milk silo between cleanings, Wein estimates, which means 400,000 cartons of contaminated milk can be shipped out around the country. And since botulism doesn't sicken its victims for forty-eight hours, it will take a while for anyone to notice.[34] This is not simply some personal nightmare: when Tommy Thompson announced his resignation as secretary of health and human services in 2004, he said in his final press briefing: "For the life of me, I cannot understand why the terrorists have not attacked our food supply, because it is so easy to do."[35]

Even apart from terrorists, the centralized food system we've built presents risks. "The industrialization of poultry is the nub of the problem" of avian flu, says Kennedy Shortridge, a Hong Kong microbiologist who has spent three decades studying influenza viruses.[36] Concentrated agriculture also manages to make us sick on a fairly regular, if less dramatic, basis. Seventy-six million Americans fall ill annually from food-borne illness; 300,000 are hospitalized; 5,000 die.[37] Salmonella is the biggest culprit, and its prevalence has doubled since the 1970s, which makes sense when you consider the enormous poultry barns and cattle feedlots that grew up in those years. Half the chicken on sale in British supermarkets is contaminated with campylobacter, the journalist Felicity Lawrence recently reported; this is, in part, because the live birds are stacked in enormous towers of cages as they await slaughter, so the waste from the top deck rains down on those below. "Look, if you are going to process poultry at that price, there's not much you can do," one microbiologist finally told Lawrence, a little impatiently. "The factories are designed to get them through fast. People want cheap food."[38]

PROBLEMS LIKE THESE—HUGE SEWAGE LAGOONS, MISERABLE animals, abused workers, vulnerability to sabotage and to salmonella—are not, perhaps, inherent problems. You could envision a huge global food system that was willing to trade a little efficiency for slightly more humane working conditions or slightly better sewage treatment.

There is a deeper issue, though, which can't be addressed without changing pretty much everything about the way we eat: we are running out of the two basic ingredients we need to grow crops on an industrial scale. These are oil and water, and in modern agriculture they mix to provide the giant harvests of cheap food we've come to count on. But they're not to be taken for granted.

Let's look at water first. Seventy percent of the water used by human beings goes to irrigate crops. Water demand has tripled in the last half century; we have slaked this thirst by pumping from aquifers, underground layers of porous rock or sand containing water, into which wells can be sunk. The diesel-driven and electrically powered pumps that make the extraction of water possible became available around the world at roughly the same time; hence it is no surprise, writes the eco-statistician Lester Brown, that we now face "the near-simultaneous depletion of aquifers."

In China, recent surveys show that the water table under the North China Plain, which produces half the country's wheat and a third of its corn, is falling fast. Every day in the countryside north of Beijing you run across people whose wells have suddenly gone dry; a World Bank study reports that wells drilled in the area now have to descend a thousand meters, more than half a mile, to tap fresh water. India is also overpumping its aquifers; studies of the wells in Rajasthan, for example, suggest the water table there has fallen more than 130 feet over the last two decades. And similar drawdowns seem to be taking place around the world. Villages in eastern Iran are being abandoned as wells go dry, and the Saudis, who used mile-deep wells to create, among other follies, a large-scale dairy industry, are now cutting back sharply on water use. In essence, Brown writes, we have created a food bubble economy, artificially inflating food production by means of an unsustainable reliance on underground water. The pumping of groundwater has generated tremendous crop yields, even compared with surface-water irrigation from dams and canals, which can't be as easily turned on and off at just the right moment. But when the water starts to run dry, that free ride is over, and farmers will have to return to growing what they can with the water that falls on their regions. For China, India, Pakistan, Mexico, and Saudi Arabia, Brown says, the question "is not whether the bubble will burst, but when."

We're used to thinking of water as key to farming. But we reflect less often on an equally critical fact: our food arrives at the table marinated in oil—crude oil. Cheap and abundant fossil fuel has shaped the farming system we've come to think of as normal; it's the main reason you can go to the store and get anything you want at any time and for not much money. And since, as we've seen, we may be both running out of oil and running out of atmosphere to store carbon, our agricultural system may be far more vulnerable than we imagine.

Agriculture is, and always has been, energy intensive. For a long time, that meant using the sun's energy to grow food that in turn powered the human and animal muscles necessary to do the work of plowing and planting and harvesting. New inventions—the scythe, the moldboard plow—made that energy go a little further. In the early twentieth century, though, the widespread use of fossil fuels changed the whole equation. Crucially, in 1909 a pair of German chemists named Fritz Haber and Carl Bosch invented a process to synthesize ammonia from atmospheric nitrogen and the hydrogen in fossil fuels; today, their process, mostly using natural gas as a feedstock, produces 150 million tons of ammonia-based fertilizer each year, which adds as much nitrogen to soil as all natural sources combined. Take that away and we'd notice. Meanwhile, almost simultaneously with the invention of artificial fertilizer, farms around the developed world were converting to tractors, replacing horsepower with oil power. In the 1890s, roughly one-quarter of cropland in the United States was used to grow grain to feed horses, almost all of which worked on farms. Cheap oil freed that land for growing food for humans.[39] When, in the 1960s, we exported this industrialized agricultural system to the Third World, we called it the green revolution.

Because of its reliance on cheap energy, the efficiency of our vast farms and the food system they underwrite is in one sense an illusion, and perhaps a very temporary one. The number of farmers has fallen from half the American population to about 1 percent, and in essence those missing farmers have been replaced with oil. We might see fossil fuel as playing the same role that slaves played in early American agriculture—a "natural resource" that comes cheap. It takes half a gallon of oil to produce a bushel of midwestern hybrid corn; a quarter of it is used to make fertilizer, 35 percent to power the farm machinery, 7 percent to irrigate the field, and the rest to make pesticides, to dry grain, and to perform all the other tasks of industrial farming.[40] There aren't many people on that farm, but there's all kinds of machinery, and every bit of it is burning fuel. Here's the math: between 1910 and 1983, U.S. corn yields grew 346 percent. Energy consumption for agriculture increased 810 percent.[41]

But farming proper is the least of it. Processing, packaging, and distributing the food around the nation and the world consumes four times again as much energy. The numbers are astounding: the average bite of American food has traveled more than 1,500 miles before it reaches your lips, changing hands an average of six times along the way.[42] One study showed that in Iowa—center of the agricultural heartland, the place Americans think of when we think of farms—the average carrot had come 1,690 miles, from California, the average potato 1,292 miles, from Idaho, and the average chuck roast over 600 miles, from Colorado.[43] None of this makes much sense except by the standards of lowest-price economics. The Swedish Food Institute, for instance, discovered that growing and distributing a pound of frozen peas required 10 times as much energy as the peas contained.[44] Say you grow a head of iceberg lettuce in the Salinas Valley of California and ship it back east: you use 36 times as many calories of fossil energy as the lettuce actually contains. Ship it to London, and you use 127 times as many calories.[45] A pound of grapes flown in from Chile effectively gives off six pounds of carbon dioxide.[46] (Needless to say, the fastest-growing part of the food business is shipment by refrigerated plane.)[47] If what you're eating comes in a package, then the calculations get really wild: to package a box of breakfast cereal requires 7 times as much energy as the cereal contains.[48] Bottled water is, of course, the champion of this kind of equation, since it delivers zero calories. The amount of water traded worldwide has doubled each decade since the 1970s; Californians alone (almost all of whom have access to clean tap water) now throw away 1.2 billion single-serving water bottles annually.[49]

The international food trade just keeps increasing. In the last four decades, the tonnage of food shipped between countries has grown fourfold, while human population has barely doubled.[50] Seventy-five percent of the apples for sale in New York City come from the West Coast or overseas, even though New York State produces ten times as many apples as the residents of the Big Apple consume. In England, farmers ship roughly the same amount of milk, pork, and lamb abroad as British supermarkets import, in what agricultural economists call a food swap. As Herman Daly once wrote, "Americans import Danish sugar cookies, and Danes import American sugar cookies. Exchanging recipes would surely be more efficient."[51] In much of the world, 40 percent of the truck traffic comes from the shuttling of food over long distances.[52]

Here's the bottom line: if the oil runs out, we won't be able to farm or trade this way any longer. And if we took global warming seriously, we'd stop doing it right now: compared with regional and local food systems, our national and international model releases five to seventeen times more carbon dioxide into the atmosphere.[53] A Japanese study found that eating local food would be the equivalent of cutting household energy use by 20 percent.[54] But what a scary proposition. Because, for all its flaws, the food system we have now manages to more or less feed most of the earth's population. If we didn't have vast factory farms, if we didn't have superefficient agriculture, then we'd starve. Modern, energy-intensive agriculture has "kept more than one billion people from hunger, starvation, or even death," observes Norman Borlaug, the scientist often described as the father of the green revolution. There are still 800 million hungry people to feed, he notes, but not to fear: "New high-yielding, disease- and insect-resistant seeds, new products to restore soil fertility and control pests, and a succession of agricultural machines can ease drudgery and speed everything from planting to harvesting."[55] In other words, pour on the oil, with a side order of biotech. We're in a box.

OR ARE WE? THIS IS A KEY POINT: WE ASSUME, BECAUSE IT MAKES a certain kind of intuitive sense, that industrialized farming is the most productive farming. I mean, if I sit on my porch whittling toothpicks with my Swiss Army knife, I can produce a hundred in a day. If I install a toothpick-whittling machine, I can produce a thousand in an hour. By analogy, a vast Midwestern field filled with high-tech equipment ought to produce more food than someone with a hoe in a small garden. As it turns out, however, this simply isn't true. If all you are worried about is the greatest yield per acre, then *smaller farms produce more food*. Which, if you think about it some more, makes sense. If you are one guy on a tractor responsible for thousands of acres, you grow your corn and that's all you can do: one pass after another with the gargantuan machines across your sea of crop. But if you're working on ten acres, then you have time to really know the land, and to make it work harder. You can intercrop all kinds of plants: their roots will go to different depths, or they'll thrive in each other's shade, or they'll make use of different nutrients in the soil. You can also walk your fields, over and over, *noticing*. As one small farmer recently wrote in *Farming* magazine, spending part of every day in the pasture gives you a "grass eye," "a keen awareness" of where small seeps of water are muddying the fields, or whether "earthworms and other soil life are properly disposing of cow pies." Yellow clover leaves signify a sulfur deficiency; an abundance of dandelions means a shortage of calcium. "Every spot or plant in the pasture," he says, "is trying to tell us something."[56] Does this sound like hippie nonsense? According to the most recent USDA Census of Agriculture, smaller farms produce far more food per acre, whether you measure in tons, calories, or dollars. They use land, water, and oil much more efficiently; if they have animals, the manure is a gift, not a threat to public health. "In terms of converting inputs into outputs, society would be better off with small-scale farmers," writes Brian Halweil. "As population continues to grow in many nations, and the amount of farmland and water available to each person continues to shrink, a small farm structure may become central to feeding the planet."[57]

But if this is true, then why don't we have more small farms? Why the relentless consolidation? There are many reasons, including the way farm subsidies have been structured, the big guys' easier access to bank loans, and the convenience for politically connected food processors of dealing with a few big operations. But the basic reason is this: we have substituted oil for people. The small farm grows more food per acre, but only because it uses more people per acre—low-input farming in Great Britain employs twice as many people per acre, according to a 2005 study.[58] Since World War I, it has been cheaper to use oil than to use people. Cheap oil has meant cheap synthetic fertilizer, big tractors, and everything else we associate with modern agriculture. You get more food per *acre* with small farms; more food per *dollar* with big ones.

What about conventional versus organic? Could we take away the fossil fuel (which means, most of all, the synthetic fertilizer), put people back on the land in larger numbers, and have enough for dinner? The proponents of conventional agriculture scoff at the idea: Dennis Avery, director of Center for Global Food Issues, says you'd need so much land to grow forage for the animals providing the manure that a world of low-input organic farmers would only work if you were "willing to destroy three billion living human beings and forcibly abort most of the babies now being born in the world."[59] However, organic farming techniques have steadily improved in recent decades, especially in their use of cover crops, or "green manures," which enrich the soil without needing animal waste.

The best data come from an English agronomist named Jules Pretty, who has studied two hundred "sustainable agriculture" projects in fifty-two countries around the world. They might not pass the U.S. standards for organic certification, but they're all low-input, using far less energy and chemicals than industrialized farming. "We calculate that almost nine million farmers were using sustainable practices on about 29 million hectares, more than 98 percent of which emerged in the past decade," he noted in 2002. "We found that sustainable agriculture has led to an average 93 percent increase in per hectare food production." These were not tiny, isolated demonstration farms; Pretty studied fourteen projects where 146,000 farmers were raising potato, sweet potato, and cassava, and he found that practices like cover-cropping and fighting pests with natural adversaries had increased production 150 percent, to seventeen tons per household. With 4.5 million grain farmers, average yields rose 73 percent.[60] When Indonesian rice farmers switched away from pesticides, he found, their yields stayed the same but their costs fell sharply.[61]

And over time, instead of eroding soil or drying up aquifers, as industrial agriculture does, small-scale, low-input farming yields new benefits. Pretty describes a hillside farm on the edge of a remote village in central Honduras, where in the late 1980s the farms were poor-quality pasture and cornfields, and people saw migrating to the city as their only hope. No child in the village had ever been to high school. But one local farmer, Elias Zelaya, was trained by a small nonprofit organization in some of the new sustainable agriculture techniques. He started inter-cropping beans with his corn; the nitrogen they fixed improved both his yield and his soil. Over the years he's added twenty-eight types of crops and trees to his small farm, along with pigs, chicken, rabbits, cattle, and horses. "The effect is remarkable," says Pretty. "The unimproved soils on the edge of Elias' farm are no more than a few centimeters deep, and beneath it is hard bedrock. But in the fields where Elias grows legumes as green manures and uses composts, the soil is thick, dark, and spongy to the step. In some places on the farm, the soil is more than half a meter deep."[62]

Many of the modern sustainable practices will seem famil-iar to American backyard gardeners. In Kenya, the Associa-tion for Better Land Husbandry found that farmers who built raised beds could produce enough vegetables to see them though the dry season. "A considerable investment in labor is required," as anyone who has double-dug tomato beds can at-test. But once they're dug, and once you've begun to enrich them with compost—well, you can grow an awful lot. Ac-cording to one review of twenty-six Kenyan communities, "Three-quarters of participating households are now free from hunger during the year, and the proportion having to buy vegetables has fallen from 85 percent to 11 percent."[63] Every year new techniques appear. Velvetbean, a green ma-nure, fixes so much nitrogen that on the Central American farms using it corn yields have risen two or three times; cer-tain cowpeas increase the yields of Thai rice farmers by as much as a fifth. This is not simple peasant agriculture; in fact, it's far more complex than just following the fertilizer or spraying schedule that the nice man from the company hands you when you fork over your cash. But farmer-run schools have sprung up in country after country to spread the new techniques, and the longer that small farmers experiment with the new ideas, the more improvement they find. Take fish ponds—you see them across Asia and Africa, newly dug pools for raising grass-eating fish like carp. In Bangladesh, I've seen them built beneath chicken coops so that the poultry waste will fall through the bottom of the cages and fertilize the weeds that the fish then consume. In Malawi, six years after farmers started building such ponds, total calorie yields had nearly doubled. In the words of one expert, "As farmers gain a greater understanding of how this new system functions, and an appreciation of its potential, they become increasingly able to guide further evolution towards increasing productivity and profitability."[64]

"I acknowledge," says Pretty, "that all this may sound too good to be true for those who would disbelieve these advances. Many still believe that food production and nature must be separated, that 'agroecological' approaches offer only marginal opportunities to increase food production, and that industrialized approaches represent the best, and perhaps only, way forward. However, prevailing views have changed substantially in just the last decade."[65]

The new farming technologies are perhaps the most exciting new "inventions" of our age—more important, in the long run, than the iPod or maybe even the Internet. They *do* sound too good to be true. But as it happens, the world has offered an unexpected large-scale test of these possibilities in the last decade, one of those strange accidents with wide-reaching consequences. The unlikely scene of this experiment is Havana.

■ ■ ■

THE PICTURES HANGING IN HAVANA'S MUSEUM OF THE REVOLU-tion document the rise (or, depending on your perspective, the fall) of Cuba in the years after Fidel Castro took power, in 1959. You can walk through gallery after gallery gazing upon the stock images of socialist glory: "anti-imperialist volunteers" fighting in Angola; Cuban boxers winning Olympic medals; five patients at a time undergoing eye surgery using a "method created by Soviet academician Fyodorov." Mostly, though, there are pictures of farm equipment. "Manual operation is re-placed by mechanized processes," reads the caption under a picture of some heavy Marxist metal cruising a vast field. An-other caption boasts that by 1990, seven bulk-sugar terminals had been built, each with a shipping capacity of seventy-five thousand tons a day. In true Soviet style, the Cubans were demonstrating a deeply held socialist belief that salvation lay in the size of the harvest, in the number of tractors, and in the glorious heroic machinery that would straighten the tired backs of an oppressed peasantry—and so I learned that within thirty years of the people's uprising, the sugarcane industry alone employed 2,850 lifting machines, 12,278 tractors, 29,857 carts, and 4,277 combines. Industrial agriculture was the cor-nerstone of communism, as dear to Castro as it is to Cargill.

But then I turned a corner and the pictures changed. The sharply focused shots of combines and Olympians now were muddied, as if Cubans had forgotten how to print photos or, as was more likely the case, had run short of darkroom chemi-cals. I had reached the gallery of the "Special Period." That is to say, I had reached the point in Cuban history where every-thing came undone. With the sudden collapse of the Soviet Union, Cuba fell off a cliff of its own and became the first place in the world to face peak oil. All those carts and com-bines had been the products of an insane "economics" under-written by the Eastern Bloc for ideological purposes. Castro spent three decades growing sugar and shipping it to Russia and East Germany, both of which paid a price well above the world level, and both of which sent the ships back to Havana filled with wheat, rice, oil, and more tractors. When all that disappeared, almost literally overnight, Cuba had nowhere to turn. The new Russia no longer wanted to pay a premium on Cuban sugar for the simple glory of supporting a tropical version of its Leninist past. The United States, Cuba's closest neighbor, enforced a strict trade embargo (which it strengthened in 1992, and again in 1996) and Cuba had next to no foreign exchange with anyone else.

In other words, Cuba truly became an island. Not just a real island, surrounded by water, but something much rarer: an island outside the international economic system, a moon base whose supply ships had suddenly stopped coming. There were other deeply isolated places on the planet, such as North Korea and Burma, but not many. And so most observers waited impatiently for the country to collapse. No island is an island, after all, not in a global world. The *New York Times Magazine* ran a story titled "The Last Days of Castro's Cuba," and nowhere did the future look bleaker than on the farm and in the market.

During the Soviet era, much of what Cubans ate had come straight from Eastern Europe, and most of the rest was grown industrial style, on big state farms. All those combines needed fuel and spare parts, and all those long rows of grain and vegetables needed pesticides and fertilizer, none of which were available any longer. In 1989, according to the United Nations Food and Agriculture Organization, the average Cuban was eating 3,000 calories per day. Four years later, that figure had fallen to 1,900. It was as if Cuba suddenly had to skip one meal a day, every day, week after month after year. The host of one cooking show on the shortened TV schedule urged Cubans to fry up "steaks" made from grapefruit peels covered in bread crumbs. "I lost twenty pounds myself," said Fernando Funes, a government agronomist. The Cubans seemed to be proving that indeed you couldn't survive without "modern" agriculture.

But that was then. Now, looking across the table, I could see that Fernando Funes had since gained back that twenty pounds. In fact, he had a little paunch, as do many Cuban men of a certain age. What happened was simple, if unexpected. Cuba learned to stop exporting sugar and instead started raising its own food again, growing it on small private farms and in thousands of pocket-sized urban market gardens—and, since the country lacked chemicals and fertilizers, much of that food became de facto organic. Somehow, just as Jules Pretty's examples from around the world predicted, the combination worked. Cubans produce as much food today as they did before the Soviet Union collapsed. They're still short of meat, and the milk supply remains a real problem, but their caloric intake has returned to normal: they've gotten that meal back.

In so doing, Cubans have created what may be the world's largest working model of a semisustainable agriculture, one that relies far less than the rest of the world does on oil, on chemicals, on shipping vast quantities of food back and forth. They import some of their food—a certain amount of rice from Vietnam, even some apples and beef from the United States, since farm-state senators have weakened our embargo. But mostly they grow their own.

Consider Villa Alamar, for instance, a planned community built outside Havana at the height of the Soviet glory days. Its crumbling, precast-concrete apartments would look at home (though less mildewed) in Ljubljana or Omsk. Even the names there speak of the past: a central square is called Parque Hanoi, to commemorate the "Vietnamese liberation struggle." But right next to Parque Hanoi is the Vivero Organopónico Alamar.

Cuba has thousands of *organopónicos*—urban gardens—more than two hundred in the Havana area alone. The Vivero Organopónico Alamar is especially beautiful: a few acres of vegetables attached to a shady yard packed with potted plants for sale, birds in wicker cages, a cafeteria, and a small market where a steady stream of local people buys tomatoes, lettuce, oregano, and potatoes for their supper. (Twenty-five crops were listed on the blackboard the day I visited.) Sixty-four people farm this tiny spread. Their chief is Miguel Salcines López, a tall, middle-aged, intense, and quite delightful man.

"This land was slated for a hospital and sports complex," he said, leading me quickly through his tiny empire. "But when the food crisis came, the government decided this was more important." Until then, Salcines said, "I was an agronomic engineer. I was fat, a functionary. I was a bureaucrat." Salcines showed off a pyramidal minigreenhouse in which he raises seedlings, in the belief that its shape "focuses energy." Magnets on his irrigation lines, he believes, help "reduce the surface tension" of the water. Give Salcines a ponytail and he'd fit right in at the Marin County farmers' market; but he is not obsessive, even about organicity. Like gardeners everywhere, he has trouble with potato bugs, and he doesn't hesitate to use what man-made pesticide he can lay his hands on to fight them. He doesn't use artificial fertilizer, both because it is expensive and because he doesn't need it—indeed, the garden makes money selling its own compost, produced with the help of millions of worms (*Eisenia foetida:* aka California reds) in a long series of shaded trenches.

While we ate rice and beans and salad and a little chicken, Salcines laid out the finances of his cooperative farm. For the last six months, he said, the government demanded that the *organopónico* produce 835,000 pesos' worth of food. It actually produced more than a million pesos' worth. Writing quickly on a piece of scrap paper, Salcines predicted that the profit for the whole year would be 393,000 pesos. Half of that he would reinvest in enlarging the farm; the rest would go into a profit-sharing plan. It's not an immense sum when divided among sixty-four workers—about $150 apiece—but for Cuban workers this is considered a good job indeed. A blackboard above the lunch line reminded employees what their monthly share of the profit would be: depending on how long they'd been at the farm, and how well they produced, they might get as much as 291 pesos this month, almost doubling their base salary. The people worked hard, and if they didn't, their colleagues wouldn't tolerate them.

What is happening at the Vivero Organopónico Alamar certainly isn't unfettered capitalism, but it's not exactly collective farming, either. Mostly, it's productive: sixty-four people earn a reasonable living from this small site, and the surrounding neighbors get an awful lot of their food from its carefully tended rows. You see the same kind of production all over the city; every formerly vacant lot in Havana seems to be a small farm. The city grew three hundred thousand tons of food last year—*nearly its entire vegetable supply*, and more than a token amount of its rice and meat, said Egidio Páez Medina, who oversees the *organopónicos* from a small office on a highway at the edge of town. "Tens of thousands of people are employed," he noted. "And they get good money, as much as a thousand pesos a month. When I'm done with this job I'm going to start farming myself—my pay will double." On average, Páez said, each square meter of urban farm produces five kilograms of food a year. That's a lot. (And they're not just growing cabbage and spinach; each farm also seems to have at least one row of spearmint, an essential ingredient for the *mojito*.)

The elephant in the room, of course, is Cuba's political system. Human Rights Watch notes in its most recent report that the government "restricts nearly all avenues of political dissent" and "severely curtails basic rights to free expression," among other unsavory habits. It's as if you went to Whole Foods and noticed a guy over by the soy milk holding a truncheon. Cuba has been headed by the same guy for more than forty-five years (and he seems intent on replacing himself with his brother). The nature of that system, and that guy, had something to do with the way the country responded to its crisis in the 1990s.

For one thing, Castro's Cuba was so rigidly (and unproductively) socialist that just slightly loosening the screws on free enterprise liberated all kinds of pent-up energy. Philip Peters, a Cuba analyst at the conservative Lexington Institute, has documented how the country redistributed as much as two-thirds of state lands to cooperatives and individual farmers and, as with the *organopónico* in Alamar, let them sell their surplus above a certain quota. There's no obvious name for this system, though it's a little like sharecropping. "It's not reform like you've seen in China, where they're devolving a lot of economic decision making out to the private sector," Peters said. "Cuba's made a decision to graft some market mechanisms onto what remains a fairly statist model. It could work better. But it has worked."

Castro, as even his fiercest opponents would admit, has almost from the day he took power spent lavishly on the country's educational system. Cuba's ratio of teachers to students is akin to Sweden's; people who want to go to college go to college. Which turns out to be important, because farming, especially organic farming, is no simple task. You don't just tear down the fence around the vacant lot and hand someone a hoe, quoting him some Maoist couplet about the inevitable victory of the worker. The soil's no good at first; the bugs can't wait to attack. You need information to make a go of it. Cuba's semi-organic agriculture is at least as much an invention of science and technology as the high-input tractor farming it replaced.

One afternoon, near an *organopónico* in central Havana, I knocked on the door of a small two-room office, the local Center for Reproduction of Entomophages and Entomopathogens. There are 280 such offices spread around the country, each manned by one or two agronomists. Here, Jorge Padrón, a heavyset and earnest fellow, was working with an ancient Soviet refrigerator and autoclave (the writing on the gauges was in Cyrillic) and perhaps three hundred glass beakers with cotton gauze stoppers. Farmers and backyard gardeners from around the district would bring him sick plants, and he'd look at them under the microscope and tell the grower what to do. Perhaps he'd hand over a test tube full of a *Trichoderma* fungus, which he'd grown on a medium of residue from sugar-cane processing, and tell his questioner to germinate the seed in a dilute solution; maybe he'd pull a vial of some bacterium—*Verticillium lecanii* or *Beauveria bassiana*—from a rusty coffee can. "It is easier to use chemicals. You see some trouble in your tomatoes, and chemicals take care of it right away," he said. Over the long run, though, thinking about the whole system yields real benefits. "Our work is really about preparing the fields so plants will be stronger. But it works." It's the green revolution in reverse.

THE POINT IS NOT THAT WE NEED TO BE CUBA. UNLESS THE VERY worst fantasies of the peak-oil researchers come true, we won't see our lives change overnight as lives in Cuba did. But could we head in that direction gradually, if we wanted to? This is the crucial question. Is there really a wealth of possibilities in our communities, or are we irrevocably tied to our global system, come what may?

One place to answer that question is a few hundred acres of floodplain alongside the Winooski River a mile and a half from the center of Burlington, Vermont's largest city. The Intervale, as it's called, is a gritty spot, literally on the other side of the tracks, and next to the city's electric power plant. For many years it served as the town's dump. "When I got here in 1980," recalls Will Rapp, "the garbage was still four or five feet high all around. There were junked cars everywhere, seepage from the sewage plant." Rapp went on to found the successful catalogue company Gardener's Supply, and he located his headquarters and showroom at the entrance to the Intervale. But he also did something even more important: he helped to form a nonprofit foundation that leased about two hundred acres of the surrounding bottomland and in turn began renting it to people who wanted to get started in farming. It was a kind of agricultural laboratory.

Remember, this is small. Two hundred acres, or about 1/1,000th the size of what one U.S. undersecretary of agriculture thinks constitutes a proper farm for a single manager to operate. To walk through the Intervale, however, is to sense a very different possible future for American agriculture. I was with a man named Buzz Ferver and a woman named Kit Perkins, who run the nonprofit trust that administers the land. It was a calendar-perfect late August morning after the first cool night of the fall—the temperature had dropped to 38 degrees, a gentle reminder that the growing season was coming to an end. We walked first through the woods, a boundary of forest along the river, full of big cottonwoods and wild cucumber, with a bike path that connected back to the center of town. But soon we came upon a more industrial scene: the Intervale compost operation, which helps underwrite the project. Trucks rumbled in and out, bringing horse manure bedded with sawdust, dairy waste, chicken manure, all the leaves and light yard waste from the surrounding county, and everything left over from making Ben & Jerry's ice cream. Bulldozers pushed the waste around, and machines sifted the compost through screens. Most of the compost is sold to other farmers by the truckload, or to home gardeners by the plastic bag, but quite a bit stays on site, helping to make the two hundred acres of farmland fantastically fertile.

We wandered through the fields of the biggest operation, the Intervale Community Farm, a CSA to which 450 member families pay a few hundred dollars up front every winter, in return for which they show up once a week to claim their share of the produce. Some pay a little less in exchange for working on the farm; today, a crew of eight was pulling weeds in the rows of onions that would be harvested late in the fall. Because the farm is organic, there's no getting around the weeds that need pulling (in fact, one of the farmers said, they'd lost control of a couple of long rows of no-till squash they'd planted as an experiment—you could barely see the butternuts ripening amid the green tangle). But everything was coming in on schedule, row after row of lovely carrots and parsnips and beets. A tape loop of predator calls was playing on a boombox to chase away the birds; a tractor chugged by, hauling a wagonload of watermelons and another picking crew sprawled on top of them. A couple of mobile chicken coops from the Lazy Ladies Egg Farm had been parked nearby, and their occupants were out happily pecking insects.

A few fields away, Spencer Blackwell was growing grain. "This valley used to be the breadbasket of America," he said, "but the varieties that do well here have kind of been lost." He's bringing them back—planting, among other things, barley for one of the burgeoning number of area breweries. Across a drainage ditch lies his field of black beans. "I let the frost kill them—they dry on the vine," he said. This year, on two acres, he's raised about a ton and a half, which net him 89 cents a pound and provides the filling for a year's worth of burritos at the town's most popular breakfast spot. He's been farming on the Intervale for five years, taking advantage of the shared equipment, such as tractors and greenhouses. But it's not just the infrastructure. Instead of isolation, the fate of most modern farmers stranded in their giant acreage, there's the accumulated know-how of his neighbors to draw on.

Like David Zuckerman, whose Full Moon Farm is just through a narrow border of trees. Zuckerman looks pretty much what you'd expect a Vermont organic farmer to look like: ponytail, baseball cap, grin. But there's nothing scruffy about the well-maintained field he cultivates with his wife, Rachel Nevitt. His operation is a CSA, too, with 150 members who take about half his produce. Another 30 percent goes to the booming Burlington farmers' market. When he's not in the fields, Zuckerman is a member of the Vermont legislature—in fact, he's the chair of the House Agriculture Committee, which makes him the second most important farm policy guy in the state. The future may be out here in this field.

The Intervale offers two bottom lines that demonstrate the real possibilities for changing the food economy. First, these two hundred acres supply *7 or 8 percent of all the fresh food consumed in Burlington.* They grow five hundred thousand pounds of salable produce, not to mention another fifty thousand pounds gleaned for local food banks. The Intervale is not some tiny pilot project, some demonstration plot. It's large enough to give you an intuitive sense of scale, a visceral idea of how much land it would take to begin feeding ourselves locally—if, of course, we changed our models. The Intervale employs about fifty people at a time; whether that's a good thing or a bad one depends entirely on how you think about the economy. But at least it indicates that Jules Pretty is right: you can grow tons of food with low-input techniques as long as you're hardworking, careful, and clever. "If Vermont were cut off from the rest of the world tomorrow, I think we could be feeding ourselves by the end of a single growing season," says Zuckerman.

Second, there are plenty of people who want to farm, if we can figure out how to make it happen. The Intervale lets novices overcome the biggest obstacles—high land prices around urban areas, lack of expertise in both growing and marketing, initial access to costly equipment. "There's an incredible resurgence of people in a directionless society suddenly wanting to find their roots," says Zuckerman. "There's real satisfaction in producing your own food." In fact, says Kit Perkins, the Intervale is not only overwhelmed with people who'd like to lease its plots, it's also had to set up a small consulting service to handle inquiries from communities around the world that are looking to start their own incubator farms. "Two hundred years ago in America, farming was glorified," adds Ferver. "That eroded to the place where farmers were forced into a marginal mindset. But here we've been able to build some respect for farmers. There's a whole lot of pizzazz."

■ ■ ■

THE INTERVALE MAY BE AN EXPERIMENT, BUT IT'S NOT A BIZARRE exception. Over the last decade, just as most of American agriculture has entered the final throes of consolidation—as Idaho has seen the number of potato farms shrink to eight hundred, as a million hogs have moved onto a single Utah farm, as subsidies and political favors have made the massive agribusiness giants ever more powerful—a reaction has begun, still fairly small but growing fast.

Take farmers' markets as an example. In September 1972, eleven sellers set up shop in Madison, Wisconsin, one Saturday morning. Three decades later, consider the spectacle that unfolds each weekend on the blocks around the state capital. According to the *New York Times* reporter R. W. Apple, twenty thousand shoppers in a slow counterclockwise drift "from stall to colorful stall, from tomatoes to bison to apples to cheese, in an almost uninterrupted river of humanity, towing wagons, pushing baby carriages, and lugging bulging canvas or paper bags." Swaths of Wisconsin countryside have been reshaped by the economic opportunity the market presents.[66] The United States had 340 farmers' markets in 1970, 1,700 in 1994, and almost doubled to 3,100 by 2002. Two years later, the number was *3,700.* Tens of thousands of farmers sell their produce at these markets, and when they do, they get to keep all the money, not the 8 or 10 percent they'd take in by selling through the industrialized food system.[67] Upscale chefs throng the Greenmarket in New York City's Union Square, but there are thirty-three other farmers' markets spread around the city, many of them in housing projects.

Community-supported agriculture farms, like the ones I visited at the Intervale, have grown with similar speed: the first American CSA was founded in Massachusetts in 1985; now there are more than fifteen hundred. And once you start looking, new farms are everywhere. In rural areas, the number of old-style farms continues to dwindle, but the total number of farms has stabilized, thanks to new small growers. Vermont's most urban county, for instance, saw 19 percent more farms in 2005, even as traditional dairies continued to fail. For every dairy, there are now two farms producing something else.[68]

A few of these operations are really over the top—in Woodstock, which is quaint Vermont squared, a farmer raises fifty Asian water buffalo, each with its own heated waterbed, the better to produce high-quality mozzarella. But most of the new farmers are as gritty as you could want. On every continent, as Brian Halweil points out, "people are farming the cities." Urban areas worldwide already produce about a third of the food they consume, though the growers get little attention from politicians and planners, who tend to view urban farms as anachronisms. In Shanghai—the city with the world's fastest train, the tallest hotel, the biggest TV screen—60 percent of the vegetables and 90 percent of the milk and eggs come from urban farms. A recent study estimated that even London could grow a fifth of the fruit and vegetables its ten million residents consume on just the 10 percent of farmland left among its sprawl.[69] Seventy-five years ago, New York City covered just as many acres as it does now, but it got most of its food from the surrounding region. That's why New Jersey was called the Garden State. You may think all that land has turned into refineries and suburbs, but you'd be wrong. A satellite map of upstate New York, say, shows vast tracts of abandoned farmland growing back into patchy forest.

Say you're a dreamer. Imagine the most ruined city in America. That would be Detroit, which has lost half its population in the last few decades. A million people have moved away; as much as a third of the city's 139 square miles consists of empty lots and dilapidated buildings, "an urban core giving way to an urban prairie," in the words of the *New York Times*. But slowly, some of that land is coming under cultivation: forty community gardens and microfarms, some covering entire city blocks, have sprung up in recent years. A farmer named Paul Weertz farms ten acres spread over seven lots, producing hay, alfalfa, honey, eggs, goats' milk, even beef cattle. His tractor barn is an old garage. In 2000, a group of architects, urban planners, and local activists convened by the University of Detroit spent six months coming up with an ambitious plan for expanding such farms, connecting four and a half square miles of the city's east side into a self-sustaining village "complete with farms, greenhouses, grazing land, a dairy, and a cannery."[70] "When you first look at this, people say it's wild and crazy," says the dean of the local architecture school. "But when you look at it closer, it's not so wild and crazy after all. What we are talking about doing are all very pragmatic things."[71]

Local food economies seem to pick up momentum almost automatically as, instead of being competitors, other farmers become allies who help spread the word. In Oregon, when older farmers found themselves "beaten down on the price" in global commodity markets, they started turning to metro Portland instead. "We were going broke, and that's about the nicest thing you can say about it," a rancher told the *Willamette Week* reporter Zach Dundas. The farmers started a cattle co-op that now sells nine hundred head of beef a week, some of it to Whole Foods and some of it in the local farmers' markets. Each family in the co-op has to go into the big city at least once a year to work the market—an eye-opening trip for ranchers who "in some cases have never seen a working parking meter before, let alone a practicing homosexual. . . . 'I was talking to these four women about the meat, and pretty soon I noticed they all had beards,' said one farmer. 'It's different than what we're usually exposed to.'" Meanwhile, new farmers are being born on one small farm after another. At Sauvie Island Organics, for instance, just north of the city, sixty young people apply each spring for three internship positions. "The CSA operations are really the new American farmer," said one former apprentice, now managing a six-acre farm blocks from a strip club in the southeast corner of the city. What does it all add up to? In 1974, Oregon had 13,384 full-time farmers. In

2002, the last time the USDA counted, that number had grown to 21,580.[72] And it could easily grow larger still. At the moment, four-fifths of America's fruit, two-thirds of its vegetables, and half its milk are raised in "metropolitan counties or fast-growing adjacent counties."[73] Under present arrangements, of course, almost all of that food enters the commodity stream, being trucked or flown off to some distant corner of the country or the world. But the numbers demonstrate that there are both fields and farmers close to where almost all of us live. It's not bizarre to imagine those farmers and those fields starting to produce what their neighbors need.

Colleges and universities are an obvious market, since they offer a captive population, and one likely to be receptive to the environmental and community impulses behind local food. At least two hundred universities have made serious commitments to local food. Some are where you might expect it: the University of Portland, for instance, spends 40 percent of its food dollars in Oregon, and Middlebury College buys a third of its food from the surrounding Champlain Valley (including a small but growing supply from the student farm-garden located outside the front door of the college's science center). The change isn't easy. A dining hall operator is used to picking up the phone and ordering trailerloads of food from some giant like Sysco; it takes a lot of patience to deal with pickups pulling up at the loading dock, and it takes more work to deal with onions that arrive round, not pre-cut. But the pressure is mounting. Sodexho, another food-service monster, lost its contract at the University of California at Santa Cruz after a student campaign in favor of local foods, a campaign that has since spread to all the UC campuses.[74]

And when it works, it really works. A few years ago, Fanny Singer matriculated at Yale. Her mother, Alice Waters, arrived for parents weekend that first fall and decided that she didn't want her daughter eating what the cafeteria served. And since Alice Waters is the chef who helped launch the local foods movement through her Chez Panisse restaurant in the Bay Area, she knew what needed to be done. Yale gave her the Berkeley College dining hall, one of thirteen on campus, to experiment with; she raised the money to convert it to an entirely seasonal and local menu. Such a change wasn't easy: the cooks were used to thawing, not cooking; the dining hall administration worried that students really wouldn't give up their hot dogs and fries. "I told them not to worry, that I'd served a lot of dinners," said Waters—and it turned out she was right. The year the program launched, lines started forming around the building as students from other Yale colleges tried to get in. They wanted the squash gratin and the beet slaw, and they didn't seem to mind that lettuce and tomato disappeared from the salad bar in October, which is when they also disappear from the fields of Connecticut. Soon students were counterfeiting Berkeley ID cards in an attempt to get some butter-braised root vegetables of their own—and when Yale hosted a conference about the project, two hundred campus food service personnel from around the country showed up to learn.[75] What impressed me most was the pride that the cooks took in their work. Most were from New Haven, which has one of the country's poorest inner cities, but they were now firmly connected to the seasons of life in the countryside around them. Their work was harder, but it clearly meant more.

It's harder to pull off the same trick in elementary and high schools. Even in rural areas, where the farm may be just down the road, public school cafeterias have long been the dumping ground for "surplus" commodity food—meaning the beef and cheese the industrial farming system couldn't unload somewhere else. (This explains the unvarying Sloppy Joe monotony of lunch lines across the country.) Many financially strapped schools have turned over their cafeterias to fast-food outlets in recent years, but that may be starting to change. New York City, which has the biggest school district in the country and a population one-eighth of whom suffer from diabetes, has banned soda machines in the hallways and asked Ann Cooper, a stalwart of the local food movement, to "reprocess" fourteen of its top recipes to include more food from the region.[76]

Other forces are starting to help, too. For years, local land trusts and nature conservancies have been among the country's most effective environmentalists, raising piles of money to protect open spaces from development. For years they picked sites based on aesthetics (a lovely view) or biology (a rare orchid). Recently, though, more and more land trusts have begun to concentrate on keeping cropland in production, connecting young farmers without the money to buy expensive land with farms whose development rights have already been paid for and thus enabling those farmers to make a living growing food. In Montana, the Clark Fork Coalition, which had spent years helping restore a river polluted by abandoned mines, changed focus recently to start an open-air meat market in downtown Missoula. They want to help ranchers move away from low-margin commodity beef and keep more of the food dollar; if that happens, the environmentalists reason, there's less chance they'll sell their ranches to vacation-home developers.[77] Projects like these can start to add up.

BUT THEY COULD ADD UP A LOT FASTER, IF THEY DIDN'T HAVE to depend on the students in the environmental studies class pestering the dining hall manager. Imagine, instead, that the federal government shifts some small percentage of America's vast farm subsidy budget away from corporate farming. At the moment, subsidies essentially underwrite consolidation: almost a third of all federal farm payments go to the largest 2 percent of farms, and almost three-quarters of the payments go to farms that are among the top 10 percent in size.[78] It's all politics—the farm program subsidizes those crops that are geographically concentrated in a few states, and hence, in essence, have their own senators: wheat, corn, cotton, soybean, and rice growers get virtually all the federal subsidy payments.[79] There is no butternut squash subsidy, no apple subsidy.

And since big farmers quickly figured out that there was more money to be made "farming the program," the nation's croplands soon reflected the politics of subsidies just as much as the reverse: Elizabeth Becker, for instance, describes in the *New York Times* the town of Denison, Iowa, where "crops that do not qualify for a subsidy are as rare as buffalo herds. . . . Orchards have been plowed under for corn. Truck gardens are a thing of the past." Where once there grew potatoes and cherries, peaches and pears, "commercial crops are down to four: feed corn, soybeans, hay, and oats. Denison has a hard time filling a farmers' market one afternoon a week."[80] The real beneficiaries, of course, are less the giant farmers than the gargantuan food processors that they deliver the ingredients to. Ever wonder why soybean products can be found in two-thirds of all processed food? It may have something to do with the fact that "about seventy percent of the value of the American soy bean comes straight from the U.S. government."[81] Ditto for high-fructose corn syrup. Essentially, we are subsidizing Cheetos.

Imagine eliminating those subsidies altogether, so you weren't tilting the playing field. Or imagine tilting it toward small, local producers, rewarding those whose farms didn't use much energy, that grew food for their neighbors. (That's one reason why people take vacations in France and Italy that consist essentially of looking at small farming villages and eating the bounty they produce.) In a few districts of England, town planners have subsidized local schools and hotels so that they'll purchase more local food; after several years, the average age of a farmer in those townships had dropped to thirty-two—the average British farmer is almost fifty-five—"and the farms are among the most profitable in the nation."[82]

Imagine, too, what might happen if the agriculture departments of the land-grant colleges, which function now as extensions of the big agrochemical companies that provide much of their funding, instead worked on local marketing schemes and low-input farming. Our scientists are as bright as the Cubans'; were their energies similarly directed, this transition would become much easier.

Easier, not easy. It will take tremendous work, and many setbacks, to remake American agriculture. One of my favorite local food projects was a café in the gritty Vermont town of Barre that bought all its ingredients locally. The Farmers Diner served ham and eggs, French fries, milkshakes, and hamburgers—and it closed its doors after a few years of trying to serve them at pretty much the same price as the guy down the road who just called up Sysco when he needed more food. Now the owner, Tod Murphy, is trying again, with a new location thirty miles to the south, in a town with more tourists. Making a go of the diner would have been a lot easier if the state still had an agricultural infrastructure, but the governor slashed $200,000 from the budget that would have helped start a new in-state slaughterhouse. He was too busy subsidizing what's left of the state's commodity dairy trade.

Sometimes the enemy is too much success. Small farmers spent twenty years spreading the idea of "organic" food. They were persuasive: by the turn of the century, sales were growing 20 percent a year. Which was enough to attract the attention of the big growers, who quickly took over the business: as of 2006, the biggest organic growers are companies like General Mills and Heinz and ConAgra.[83] It's true, one assumes, that they don't spray their "organic" lettuce with pesticides, though it's also true that they keep lobbying the government to "relax" organic standards to allow more "flexibility." But in every other respect they resemble every other agribusiness grower. Stonyfield Farm buys organic milk powder for its yogurt in New Zealand. "Once you're in organic you have to source globally," says Gary Hirshberg, the company's founder.[84] Burkhard Bilger of the *New Yorker* recently traveled to California's Central Valley to watch the organic tycoon Todd Koons grow mâche lettuce. Having leveled his vast fields with GPS and laser equipment, Koons has modified special harvesters to cut his crop. "It's a brave new world over here," he says. "The machines are bigger, we drive 'em faster, and we drive 'em larger." The mâche is packed in individual bags, designed with ten layers of plastic. "As the lettuce sits on the shelf, the gases in the bag are constantly consumed, released, and replaced. Oxygen, nitrogen, and carbon dioxide molecules bond with the polymers on one side of the plastic and are released on the other. Every type of salad requires a different type of bag, tailored to its respiration by gas chromatography and computer analysis."[85] But hey, it's organic.

Local bakers were making a comeback, too, until supermarkets figured out how to make vast quantities of dough in some central plant, freeze it for months, and then "bake" it fresh at their branches. They created, in the words of one food writer, "artisanal bread without the artisan," driving bakeries out of business in many towns.[86]

"Local" will be harder to co-opt, because Del Monte and its ilk simply can't grow different food in every market; if they tried, their economies of scale would disappear. "Local" steps far enough outside current conventional economics to represent a real challenge.

The deepest problem that local-food efforts face, however, is that we've gotten used to paying so little for food. It may be expensive in terms of how much oil it requires, and how much greenhouse gas it pours into the atmosphere, and how much tax subsidy it receives, and how much damage it does to local communities, and how many migrant workers it maims, and how much sewage it piles up, and how many miles of highway it requires—but boy, when you pull your cart up to the register, it's pretty cheap. In the 1930s a family might have spent a third of its income on food; middle-class Americans now spend more like a tenth. Even in Italy, one recent study found residents spending more on cell-phone service than on food shopping.[87] And food is cheap not just in terms of money, but time. Mostly we eat processed food; cooking is something that happens on the Food Network. In fact, fresh-food sales fall every year; per capita consumption of eggs, milk, fresh vegetables, and wheat flour was far higher in 1950 than a generation later.[88] Our food is cheap, and fast, and easy.

The problem is what that cheap, fast, easy food doesn't deliver. We get all the calories we need (and more that we don't), but our money doesn't bring us much in the way of satisfaction, precisely the commodity high-powered ever-growing modern economies have done so little to provide. Where food is concerned, one way to think about satisfaction is in terms of taste. Consider how you feel after a cross-country trip—a little tired and limp and wan. Well, that's how the lettuce feels. Eighty percent of our tomatoes are harvested and shipped green, and then artificially ripened upon arrival at their retail outpost. Yum![89] A chicken that has never stood up in its entire short life won't taste like much, nor will a salmon reared in a cramped pen and fed food coloring to turn it pink. The supermarket crammed with its thousands of brightly packaged offerings is a mirage: if you could wave a wand and break everything down into its constituent ingredients, a pool of high-fructose corn syrup would fill half the store. Real food really does taste better; that's why, say, the Slow Food movement, which started in Italy and spread around the world, has grown so rapidly.

The idea that better-tasting food is a yuppie indulgence, however, is simply wrong. A recent survey of organic food buyers found Asians, Native Americans, Hispanics, and African Americans to be more likely than Caucasians to seek out organic food.[90] When the *Los Angeles Times* set out to survey farmers' markets across the city, they found that some of the busiest served ethnic communities and that at some markets payment was accepted in food stamps as well as in cash. If strong local food networks developed further, then prices would keep coming down as middlemen were eliminated. When I buy my neighbor Ben Gleason's grain to make a loaf of bread, I pay barely more than I do for the regular flour in the next bin, but he gets almost all of the money. If you buy a loaf of supermarket bread instead, the farmer gets 6 cents of each $1 you spend.[91] If you pay $1.57 for a head of red-leaf lettuce in the store, chances are the farmer got about 19 cents of that—a 726 percent markup.[92] CSAs deliver vegetables at something like half the price supermarkets charge. There's lots of margin that should make it possible for local food to work for everyone.

But there will always be a cost in terms of time, of effort. No food system will ever require less participation than our present one, not unless Jetsons-style food pills actually hit the shelves. If you belong to a CSA, you have to go to the farm and pick up the box of vegetables—and then you have to do something with twenty pounds of produce, some of it unfamiliar. When I spent the winter buying locally, dinner took more time. I had to get to the farmers' market, or sometimes to the farm; I had to cook soup and make bread—neither of which is very hard, but both of which are now skills that many people either don't possess or don't use. And sometimes we got a little tired of eating the same things. By February, our eleven-year-old daughter was using the words "icky" and "disgusting" fairly regularly, always in connection with root vegetables. Not potatoes, not carrots, but turnips, parsnips, rutabaga. It is a little hard to imagine how people got through winter on the contents of their root cellars alone.

Which is why I was glad for the Ziplocs full of raspberries and blueberries my wife had frozen in the summer, and even gladder for the high-tech apple warehouse just down the road in Shoreham. Here's the thing about apples: the best ones rot pretty fast. The great apples of the Northeast, your Cortlands, your Empires, your Northern Spy, above all, your Macintosh, are soft, ephemeral. That crisp bite that sprays your tonsils with juice soon turns to mealy mush. For generations, people solved that problem by converting them into cider—hard cider, for freezerless storage. (That's what most of the myriad apple orchards around New England were planted for.) But there's another solution if, like my neighbor Barney Hodges, you have a storage shed where you can pump in nitrogen. "We push the oxygen level down from its normal 20 percent to just under 3 percent. The apple's respiration is slowed down to the point where the ripening process is nearly halted," he explains. Every few weeks he cracks open another room in the warehouse, and it's as if you're back in September—the apples in his Sunrise Orchard bags head out to local supermarkets, where he frets that they won't be kept cool. Here's the take-home message: local farming can be as technologically inventive as industrial agriculture. Maybe more so, since it relies less on the brute force of petroleum. And also this: if you get your hands on nice apples, don't leave them in a pretty ceramic bowl on the counter. Put them in the refrigerator!

February. By now, pleasant routine is setting in: eggs in the morning, soup and a cheese sandwich for lunch. And for dinner, some neighbor that until quite recently was clucking, mooing, baaing, or otherwise signaling its pleasure at the local grass and hay that it was turning into protein. Also potatoes. And something from the freezer—it's a chest-type, and in a dark corner, so you basically just stick a hand in and see what vegetable comes out.

And oh, did I mention beer? Otter Creek Brewing, a quarter mile down the road from my daughter's school, makes a stellar witbier, a Belgian style, naturally cloudy, with raw organic wheat from Ben Gleason's farm. It's normally sold in the summer, but I've hoarded some for my winter drinking. "We'd love to use local barley for the rest of our beers," says Morgan Wolaver, the brewery's owner. But someone would have to build a malting plant to serve not just Otter Creek but the state's seven other microbreweries. Perhaps right next to the oat mill . . .

March. I can see spring in the distance. There's still feet of snow in the woods, but the sun is September strong, and it won't be long till down in the valley someone is planting lettuce. There's so much that I've eaten and not described: the venison burgers at the local bar, the Cryovac'ed Lake Champlain perch sold at Ned's Bait and Tackle (though you should eat it only once a month if you're of childbearing age).

But there's one place I must describe, both because it's provided many of my calories and because it embodies the idea of a small-scale farmer making a decent living growing great food. Jack and Anne Lazor bought Butterworks Farm in Vermont's Northeast Kingdom in the midseventies, after a stint of working at Old Sturbridge Farm in Massachusetts. There they dressed in colonial costumes and milked cows by hand and talked to the tourists. But, as they eventually figured out, they weren't actors; they were real farmers. Slowly they've developed one of the state's premier dairies: their organic yogurt is nearly a million-dollar business, expanding steadily year after year after year; I've been living off their dried beans, too, and their cornmeal. It's great fun to sit in their kitchen eating bacon and eggs while Anne mixes up some salve for the teats of her cows and the Lazors describe their life. The talk's a mix of technical detail (they milk Jerseys, not the more common Holsteins, which means less milk but higher protein, so their yogurt needs no pectin to stay firm) and rural philosophy. "We have such a 'take' mentality," Jack says. "It's part of our psyche, because we came to this verdant land as Europeans and were able to exploit it for so long."

But here the exploitation feels more like collaboration. We stroll over to his solar barn, where the forty cows in the herd loiter patiently, mulling over the events of the day. "That's Morel, that's Phooey, that's Vetch, that's Clover, that's Jewel . . ." The vet wanders in, to report that he's figured out what's wrong with Emily: milk fever, easily treated. ("Since this place is organic, everything in my truck is pretty useless," he says. "All my antibiotics, I just leave them behind. The weird thing is, though, with the bigger industrial dairies, where I can use all my medicines, I'm visiting them three times a week. Here it's once a month.") It's very calm in here, no sound but cud being chewed, and it's warm out of the late-winter wind. Jack, who's a talker, is explaining how Vermont could market itself as "the natural state," and how he's hoping to market *masa harina* for making tortillas next year, and so forth. I'm sort of listening, and mostly just absorbing the sheer pleasure of the scene—that this place works, that I've been connected to it all winter long, that it will be here, with any luck, for the rest of my life.

Eating this way has come at a cost. Not in health or in money (if anything, I've spent less than usual, since I haven't bought a speck of processed food) but in time. I've had to think about every meal, instead of wandering through the world on autopilot, ingesting random calories. I've had to pay attention. But the payoff for that cost has been immense, a web of connections I'd never known about. I've gotten to eat with my brain as well as my tongue: every meal comes with a story. The geography of the valley now means something much more real to me; I've met dozens of people I wouldn't otherwise have known. Yes, in the wake of my experiment I'm back to oranges and Alaska salmon and the odd pint of Guinness Stout. But the winter permanently altered the way I eat. In more ways than one, it left a good taste in my mouth.

That good taste was *satisfaction*. The time I spent getting the food and preparing it was not, in the end, a cost at all. In the end it was a benefit, *the* benefit. In my role as eater, I was part of something larger than myself that made sense to me— a community. I felt grounded, connected.

It is to such questions of identity that we must now turn.

3 | ALL FOR ONE, OR ONE FOR ALL

The story of the last five hundred years is the story of continual emancipation. The people of the modern world have freed themselves from innumerable oppressions: absolute monarchy, feudalism, serfdom, slavery. Five hundred years ago, if you were a European, you most likely rested in the bosom of the church, as a small part of the Great Chain of Being that was medieval Christendom. You were born in a village, and there you would likely spend the rest of your life; the world outside was unsafe, the lair of bandits and wild animals. "In the medieval era," the historian Georges Duby has observed, "solitary wandering was a symptom of insanity. No one would run such a risk who was not deviant or mad."[1] Your spouse would come from a small pool of eligible partners, and once married you would in all likelihood stay that way. You inherited your profession from your parents and passed it down to your children.

Many factors dissolved this ordered world. Most notably, the new religious idea of the Protestant movement—that each of us was responsible for his or her own salvation—began to erode the old idea of the one true church. The work begun by the Reformation was finished by fossil fuel, which freed farmers from the land, liberated us from days of manual labor, and granted us a mobility that expanded human horizons. People *moved*. And they communicated across distances as the telegraph and telephone and radio and television and the Web snatched ideas out of thin air and delivered them to every home. As Marx and Engels put it in their classic summary: "All fixed, fast-frozen relations, with their train of ancient and venerable prejudices and opinions, are swept away; all new-formed ones become antiquated before they can ossify. All that is solid melts into air."[2]

All of these liberations have brought benefit, often great benefit: they have helped produce the ideas we hold dearest, such as democracy; they helped spur the civil rights and women's revolutions; and they have made us much, much richer. But most of them also carried costs, sometimes harder for us to see. We surrendered a fixed identity—a community, an extended family, deep and comforting roots—for, quite literally, the chance to "make something of ourselves." Now we create our own identities. We build from scratch the things our ancestors once took for granted. This liberation is exhilarating, and it is daunting; it is exciting, and it is lonely.

"Making something of yourself" is, more than anything else, an economic task. Adam Smith, describing the invisible hand of the market, could not have been more explicit: free economies worked as if guided by a higher power, a replacement for the authority that had ordered medieval life. The interests of each of our own individual selves added up to social good—to longer lives, fuller tables, warmer houses. *The community was no longer necessary to provide these things*; they would appear as if by magic. And they did appear.

In recent decades, however, this process of liberation seems to me to have come close to running its course. What ties are left to cut? We change religions, spouses, towns, professions with ease. Our affluence isolates us ever more. We are not just individualists; we are hyper-individualists such as the world has never known.

Consider, for instance, how suburbanization changed us. By

the 1990s, observes the journalist James Howard Kunstler, "the dirty secret of the American economy was that it was no longer about anything except the creation of suburban sprawl and the furnishing, accessorizing, and financing of it."[3] Does that sound like an exaggeration? The statistics are even more stark: according to the U.S. Census Bureau, the average density of cities, suburbs, and towns in 1920 was about 10 persons per acre; by 1990, it had dropped to 4 persons per acre, even as the U.S. population doubled. The average new house has doubled in size since 1970, even as the number of people living in it has steadily shrunk, and the average density of the most recent housing developments in America is only two people per acre. "We did this," explains the writer Jeremy Rifkin, "by occupying eight times more developed land than we did more than eighty years ago."[4]

Simple mathematics tells you that such changes lower your chances of bumping into the other inhabitants of your neighborhood—or, indeed, of your own home: builders are now consciously designing houses to make sure people stay to themselves. As the *Wall Street Journal* reported recently, "Major builders and top architects are walling off space. They're touting one-person 'Internet alcoves,' locked-door 'away rooms,' and his-and-her offices on opposite ends of the house. The new floor plans offer so much seclusion, they're 'good for the dysfunctional family,' " says Gopal Ahluwalia, director of research for the National Association of Home Builders. Indeed, at the industry's annual Las Vegas trade show, the "showcase 'Ultimate Family Home' hardly had a family room." Instead, the boy's personal playroom had its own forty-two-inch plasma TV, and the girl's bedroom had a secret mirrored door leading to a "hideaway karaoke room." "We call this the ultimate home for families who don't want anything to do with one another," says Mike McGee, chief executive of Pardee Homes of Los Angeles, builder of the model.[5]

This transition from individualism to hyper-individualism has also been felt in the political arena. In 1987, the British prime minister Margaret Thatcher announced, "There is no such thing as 'society.' There are just individuals and their families."[6] Talk about everything solid melting into air! Adam Smith himself would have been taken aback. But across much of the rich world we have decided, again quoting Thatcher, that "there is no alternative." Our liberal politicians dismantle welfare programs; our conservative politicians cut taxes as if taxation were an obvious affront. The "public realm"—things like parks and schools and Social Security, the remainders of the ordered communities from which we came—is under steady and increasing attack. Instead of health insurance, Americans are offered "health savings accounts" so that they can "take care of themselves."

This ideological change has sunk deep in almost every realm. Take Christianity, the faith that upward of 85 percent of Americans (including me) profess. An evangelical pollster, George Barna, recently asked a sampling of Christians a list of questions, the answers to some of which demonstrated a fairly pervasive biblical illiteracy (only 40 percent of respondents could conjure up any five of the Ten Commandments. A scant half of Americans can name any of the four Gospels. Twelve percent of Americans are confident that Joan of Arc was Noah's wife.) But more interesting was this finding: 75 percent of American Christians think the saying "God helps those who help themselves" can be found in the Bible. The sentiment is actually from that paragon of individualist vigor Benjamin Franklin, and the Bible of course says pretty much the opposite. Every time Jesus tries to sum up his message, he falls back on the formula "Love your God, and love your neighbor as yourself." That is, he posits a life built *around others*.

But that life is hard for us to imagine. We're more at home now in the kind of scene a reporter found at one booming mega-church outside Phoenix: a drive-through latte stand, Krispy Kreme doughnuts at every service, and sermons about " 'successful disciplines for living'—how to control your children, how to reach your professional goals, how to invest your money, how to reduce your debt." (On Sundays, arriving children were handed X-boxes to play with by themselves.) Or consider a recent week's listing of Christian best-sellers. For every challenging text like Rick Warren's *The Purpose Driven Life*, there were two like *Your Best Life Now* by Joel Osteen, the pastor of America's mega-est church, which recently bought a sixteen-thousand-seat basketball arena in Houston for its services. As one marketing expert explained, "He's not in the soul business—he's in the self business."[7]

It may be true that "God helps those who help themselves," both financially and emotionally. (Certainly fortune does.) But, from a Christian perspective, Franklin's statement is at best a subsidiary, secondary truth. And this strain of belief matters mightily, because it's one reason that so many Christians have backed the harsh economic policies of recent administrations. This is the scripture that begins with Adam Smith, not Adam.

And if politicians and clergymen have drunk deeply of it, orthodox economists have all but drowned. They are "forced to ignore the possibility that irrationality, prejudice, love, community solidarity, idealism, upbringing, and even enlightened self-interest might help explain the way people behave," writes the English critic Richard Douthwaite, "because if they abandoned their twin simplifying assumptions of rationality and pure self-interest . . . the world would remain so complicated that they would not be able to say anything about it." Indeed, there's suggestive evidence that economists are self-selected by this very exaltation of individualism. Consider Douthwaite's description of an experiment carried out at Cornell University: first-year graduate students from many different disciplines were given a sum of money and asked to divide it between two accounts, one "private" and the other "public." They were told that they'd be able to keep the money in their private accounts at the end of the experiment, but that money in the public account would be pooled, its total increased by a certain percentage, and then divided out equally among all participants. For the group as a whole, it was obviously best if everyone put all their money in the public account—this would create the maximum sum to be increased by the bonus percentage, and everyone would prosper. For the individual, though, the best course was to put all the money in one's own account and then take a share of the pool provided by the suckers. When the results were analyzed, economics students had contributed, on average, only a fifth of their money to the public account, while other students had put in half.[8]

Yet the message that we've passed some negative crucial threshold seems to be taking hold even among economists. Eminent figures within the profession are building, as we've seen, an increasingly sturdy architecture of environmental economics, and are exploring psychology and sociology to address basic issues of human satisfaction. Now economics students are beginning to demand even faster change. In the spring of 2000, hundreds of students at the Sorbonne, France's highest-powered university, signed a petition demanding reform within the profession, which they said had become "enthralled with complex mathematical models that only operate in conditions that don't exist." Their rallying cry was "We wish to escape from imaginary worlds!" Within weeks, 750 students at Cambridge and Oxford signed on; before long, students were distributing "alternative" readings during sessions of Harvard's introductory economics course.[9]

Maybe the most important part of the French students' protest was the name they chose for their movement. They wanted, they said, a "post-autistic economics." "Autistic" seems to me a useful word not just for the closed-in profession of economics but also for the world it has helped to create. That world is composed, more and more, of individuals in isolation from each other, each following his or her own path. Plenty of data back this up. Every study of the phenomenon shows Americans spending less time with friends and family, either working longer hours, or hunkered down in their "Internet alcoves." And there's anecdotal evidence, too. Consider the most influential new program on television in the last decade, *Survivor*, which ushered in the reality show craze. Along with its uncountable offspring, it operates from the premise that the goal is to end up *alone* on the island, to manipulate and scheme until everyone else goes away and leaves you by yourself with your money.

The Soviets and the Chinese failed in their twentieth-century efforts to make the New Man. But in a sense we succeeded, evolving by century's end this new species of hyper-individualist. Our public policy has followed naturally from this individualism. For example, economists almost always reject as inefficient laws that make it harder for companies to shut down a plant—that require, say, a year's notice for laid-off employees. That's because they consider a geographically mobile society to be more efficient, moving people from where they are less productive to where they are more so. Since productivity is the goal that counts, never mind the fact that when people live near where they grew up, within reach of family and old friends, their lives are more stable and their marriages are less likely to falter.[10] In fact, the more individualistic a society, the higher the divorce rate, which may explain why in those dynamic states of the Sun Belt, people divorce twice as much as the inhabitants of old-fashioned New England.[11] "Similarly," notes Richard Layard, "if people are highly mobile, they feel less bonded to the people among whom they live, and crime is more common."[12] The increased mobility of the past few decades is one reason that the average person in her twenties or thirties is half as likely to join a group of some kind as her grandparents.

What's especially odd is that this decline (and a similar decline in voting) took place even as far more people were well-educated. Education usually increases civic participation. But it hasn't been enough to combat the rapid increase in isolating individualism; even education isn't as powerful as what one group of psychologists called "the social toxin corroding America's civic life."[13] The political scientist Robert Putnam, whose book *Bowling Alone* (2000) did more than anything else to document this trend, tried to apportion blame: his data indicate that 10 percent of the decline comes from increased pressure at work, especially on two-career families, and that another 10 percent can be chalked up to suburbanization (how are you going to lead the Cub Scout pack if it takes you an hour to drive home every night?). Twenty-five percent comes essentially from television, and the way it and other new technologies have privatized entertainment. But Putnam attributes half the damage to a "generational shift, with younger Americans far less interested in giving their time to others and advancing non-pecuniary social goals"—that is, to the development of what I've been calling hyper-individualism.[14] Hell, even the U.S. military now recruits under the slogan "An Army of One," the antithesis of every old idea about the brotherhood of soldiers.

We've been well and truly sold on the idea of the individual; 55 percent of Americans under the age of thirty think they will end up being rich.[15] And if you're going to be rich, what do you need anyone else for? You can see the political results of Looking Out for Number One in the deterioration of all the institutions of our common life. America, once the healthiest nation on earth, now ranks twenty-seventh, below all the nations of Western Europe and even countries like Cyprus and Costa Rica. Our public education system used to be the envy of every nation, but we now lag behind twelve of the eighteen developed nations in fundamental literacy skills; 16 percent of our fifteen-year-olds fall below standard educational benchmarks, compared with 2 percent of Japanese and 5 percent of Canadians. Modern environmentalism was invented in the United States—we pioneered everything from national parks to clean-air legislation—but an index prepared by Columbia University found that America ranked 51st of 142 nations in environmental sustainability. We have the highest percentage of our population in prison. Spending on public works, such as highways and bridges, is falling; more parks and libraries are closing than opening. The *Economist* recently tried to sum up all such measures into a single quality-of-life index. Even though America trails only Luxembourg in gross domestic product per person, it comes in thirteenth in total quality of life.[16] And that's now. It would be hard to argue that any of these trends shows much promise for generations yet to come; in any case, the future is beyond the immediate scope of a hyper-individualized life.

Our commitment to this hyper-individualism allows us to tolerate, and even celebrate, inequality so gross that it's almost as much farce as tragedy. The gap between the rich and everyone else is not a cause for concern, but for celebration; its beneficiaries are often hailed as our exemplars. Trump! In 1973 the CEOs of large corporations earned thirty-five times as much as the average worker; now they earn two hundred times as much.[17] "Sometime in the late 1970s," observes the journalist Jim Lardner, "our economy began to . . . send most of its rewards to those who already had the most. The result is a concentration of income and wealth that is not only higher than it has been since the 1920s, but higher than that of any of the world's other populations." And the further result is that more and more Americans no longer live in the rich world; instead, they struggle to get by.[18]

It's hard for most of us to really take this in. We've believed for a very long time that America stands tallest among nations. In 2003, Alan Greenspan, the chairman of the Federal Reserve, was offering his usual oblique testimony to the Congress about the state of our economy. Accustomed to deferential treatment, he was doubtless surprised when Congressman Bernie Sanders, of Vermont, challenged him. "I think you just don't know what's going on in the real world," Sanders said, offering statistics about inequality and insecurity among Americans. Greenspan replied, in the way that has shut up most of us, "Congressman, we have the highest standard of living in the world."

"Wrong," said Sanders. "Scandinavia has a higher standard of living." Indeed, it does, as do many other European countries and Japan—places where individualism is less hyper.

For a moment, Greenspan was at a loss. Well, he finally said, "we have the highest standard of living for a country our size." Which is true, since the only more populous nations on earth are China and India, and Indonesia and Brazil follow us on the list.[19]

FROM PROBLEM TO PLAN. IF HYPER-INDIVIDUALISM IS DAMAGING our lives, what can we do about that?

In an earlier day, the answer for many would have involved a sharp turn to the left. But one real benefit of living in the twenty-first century is that the twentieth taught us an awful lot about what didn't work. Our lives may not be making us particularly happy, but the institutionalized anti-individualism that marked the Soviet and Maoist experiments was infinitely worse. Not only did they fail to compete economically with market economies, they failed in every other way—environmentally, socially, morally. I can remember visiting hospital wards in Siberia and meeting women who had had ten abortions, in part because the centrally planned government couldn't produce enough condoms that didn't break. Hulking ancient factories, whole regions off-limits because of chemical pollution: the former Soviet Union is the most toxic place on earth. In China, you can feel the relief, even decades later, that the Cultural Revolution is over and that people are pretty much left alone. It's a great luxury for us to not even have to entertain the possibility that state socialism might be the way out of our troubles.

The contemporary liberal answer to our predicament is continued economic growth, but with the benefits distributed more fairly and more of them put back into the public realm. We should try, in other words, to turn back the clock a couple of decades in our political and economic life, and then correct our trajectory slightly so that we stay highly (but not, perhaps, hyper-) individual. While this would certainly be an improvement on what we're doing now, it can't solve the problems of peak oil and global warming. And in any event it can't fundamentally alter the dynamic of dissatisfaction that I've been describing.

But there is a more hopeful version of the future: *a shift to economies that are more local in scale.* Local economies would demand fewer resources and cause less ecological disruption; they would be better able to weather coming shocks; they would allow us to find a better balance between the individual and the community, and hence find extra satisfaction. That is why I spent a winter eating locally. A tomato from the small farmer at the end of your suburban road takes less fuel to transport, and a tomato from the farmer at the end of your suburban road tastes better. But it's more than that—it's better because it comes from a . . . farmer down at the end of your suburban road. Getting that tomato—from his farmstand, from a farmers' market, from your CSA share, even from a bin at an enlightened supermarket—requires you to live with a stronger sense of community in mind. Requires that you reorient your personal compass a little bit. Requires that you shed a certain amount of your hyper-individualism and replace it with a certain amount of neighborliness. It *doesn't* require that you join a commune or become a socialist. If we let go of a little bit of our individualism (at the moment, we have plenty to spare), we may recover something we've been missing.

Here's a suggestive piece of data about what that something might be: sociologists studying shopping behavior reported recently that consumers have *ten times as many conversations* at farmers' markets as they do at supermarkets. An order-of-magnitude difference.[20] A simple change in economic life—where you shop—produces an enormous change in your social life. You go from being a mere consumer to being a *participant*, talking about what you like and dislike, expanding your sense of who's in your community and how it fits together.

The argument that works for tomatoes also works, as we shall see in the next chapter, for many other commodities, from energy to entertainment. I don't foresee a coordinated change in our economies, but a gradual one, faster in some places than in others, pulled by personal desire and pushed by environmental necessity. Government policy could help spur it along: those farm subsidies could be transferred from giant soybean plantations to the guy with the small wheat field down the road. But changes in our sense of what we want from the world will be at least as important as changes in the tax code, and at least as hard to achieve.

TO ILLUMINATE THE GULF BETWEEN THE INDIVIDUAL AND THE community, let's add a few more words to the millions already written about the most successful example of our current economic paradigm, that temple of More known as Wal-Mart.

Almost no one who has studied the issue continues to claim that Wal-Mart or its big-box brethren are good for the *communities* where they locate. By now the sequence of events is depressingly clear: the big-box store out by the interstate drains the life out of downtown, shuttering businesses left and right. In the few years when Wal-Mart was expanding fastest in Iowa, the state lost 555 grocery stores, 298 hardware stores, 293 building supply stores, 161 variety shops, 158 women's clothing stores, and 116 pharmacies. The jobs offered by the new Supercenters don't make up the difference: academics estimate a new Wal-Mart eliminates a job and a half for every job it creates. And not only are those new jobs ill paid, providing minimal benefits, and often abusive (the chain has had to settle an almost endless series of class action lawsuits for everything from sex discrimination to the practice of locking workers in at night), they also drive down everyone else's wages and benefits as employers try to compete across an array of retail categories that begins with Tupperware and cheap underwear but ranges from airline tickets to flower arrangements to insurance. Meanwhile, taxpayers are covering the health care costs of uninsured Wal-Mart workers and buying school lunches for their children. All in all, as University of Pennsylvania researchers concluded in a particularly comprehensive study, counties with Wal-Marts have grown poorer than surrounding counties, and the more Wal-Marts they had, the faster they grew poor.[21] None of this even touches questions about what Wal-Mart has done to transfer American jobs abroad, or to sponsor sweatshops around the world. Suffice it to say: *communities* suffer.

On the other hand, *individuals* benefit, at least as consumers. Wal-Mart sells stuff cheap. That is its single mission. "During the weekly meeting of company officers," reports the *New York Times*, CEO Lee Scott "asks embarrassing questions like: 'Why does Target make a better coffee maker and sell it for $19.95?' . . . Before the meeting is over, the buyer is expected to get on his BlackBerry or his phone and not only find out why but, ideally, to have found the same or better coffee maker. He is also expected to bargain with shippers so the company can sell it for less. Oh—and to place an order. An announcement that the coffee maker will be in stores the next week is the kind of line that gets applause, and a nod from Mr. Scott."[22] Wal-Mart can offer those low prices precisely *because* of the damage it does to communities: if it paid more for employee health care, or boosted wages, or behaved responsibly in any way, that coffeemaker might cost $29.95.

Because economists think of human beings primarily as individuals and not as members of a community, they see this superefficiency as an uncomplicated blessing. A couple of years ago, when Wal-Mart announced plans to open a bunch of new stores in Vermont, an economist at the state university, Art Woolf, wrote an op-ed piece for the *New York Times* excoriating activists who were trying to preserve the state's communities. Communities were not his issue—individual consumers were; he titled his essay "Green Mountain Shoppers, Unite." Woolf calculated that a full complement of Wal-Marts would save Vermonters $36 million annually.[23] This works out to about $58.14 apiece for us. That's real money. And, of course, there's the pleasure—real, for some people—of getting to buy an amazing array of merchandise that's hard to come by in rural communities. So we each get to calculate: is that individual gain worth selling out the community at large?

FOR WAL-MART TO PROSPER, WE MUST THINK OF OURSELVES AS individuals—must think that being individuals is the better deal. But the point that I want to make from here on in is just the opposite: think of yourself as a member of a community, and you'll get a better deal. You'll build a world with some hope of ecological stability, and where the chances increase that you'll be happy. You may not have quite as many small appliances, because they may cost a few dollars more, but you'll be happier.

The economist Richard Layard, in his pathbreaking book *Happiness*, lays out the matter almost as an equation. "Both income and companionship have declining marginal returns," he says. The evidence shows that "increases in income produce large hedonic gains in developing countries," small and variable gains in Europe, and, "at least over a fifty-year postwar period, negative gains in the United States." Community follows precisely the opposite pattern: increased companionship "yields more happiness in individualistic societies, where it is scarce, than in collectivist societies, where it is abundant." What this means is: if you are a poor person in China, you have plenty of friends and family around all the time; perhaps there are five people living in your room. Adding a sixth doesn't make you much happier. But adding enough money that all five of you can eat some meat from time to time pleases you greatly. By contrast, if you live in a suburban American home, buying another coffeemaker adds very little to your quantity of happiness—indeed, trying to figure out where to store it, or wondering whether you picked the perfect model, may decrease your total pleasure. But since you live two people to an acre, a new friend, a new connection, is a big deal indeed.[24] We have a surplus of individualism and a deficit of companionship, and so the second becomes more valuable.

Humans seem to be genetically wired for community. As Layard points out, all primates live in groups and get sad when they're separated: "an isolated individual will repeatedly pull a lever with no reward other than the glimpse of another monkey."[25] Why do people so often look back on their college days as the best years of their lives? Usually, it's not because their classes were so fascinating. More important is the fact that they lived more closely and intensely in a community than ever before or since (college is the four years in an American life when we live roughly as we've evolved to live). Every measure of psychological health points to the same conclusion: people who "are married, who have good friends, and who are close to their families are happier than those who are not," says the Swarthmore psychologist Barry Schwartz. "People who participate in religious communities are happier than those who are not." Which is striking, Schwartz adds, because social ties "actually decrease freedom of choice." To be a good friend is hard work.[26]

Of course, it's obvious to most of us that having friends is better than not; but the data show that for people in the rich world, having connections with others is *much* better than having more money. The math of the various quality-of-life indexes is daunting, but the results are clear: in the rich world, says Layard, "feelings about people contribute more to subjective well-being than feelings about money, whether spent or saved."[27] It's not so hard, then, to figure out why happiness has declined here even as wealth has grown. In the two decades between 1974 and 1994, the percentage of Americans who said they frequently visited with their neighbors fell from almost a third to barely a fifth, a number that has continued to fall in the last decade. We simply worked too many hours earning, we commuted too far to our too-isolated homes, and there was always the blue glow of the tube shining through the curtains.[28]

Do we just *think* we're happier in communities? Is it just some sentimental affectation? No; the body reacts to community in measurable ways. Staggering ways. According to Robert Putnam, if you do not belong to any group at present, joining a club or a society of some kind *halves the risk that you will die in the next year.*[29] A 1997 Carnegie Mellon University study found that, when researchers (somewhat disgustingly) sprayed samples of cold virus directly into subjects' nostrils, "those with rich social networks were four times less likely to come down with illness than those with fewer friends." The National Heart, Lung, and Blood Institute found that middle-aged women with large social circles had a 23 percent lower incidence of coronary artery disease. People above the age of eighty with "poor social networks" had a 60 percent higher than average chance of dementia.[30]

So: economic health improves if we constantly shift people "from places where they are less productive to ones where they are more productive," but your actual physical health suffers. If you buy everything at Wal-Mart, it's cheaper, and perhaps you'll get to know the designated "greeter" with her scripted speech. But if you go to the farmers' market, you'll have ten times as many conversations. And what if you go to the CSA farm to pick up your share of produce and do your share of weeding? Could it possibly be better to pull dandelions with your neighbors once a week? After all, we've "escaped the drudgery" of farm work—that's one of the great theoretical achievements of our century. And it *is* drudgery for migrant workers who spend all day, every day bent in the sun. But when the psychologist Mihaly Csikszentmihalyi, whose works on "flow" helped launch the study of human satisfaction, studied dozens of activities to see what actually made Americans happy, he found that volunteer work of all kinds generated "high levels of joy, exceeded only by dancing." Why? The most common answers included "I meet people and make friends through it." "It's the satisfaction of seeing the results." "It broadens my experience of life." 'It gets me 'out of myself.' "[31] This sounds silly and soft-headed to some of us, but only because we've so internalized the economist's ideal of the human being as a self-contained want-machine bent on "maximizing utility." Think about your own life: which moments mattered most? Didn't most of them entail being involved in something larger than yourself? Either out in the hugeness of the natural world, or working together with those around you toward some common end, often for no material gain?

You can run this experiment backward, too. If community makes us healthier, its erosion should have the opposite effect. The incidence of depression exploded in the twentieth century. According to a study done in 1985, only 1.3 percent of people born in 1910 had had a major depressive episode in their lifetime, despite the fact that they had lived for seventy-five years. Depression was a rarity, like esophageal cancer or being hit by a bus. It happened, but not often. In contrast, the same study found that those born after 1960 had a 5.3 percent chance of a major depressive episode, even though they'd been alive no longer than twenty-five years. "Each succeeding cohort in each area had a higher rate of depression than cohorts before it," the researchers observed. "There were huge differences . . . suggesting a roughly ten-fold increase in risk for depression across generations."

The increases are not an artifact of increased knowledge about depression; the researchers couched their questions in general, nonmedical terms, such as "Was there ever a time in your life when you tried to kill yourself?" Instead, depression is clearly more like diabetes, surging because of some dramatic change in human circumstance in recent decades. It is not hard to conclude that that change might be the erosion in community, in contact, in connection. It's hard to find a control group in this country that hasn't experienced the great uptick in individualism—it's like trying to find a community without television so you could research its social patterns. But one set of studies is quite fascinating. The Old Order Amish of Pennsylvania, who live a life poor in appliances but rich in community, had a depression rate about one-tenth that of their neighbors.[32] It's not that the Amish are trouble free: they have drug abuse, wife beating, and social tension, just like every community on earth. But that's the point—they have a community, something more than the individual self to fall back on, to cushion the blows that life throws.

We are unlikely to become Amish; most of us have gained a good deal from the changes of the twentieth century. But those gains have passed the point of diminishing returns. We are far more complex than the standard utility-maximizing economic models indicate. We don't need to become Amish, but we do need to start building an economy that works for our current needs, rather than constantly readjusting our lives to serve the growth of the economy. As Richard Layard concludes in his majestic work on happiness: "The current pursuit of self-realization will not work. If your sole duty is to achieve the best for yourself, life becomes just too stressful, too lonely—you are set up to fail."[33] It is, he adds, "a deep fallacy of many economists to think of human interaction as mainly a means to an end, rather than also an end in itself."[34] When you go to the farmers' market, in other words, you're not just acquiring tomatoes; you're making friends.

WHEN WE HAD A LOT OF COMMUNITY AND NOT MUCH STUFF, IT made sense that we aimed for stuff. But why do we keep aiming for it? Why don't we realize that we have enough, and turn our attention elsewhere? To answer that question, we need to discuss another pervasive aspect of our economy: advertising. At first, advertising was fairly straightforward: this horseless carriage was superior to that one. For a while after that, advertising worked in devious ways that were still fairly straightforward: if you bought this car, you'd have sex a lot. But eventually advertisers figured out (long before sociologists or psychologists or anyone else) that we lacked community, and they set about promoting the idea that the particular stuff they were selling would satisfy those social longings. That's truly devious, and truly powerful. As James Twitchell writes in his celebration of this phenomenon, *Branded Nation,* "Much of our shared knowledge about ourselves and our culture comes to us through a commercial process of storytelling called branding . . . ten percent of a two-year-old's nouns are brand names." What branding does, says Twitchell, is "give the consumer something to hold on to."[35]

No wonder, then, that, in the words of the University of Massachusetts media researcher Sut Jhally, "Advertising is so attractive to us, so powerful, so seductive. What it offers us are images of the real sources of human happiness,"[36] for example, community and friendship and family. And if it could deliver those things—if buying Pepsi could make you part of a meaningful human community called the Pepsi Generation—then the twentieth century would have worked better than it did. We'd all have been overjoyed. Since, however, Pepsi can't do that, any more than Tiffany or Ford or Michelob, we've gotten stuck in our current cul de sac. Branding works its magic only up to the point of sale, and then actual human need returns, unfulfilled; the advertiser is always pleased to offer a new round of promise and failure, but after a century it's probably time to pursue some other strategy. That other way involves making the transition from globalized to local economies.

The transition would yield many benefits. Imagine what could happen to our relationship with time. It is well known that since the 1960s Americans have been working longer and longer hours. Between 1973 and 2000, the average American employee added 199 hours to his annual schedule—that is, the equivalent of five forty-hour weeks. Why? The economist Juliet Schor points out that new technologies, instead of freeing us from labor, provided firms with "new opportunities for making money. . . . As they seized them, they required long work hours from their employees." Since we were each individuals, working without any safety net such as national health insurance, we felt deeply insecure, and unwilling to risk a good job if we had one.[37] (Even people with crappy jobs often found themselves forced to put in unpaid overtime, as lawsuits against companies like Wal-Mart have made clear.)[38] Instead, says Schor, "people responded to their stressful working lives by participating in an orgy of consumer upscaling. . . . Over the last thirty years, real consumption expenditures per person had doubled."[39]

Now, much of this new spending is not for Jacuzzis and high-definition TV sets. Much of it simply buys the services that make it possible for us to work those long hours—more child care, more prepared meals. People who are strapped go to McDonald's. Meanwhile, says the writer Jon Rowe, "upscale parents are contracting out the task of putting on birthday parties, helping kids with homework, even teaching them how to ride a bike."[40] The National Association of Professional Pet Sitters has six thousand members.[41] The results of all this work, given what we now know about the deeper economy, are predictable. The more hours you work, the less satisfied you become with your life, even though you make more money. The amount of time that parents spend with their children has steadily decreased, a trend "reliably linked to lower levels of average happiness and life satisfaction" for kids, says Layard.[42] Indeed, children in affluent suburbs are more likely to be depressed even than those living in inner-city poverty.[43]

The more hours you work, the bigger your ecological footprint, too. That's because you're spending more money and spending it carelessly: with no time to go to the farmers' market, let alone to cook what you buy there, you drive through the drive-through instead. The numbers are substantial: an American working twenty to forty hours a week requires about twenty-three acres of the earth to support him; someone working more than forty hours requires nearly twenty-eight acres.[44]

Now try the following thought experiment, which Schor suggests. Between 1969 and 2000, she reports, overall labor productivity increased about 80 percent, so that the average worker in 2000 could produce nearly twice as much per hour as the average worker in 1969. "Had we used that productivity dividend to reduce hours of work," Schor points out, "the average American could be working only a little more than twenty hours a week."[45] The math isn't that linear, of course, but it gives some sense of scale. And there are those of us yet alive who can actually remember the year 1969 and so can testify that it was not a dark era of unrelieved poverty. True, we drove smaller cars and lived in smaller houses and ate out less. On the other hand, we ate together more. And we were working forty-hour weeks then. If those hours had been substantially reduced, there would now be more time for almost everything, from talking to your spouse, to sleeping in, to volunteering at the local hospital. You could grow some more of your own food, and have time to cook it, using other ingredients you got from your neighbors. You would have less money, but also less need for child care, for work clothes, for the expense of commuting. We actually have some record of what such a change might mean to a community: in 1930, in the teeth of the Depression, the cereal entrepreneur W. K. Kellogg put his workers on a six-hour day at full pay. Productivity increased dramatically, helping pay for the experiment. Meanwhile, the company town's parks, community centers, churches, and YMCAs all flourished. Researchers who interviewed the townspeople found that their interests had grown and changed: they now asked themselves, "What shall I do?" not just "What shall I buy?" Indeed, workers looked back on the eight-hour day with a shudder. "I wouldn't go back for anything," said one. "I wouldn't have time to do anything but work and eat."[46]

Building such a world again won't be easy: the logic of the global market militates against it, as does the self-interest of those at the top of the economic pyramid, who are making huge gains from globalization and have the political clout to ward off most challenges. If we are to reverse the trend of overwork, change will probably begin with small and voluntary schemes like those that have begun to change the food market. A number of towns around the country, for instance, have begun to experiment with time-bartering networks. If you help an elderly neighbor cook her meals, you are rewarded with a certain number of "time dollars," which guarantees that "somewhere down the line a neighbor will help you in return."[47] In a traditional, well-functioning community, such arrangements are unnecessary; people do the calculations intuitively, on the fly. I remember spending a day working in the field of an Amish farmer in Ohio, cutting corn and taking it to the silo. The field was full of men in white shirts: all the neighbors would converge on one field to help, then move on to the next field the next day. No one was keeping score, but I imagine all of the men knew roughly that they would get out what they put in. (And it was a good deal more fun than working alone, besides which there was the huge and delicious midday meal that their wives had gotten together to prepare.)

It's important to realize that working together is not some freak Amish trait—it's what all people did before they had machinery powerful enough to enable them to work alone. Douglas Harper, in his book *Changing Works*, a fine oral history of upstate New York farming, interviews a dozen farmers old enough to remember what life was like before big tractors and combines. "It's all changed," said one old-timer. "We would pitch in and go help. Everyone wasn't so busy then. Oh, they had time or something. I don't know what it was. Now they got so damn much going on, you're going so far and so fast and so furious that everybody is going with their shirt-tail straight out and don't have time to say hello. You don't have any neighbors. You don't have any neighbors now." Another local farmer agreed. "You hardly ever see your neighbors any more. Just like the Bakers over here—their land joins on ours. We wave when we go by and they wave when they go by. We're lucky if we talk to them once or twice a year." What happened? Harper asked. Well, the farmer explained, it was just that once everyone had a big efficient piece of equipment all their own, "there was no need, no call, really to go see them. . . . I don't think anyone has anything against anyone—you just don't have any need to be there."[48]

We don't *need* each other for anything anymore. If we have enough money, we're insulated from depending on those around us—which is at least as much a loss as a gain. By some surveys, three-quarters of Americans confess that they don't know their next-door neighbors. That's a novel condition for primates; it will take a while to repair those networks.

JUST AS OUR INCREASING "PROSPERITY" HAS SOMEHOW MAN-aged to produce less time, it has also magically undercut our security. Security is as basic a human need as there is, and its lack is already the defining feature of our age.

Imagine the average human existence until a few hundred years ago: poor, often unhealthy. And deeply stable. People were psychologically secure—they knew who they were, and what that meant. And physically secure—they lived surrounded by kith and kin, the people who would support them when they couldn't support themselves. It's quite possible that this was too much security, rooted as it was in class and caste division, in a permanent and fixed universe often stifling. Either voluntarily, or because the world was changing and we had no choice, we in the West traded much of that stability away for independence and dynamism, wagering that we'd be better off. Freedom and mobility and self-reliance have indeed produced great wealth and great character. The ability to risk and fail is at the heart of our new individualist identity— indeed, it's one of the things that sets Americans apart. Still, we need some degree of security to avoid going crazy, as we realize when events turn sharply sour. The Depression was so wide and deep that it mocked the idea that individual effort would save us. In response, we enacted programs like Social Security and, a generation later, Medicare that tried to set a floor through which we could no longer fall.

As the memory of privation faded, however, so did those commitments. If, as Margaret Thatcher insisted, "there is no society," only individuals, then why would we be responsible for each other? As our societies age, the choices become steadily more stark. We can again pledge our solidarity with one another, in which case we will need to pay more in taxes to keep Social Security strong and Medicare solvent. Or we can insist that higher taxes are too much of a burden, on us and on the economy, and we can opt for an even more radical independence. President George W. Bush has made an "ownership society" the focus of his two terms: "If you own something, you have a vital stake in the future of our country," he told a crowd in the summer of 2004. "The more ownership there is in America, the more vitality there is in America, and the more people have a vital stake in the future of this country." In practice, he proposed that we own our retirement savings in individual accounts instead of relying entirely on Social Security, that we have "health savings accounts" instead of the national health insurance employed by the other Western democracies, and so on. Such plans, said the economist Victor Canto (writing in the conservative *National Review*), would be more efficient, and more in keeping with how we view ourselves: they "will strengthen the link between reward and effort. Americans, in other words, will have a greater chance of capturing the full benefits of their actions if the Bush plan plays out."[49]

So far Americans have been wary about taking the plunge. Having curtailed welfare for poor people during the Clinton administration, we've been unwilling to surrender our own benefits; Bush's plan to revamp Social Security never gained much traction. On the other hand, we keep electing Congresses that keep cutting taxes, and if that continues long enough, at some point the whole question will be moot. It's a battle between two different ways of perceiving the world, and we can't make up our minds, so for the moment we're having our cake, and eating it, and letting the Chinese bake us more (a task they may eventually tire of). But it's not just government programs that are becoming less dependable: more and more private companies are defaulting on their pensions, arguing that if they keep their promises they won't be able to compete with companies or countries that promise nothing. The same with health care. In 1988, two-thirds of large American employers offered health benefits to retirees; the portion had fallen to one-third by 2004. As a result, older people "have become the fastest-growing portion of the work force," staffing the Sam's Clubs and Home Depots of the nation to make up for their lost benefits.[50]

We've overshot once more—given up so much security that the result is making us less happy, not more. We have lost sight of our priorities, of the fact that "people tend to want security more than they want higher income," in Layard's words. A series of Roper surveys from the early 1990s showed that when asked to list the "very important aspects of money," nearly four-fifths of respondents listed "security." Security outdistanced even "being able to help your children," which was mentioned by less than two-thirds.[51] And this is just the beginning. What will we feel like as global warming really kicks in and we start to realize that the basic physical stability of the planet, which we've counted on for ten thousand years, has been permanently undone? How did your worldview shift if you lived through Hurricane Katrina? What will it feel like if peak oil asserts itself and we realize that the truck may not always show up to fill your furnace?

In a changed world, comfort will come less from ownership than from membership. If you're a functioning part of a community that can meet at least some of its needs—for food, for energy, for companionship, for entertainment, for succor—then you're more secure. It is toward the gradual building of such communities that we will now turn.

I'M NOT SUGGESTING AN ABRUPT BREAK WITH THE PRESENT, BUT a patient rebalancing of the scales. The project will not be fast, cheap, or easy. Fast, cheap, and easy is what we have at the moment; they are the cardinal virtues upon which our economy rests (and if they also happen to be the very adjectives you don't want attached to your child, well, that should give you a little pause). The word we use to sum up these virtues is "efficiency," and on its altar we have sacrificed a good deal: our small farms were inefficient compared with factory farms; our local retailers were inefficient compared with Wal-Mart; having free time is inefficient compared with working more hours. Relationships were inefficient compared with things. And, in a certain, limited sense, each of these ideas is correct. If you leave certain factors (pollution, say, and unhappiness) out of account, we've built a society more efficient than any the world has ever seen.

But the time has come to throw some grit into the works. To make the economy less efficient, heretical as that sounds. These changes I'm discussing are not, as far as I'm concerned, ideological. They aren't liberal or conservative, Democratic or Republican; social conservatives and environmentalist progressives could find common ground in them. At the risk of betraying my background as a Sunday school teacher, let me say that these changes seem to me, at least in some measure, to be compatible with strong faith.

Consider an obvious example that makes this point clear. The most inefficient idea our society ever embraced was originally a Jewish inspiration: the Sabbath, a day set aside for relationships with family and with God and with the world around us. For much of American history, things stopped on the Sabbath. Strange as it now sounds, *you couldn't go shopping.* The seventh day offered a chance to rebalance your life a little. Certainly you could mount reasonable arguments against blue laws—they favored one religion's observance over another's, for example. But that wasn't what brought them down. What brought them down was precisely the understanding that they were inefficient—that they reduced the amount of business that could get done, the amount of money that could be made. Indeed, in 2004 the Virginia legislature mistakenly reinstated a law giving employees the right to ask for Sunday off. A court finally stayed the mistaken law, bringing much relief all around. "The gun has at least been removed from their hand and put back in the holster," said Hugh Keough, president of the Virginia Chamber of Commerce.[52] The blue laws were "liberalized" to free us for more work, more consumption; the biggest supporter of their repeal was the Chamber of Commerce. Tell me whether that's left or right.

Here's another story, entirely secular. A few years ago, in Portland, Oregon, residents of one neighborhood decided that they didn't really know each other. (This is not surprising; studies have shown that as urban neighborhoods became more heavily used by cars instead of pedestrians, the average person saw the number of friends and acquaintances she had in her neighborhood drop from nine to four.)[53] So the residents decided to reclaim a local intersection as their own public square. They didn't stop traffic, but they cobblestoned the crossing, painted it bright red and blue and yellow, and put up a "tea station" on one corner where neighbors could have a free cup of hot tea any time, day or night. Soon there were message boards and benches on the corners, and people were planting butterfly gardens at the edge of their yards to offer more color and life; the idea spread to lots of other Portland neighborhoods, and the city passed an ordinance allowing any group of residents to do the same.[54] Like the Sabbath, it was grit in the works, because cars had to slow down at these redesigned intersections. Efficiency was compromised. But something was gained—and again it's impossible to say whether the result is liberal or conservative. It's *neighborly*.

THE REST OF THIS BOOK WILL EXPLORE THE ECONOMICS OF neighborliness. It's easy to dismiss the idea as sentimental, nostalgic, some Norman Rockwell old-town-green fantasy. It is not; economies can be localized as easily in cities and suburbs as in rural villages (maybe more easily), and in ways that look as much to the future as the past, that rely more on the solar panel and the Internet than the white picket fence. In fact, given the trendlines for phenomena like global warming and oil supply, what's nostalgic and sentimental is to insist that we keep doing what we're doing now simply because it's familiar. The good life of the high-end American suburb is precisely what's doing us in.

Localism, by contrast, offers a physically plausible economy for the future, and a psychologically plausible one as well: an economy that might better provide goods like time and security that we're short of. Indeed, by increasing the conviviality of the average life, we might even reverse some of those trends away from happiness and satisfaction that seem so disturbingly entrenched. We would not discard individualism for some drab collectivist future; instead, we would re-embed individuals in some context where our impulses make more sense and do less damage.

To understand the importance of this last point, consider the book *American Mania*, by the neuroscientist Peter Whybrow. Whybrow argues that many of us in this country are predisposed to a kind of dynamic individualism; our gene pool, after all, is overstocked with people possessed of enough ambition and wanderlust to bring them to these shores. This served us well in settling a continent and building our prosperity. But it never got completely out of control, says Whybrow, because "the marketplace always had its natural constraints. For the first two centuries of the nation's existence, even the most insatiable American citizen was significantly leashed by the checks and balances inherent in a closely knit community, by geography, by the elements of weather, or, in some cases, by religious practice." You lived in a society—a habitat—that kept individualist impulses in some check. But that has changed in the past few decades, as the economy nationalized and globalized. As we met fewer of our neighbors in the course of a day, as we became ever more hyper-individualist in our economic lives, those bonds fell away. "Operating in a world of instant communication with minimal social tethers," Whybrow observes, "America's engines of commerce and desire became turbocharged."[55]

This remarkable efficiency seemed to flow straight out of our economic models. But Adam Smith, watching the butchers and bakers of his English village making each other richer through the invisible hand of economic exchange, never imagined that the skids would be so thoroughly greased. If you read the original texts, Whybrow insists, "Smith's economic philosophy was predicated on a dynamic balance between commercial liberty and a set of social structures that are rapidly eroding in America." Smith worried that too much envy and avarice would destroy "the empathic feeling and neighborly concerns that are essential to his economic model," but he "took comfort in the fellowship and social constraint that he considered inherent in the tightly knit communities characteristic of the 18th century." Businesses, for instance, were built on local capital investment and "to be solicitous of one's neighbor was prudent insurance against future personal need."[56] For the most part, people felt a little constrained about showing off wealth; indeed, until fairly recently in American history someone who was making tons of money was viewed with mixed emotions, at least if he wasn't giving back to the community. "For the rich," Whybrow observes, "the reward system would be balanced between the pleasure of self-gain and the civic pride of serving others. By these means the most powerful citizens would be limited in their greed."

Once economies grow past a certain point, however, "the behavioral contingencies essential to promoting social stability in a market-regulated society—close personal relationships, tightly knit communities, local capital investment, and so on—are quickly eroded."[57] You don't need the local bank; indeed, the local bank has probably been taken over by something called OneTrust headquartered in an office park someplace in the Sun Belt. Consider the three heirs to the Wal-Mart fortune, who are among the ten richest people on earth. They're worth $90 billion. But according to *Fortune*, the town of Bentonville, Arkansas, where their family began to make its fortune, runs a budget deficit and can't afford a new sewage treatment plant. The family is too "thrifty," as one local official puts it.[58] A better way to say it might be that they don't really live there, residing instead in the placeless world of the wealthy, where they're unlikely to meet their neighbors. If they don't much care about Bentonville, what do they care about your town, your state, even your country? And the Waltons are simply an extreme example. Recent statistics show that, Warren Buffett and Bill Gates notwithstanding, Americans making $50,000 to $100,000 give away two to six times as much of their money (in percentage terms) as people who make more than $10 million.[59]

Local economies offer one possible way around the gross inequalities that have come to mark our societies. Instead of aiming for more growth and hoping it will trickle down, we may be better off if we live in enough contact with each other that the affluent start again to feel some responsibility for their neighbors. This doesn't mean relying on noblesse oblige; it means taking seriously the idea that people, and their politics, can be changed by their experiences. It's easy to be a selfish jerk when you're one in 300 million; it's harder (though certainly not impossible) to be a selfish jerk if you live in a community, if you understand that these are the people with whom you will spend your life. Biological anthropologists have noted that our species spent 99 percent of its history in small hunter-gatherer bands, "the perfect setting for the emergence of cooperation: the identities of the other participants are known, there are opportunities for multiple iterations of games (and thus the ability to punish cheaters), and there is open-book play (players acquire reputations)." Such bands were therefore highly egalitarian.[60]

We're not headed back to roaming bands, but we may be able to re-create at least some of the institutions that marked, say, Adam Smith's Britain, and hence create some of that moderating sense of responsibility. I remember talking one day with Will Rapp, one of the organizers of the Intervale farm project in Burlington; he and his colleagues wanted to expand with a small plant that could do value-added processing—making local tofu for the city's vegan horde—and thus allow a few local farmers to start raising soybeans. "But we need people to invest who will take a three percent rate of return, not a fifteen percent rate of return," he said. Last fall in Los Angeles, for instance, the corporate owners of the city's great newspaper, the *Times*, wanted to slash the reporting staff to keep the paper's profit margin above 20 percent. Local civic leaders tried to buy the *Times*, saying they'd be happy with a 5 percent return on a good newspaper. High rates of return usually mean squeezing someone or something—the chicken plucker, the ozone layer, the city desk. We can all do that squeezing at a distance where we don't see the results, but it is a little harder to do so close to home.

The superrich aren't the only ones who have stopped paying

attention to community. Almost all of us now take our cues about how to live less from the people around us than from the people we see on television; we live not in our own cities and towns but in the generic Southern California nowhere that streams in through the coaxial cable. Juliet Schor observes that "because television shows are so heavily skewed to the lifestyles of the rich and upper middle class, they inflate the viewer's perceptions of what others have, and by extension what is worth acquiring—what one must have in order to avoid being 'out of it.'" Eighty-four percent of Americans, researchers found, wanted to be in the top 20 percent of income distribution; only 15 percent said they would be satisfied "living a comfortable life" in the middle class.[61] When the people you spend time with, even if it's pretend time, all live in suburban palaces or three-thousand-square-foot Manhattan apartments, their lives set the new normal. It's no wonder we endlessly keep shopping even though shopping isn't making us happier. If we spent more time with real-life neighbors in their actual homes, we might adjust our desires down a notch—merely keeping up with the Joneses is sane, compared with keeping up with *The OC*.

This same return to the reality of actual communities might make it easier for us to deal with other problems, too. In his powerful book *The Moral Consequences of Economic Growth*, Benjamin Friedman offers many examples to prove his point that in times of economic expansion people become more open, tolerant, and generous, pushing public policy in benevolent directions. But he also allows that there's one great counterexample: the Depression, when economic privation bred solidarity that produced the New Deal. "Enough Americans from different walks of life saw one another in distress that they may well have felt as if they were now, for practical purposes, part of one larger community," Friedman notes.[62] If we can no longer count on endless economic growth to make us tolerant and generous, and since we don't want another Depression even if it would have an excellent effect on morale, we will need to find another source for those necessary virtues. We'll need a shift toward an economy that connects us more closely. It's a hopeful sign that local and state governments across the country have enacted "living wage" laws designed to provide at least a little margin of comfort for the working poor. Congress has long refused to raise the federal minimum wage past $5.15 an hour, accepting the orthodox economic argument that a mandated rise in pay interferes "with the flow of supply and demand." But as Jon Gertner pointed out in 2006 in the *New York Times*, "Most wage campaigns arise from the bottom, from residents and low-level offices and from cities and states—from everywhere except the federal government." Advocates are currently targeting Arizona, Ohio, Montana, Oklahoma, even Arkansas, the home of Wal-Mart.[63] It's hard to pretend that the people you see around you every day should live and die by the dictates of the market.

THE SOCIAL ARRANGEMENTS THAT ADAM SMITH COUNTED ON to balance his new economics—the sturdy communities where the baker and the butcher actually knew each other, and where they had to show themselves good citizens because they wanted credit from the banker—turned out to be fragile. When the forces of economic liberty Smith helped to unleash began to erode those social arrangements, many people celebrated instead of mourned. Living in a community comes with drawbacks; small societies can be parochial, gossip-ridden, discriminatory. There was something liberating about escaping them, about being on your own. That's the story of much of American literature, with Huck lighting out for the Territory.

Instead of a happy mean, though, we've swung to the hyperindividualism that pervades our culture. It's easy to sell, from the left as well as the right. How deep does it go? The *Wall Street Journal*, which has spent twenty years insisting that global warming is a left-wing hoax, recently ran an article titled "The

Global Climate Change Island Guide," rating forty vacation destinations by their exposure to climate risk. (Avoid Sulawesi, where warming waters mean "coral reefs have experienced major bleaching in recent years, leading to new fees for diving at one marine park." Also St. John, where the reef is so damaged that a dive operator "plays down the coral, instead selling customers on the chance to pet a sting ray.")[64] If we've reached the point where planetary ecological collapse is viewed in terms of the problem it presents for our vacation plans, then we may have passed some sociological tipping point, become so completely individualized that there's scant chance of recovery.

But I think the statistics about happiness and satisfaction indicate that, deeper down, we know we've been overliberated. There are communitarians and social conservatives and progressives for whom "community" has become a magic word, a mystic goal. But it is our *economic* lives, even more than our moral choices, that play the crucial role in wrecking or rebuilding our communities. We need to once again depend on those around us for something real. If we do, then the bonds that make for human satisfaction, as opposed to endless growth, will begin to reemerge.

Every new farmers' market is a small step in this direction. It requires new connections between the people who came together to found it, the farmers who come in from the country to meet their suburban and urban customers, the customers who emerge from the supermarket trance to meet their neighbors. The market begins to build a different reality, one that uses less oil and is therefore less vulnerable to the end of cheap energy. But, more important, the new reality responds to all the parts of who we are, including the parts that crave connection. One-tenth the energy; ten times the conversations—that's an equation worth contemplating.

4 | THE WEALTH OF COMMUNITIES

When you think about Vermont, Barre is not the town you're imagining. Main Street has seen better days. There are few covered bridges, and fewer rusticators in J.Crew. There is a heroin problem. The town's peculiar local geology—it is the self-proclaimed "granite capital of the world"—has given rise to a peculiar local economy. For nearly a century, Rock of Ages Corporation has been one of the town's biggest employers, providing tombstones for a nation. Barre is, literally and figuratively, gritty.

The second chapter of this book used food as a template to begin laying out the possibilities for a local economy; in this chapter I'll try to extend that analysis to many more commodities, from energy to timber to money itself. But I want to start with a commodity—communication—that seems ephemeral. And I want to start in a place that seems unlikely. Not just gritty Barre, but one of its grittier corners.

Thunder Road, "the nation's site of excitement," sits just down the hill from the quarry, and on summer Thursday nights (because quarrymen used to get paid on Thursday afternoons) it vibrates with the noise of cars dopplering around the half-mile track, the whine rising and falling as they flash by the grandstand straightaway. It's glorious fun—the booth selling homemade videos of last year's best crashes, the "battle flags" of last year's champion cars flapping over the infield. The stands hold ten thousand people on a big night, and most nights are big. Ten thousand—one Vermonter in sixty—is more people than gather anyplace else in the state.

"After the war, that's when all this started," says Ken Squier, who built Thunder Road. Car racing may be big-time now, but it began as a local sport, and not just down South. "The soldiers came back from Okinawa, from Iwo Jima, from the Bulge. They were not going to play a children's game like baseball. This was their thing. It was always the people's sport. Always the sport for the unshined shoes."

I could listen to Ken Squier most of the night. He's a talker, and he comes by it honestly, having spent the better part of six decades in front of the microphone at the radio station his father helped build—"WDEV, Radio Vermont . . . the friendly pioneer . . . 550 AM, 96.1 on your FM dial." Naturally he broadcasts races from Thunder Road, at least on those Thursdays when the Red Sox aren't playing at the same time. And of course he discusses the races in loving detail on his morning sports wrap. He even has a weekly auto-racing hour hosted by one of his sidekicks, Dave Moody. When Disney and ABC do the same, they call it synergy.

But here's the odd part. When Dave wraps up the auto-racing show on Monday evening, the next thing you hear on WDEV is "Dinner Jazz": two hours of Cannonball Adderley and Miles and Coltrane and Dave Brubeck, brought to you by the same advertisers (Lenny's Shoes and Apparel, the Shore Acres Restaurant, LaMoille Valley Ford) that also bring you, at various times during the week, the bird-watching hour, "Music to Go to the Dump By," and the station's own bluegrass band ("We don't want to be strangers. . . . We're the Radio Rangers . . . from WDEV"). For two hours every morning, the talk show host Mark Johnson covers local Vermont issues; on Fridays he sits in the lobby of the state legislature with his portable transmitter, buttonholing one committee chair after another and grilling them pretty hard. Some nights in the winter, the station carries two different girls' high school basketball games back-to-back, or hockey from Norwich University. There's some gospel preaching on Sunday morning, and *Dairyline* with the latest hundredweight prices during the five o'clock hour so you can hear it during morning milking. There's a conservative talk show for an hour in the morning, of course—and in the afternoon, there's an hour of left-wing talk, hosted by the Socialist senator Bernie Sanders and by Anthony Pollina, of the state's Progressive party.

In other words, WDEV is a very strange signal. Forget the red states and the blue states; this station exists in a kind of purple state. Many parts of its schedule sound like things you can hear elsewhere. If you've got satellite radio, you can get bluegrass twenty-four hours a day, and nineteen flavors of jazz. Modern radio stations aim for a particular niche—say, thirty-five-year-old males who want sports around the clock. But it's a rare place in our society where Thelonious Monk and stock-car racing coexist.

Radio is, like food, a large part of most people's lives: 77 percent of the population listens to radio an average of at least three and a half hours a day, making it very nearly ubiquitous. And like food, radio used to be mostly local, hemmed in by mountains, limited by signal strength. The FCC allowed a couple of dozen 50,000-watt AM powerhouses, like WLS in Chicago, KSL in Salt Lake, and WBZ in Boston; at night, these could be heard over half the country. But for the most part radio served a *place,* and stations could get their licenses renewed every three years only if they served that place well—well enough, anyhow. They had to regularly survey citizens and community leaders to determine local needs, and then create programming that addressed those needs. As the FCC ruled in 1928, "The commission is convinced that the interest of the broadcast listener is of superior importance to that of the broadcaster. . . . Such benefit as is derived by advertisers must be incidental and entirely secondary to the interest of the public."[1] To our ears, that sounds pretty radical, but it's the basic law that governed broadcasting for fifty years.

Times have changed, however. Vermont alone has seventy-eight radio transmitters: the dial is pretty crowded even in this small state. On paper, that kind of looks like it used to. But virtually none of those stations is truly local. In the last couple of decades, radio has centralized itself even faster than farming. Major media players were able to persuade Congress to "deregulate" broadcasting, allowing one owner to control strings of frequencies. Soon, companies like Clear Channel and Infinity were the aural equivalent of Cargill and Archer Daniels Midland, able to buy up vast webs of stations. Clear Channel alone owns 1,200 of the country's stations, from KASH Country in Anchorage to Classic Rock WAIL in Key West. Radio has been a highly profitable business for them, because it's highly efficient: one guy sitting in a corporate studio somewhere in Texas can spin the latest Mariah Carey for an entire nation, and one sales force can market ads coast to coast.

Of course, as usual, there are costs. Compare the old FCC standard with what the former Clear Channel CEO Lowry Mays told *Fortune* a few years ago: "We're not in the business of providing news and information. . . . We're simply in the business of selling our customers products." When a train car overturned in Minot, North Dakota, a couple of years ago, spilling a large quantity of ammonia and sending up a cloud of poison gas, local officials quickly tried to contact the town's eight radio stations to send out the alarm—only to find that there was no one actually working in six of them. They were simply relaying a satellite feed from Clear Channel headquarters in Texas; there was plenty of country music and golden oldies and Top 40 and right-wing chat, but no one to warn about the toxic cloud drifting overhead.[2]

We are the most comprehensively entertained people in

history. Between our hundreds of channels of television, and radio, and Internet radio, and our legally and illegally down-loaded tunes, there is no vaguely musical sound emitted by anyone on the planet that is not available (for a vanishingly low price) at any time of the day or night. But, oddly, it's gotten a lot harder to hear much about your immediate vicinity. That's one reason that people rose up a few years ago to fight the FCC when it moved to make the world even safer for the Clear Channels, removing some of the few remaining restrictions on corporate ownership. It was supposed to be one more quiet backroom deal, but pretty soon activists of every stripe were fighting the regulation. When Bernie Sanders held a hearing in Vermont, for instance, there weren't enough seats for all the people who wanted to testify; Congress got so many e-mails that the Senate actually tried to reject the new regulations. Michael Powell, the shocked and peeved chairman of the FCC, whined to the *New York Times* in September 2003 that "there was a concerted grassroots effort to attack" the law. "I've never seen that," he added.

Here's another way of saying it. A couple of clicks up the dial from WDEV, you come to a Clear Channel Vermont station, one of half a dozen area signals controlled by the $8 billion corporation. It styles itself The Zone, and it carries Rush Limbaugh. After Rush, it carries *The Don & Mike Show.* Not long ago, I listened to Don and Mike for an hour. They tried to fry an egg on the sidewalk because it was so incredibly hot (in Washington, D.C., where they're located; in Vermont it was raining). They also had a big discussion about a porno film they'd recently watched on a cable channel and whether or not it was gross that the male actor had an uncircumcised penis. This turned disputatious, and either Don or Mike told either Mike or Don to kiss his ass. "Kiss the inside of my ass. Kiss the eye. Kiss the eye!" Then a woman came into the studio who had tanned the words "Don" and "Mike" onto her breasts in order to win a hundred dollars. There was more dispute, this time about whether or not she'd tanned them low enough, "across the round part, the aureole."

An economist would argue that we've chosen this world, just as we've chosen to eat at long distance—that if we wanted to listen to local radio, local radio would ipso facto exist. True, something in dirty talk appeals to many of us, and community often seems like more work than it's worth. Our choices have in some ways built our world. On the other hand, it's hard to test whether these are the choices we really, or still, want to make. If most every radio station in your town is owned by some big broadcaster, you need many millions of dollars to buy a frequency, supposing one is available.

Almost the only other way to own a radio station is to inherit it from your father, which is how Ken Squier came by his. "This was a print shop in 1930," he says, waving his arm around the small suite of offices in downtown Waterbury where WDEV still operates. "They published the *Waterbury Record*. My father was working here for Harry Whitehill, who was also the customs collector for northern Vermont. In those days that meant chasing liquor, and Mr. Whitehill spent quite a bit of time up at St. Albans near the Canadian.border, where they happened to have the first commercial station in the state. And one day he came home and said to my dad, 'Lloyd, more people can hear than can read. I think we ought to have a radio station, too.'"

Soon the station was on the air three hours a day; before long, it was carrying live chats from the governor's office and broadcasting the state basketball championship. And the local towns got an hour a week, so there was the Morrisville hour, the Montpelier hour. "My father met my mother because she came for the Hardwick hour," Squier says. "All the towns took it very seriously." WDEV offered full-service radio in part because doing so paid off nicely, and in part because Whitehill and Squier Senior saw it as their responsibility. In fact, the idea of businessmen owning radio stations was controversial. In the 1920s, as the medium got off the ground, licenses went mostly to colleges, to labor unions, and to civic-minded groups: these seemed the obvious rightful custodians of the public airwaves. But in the 1930s, as it became clear what a gold mine broadcasting could be, private owners managed to convince Congress that their "well-rounded" programming should get the edge over "narrow special interest." Washington did demand, however, a modicum of accountability, in the form of the "community service" requirements I described above. "Right from the very beginning you were supposed to assess your community," Squier says. "The government told you to assess the needs, and say how you were going to fulfill them, and if you didn't they would take your license away from you."

Not anymore, obviously. "Literally now, if you can prove you haven't been busted for drugs and you've got the money, you get a place on the dial," Squier says. "They pay lip service to need and necessity, but that's horse pucky." Indeed, Clear Channel brags a good deal about its "public service," which mostly involves running those free ads from the Ad Council. That's different from the idea that the radio station is there to actually serve a community. "A few years ago a big flood hit Montpelier," Squier says, "and after a couple of days they asked Governor Dean how he was keeping track of what was happening. And he said, 'Well, I'm listening to WDEV.' We took all our sales staff and turned them into reporters for that period. We dropped all our commercials for three days. We had someone on the scene when the railroad bridge down here moved on its moorings. That's what we're supposed to do.

"No Vermonter will ever hold a radio station license again," he continues. "They'll go to the big companies with the liquidity." Which will pay the capital costs by *not* using the sales staff to cover the three-day Montpelier flood, and *not* broadcasting back-to-back high school girls' basketball games, and *not* mounting a microphone on a bicycle to cover the local marathon, and *not* going live to the woods on the opening day of deer-hunting season.

We tend to sentimentalize "community," to imagine, say, folks greeting each other on the way to the courthouse to sign up for jury duty. Of course, real communities have real problems, even in Vermont. A couple of summers ago, a Vermont state trooper named Michael Johnson was trying to stop a car driven by a suspected drug dealer. He was putting a spike strip down on the interstate that runs past Barre to puncture the car's tires when the dealer drove into the median and ran him over. A few nights later, Squier ran the main feature at Thunder Road in his honor; state troopers drove the pace car and jugs circulated through the grandstand to collect money for Johnson's three kids. The next morning Squier was on the radio fulminating about the need to start executing heroin dealers. Red meat, understandable in the circumstances, and just what you expect from radio—but the next day, Squier invited a local lawyer onto his program to argue against the death penalty. "If you ever saw someone get executed, you wouldn't be so glib about it," he told Squier.

"I don't think you're right about that," Squier said. "But maybe you are." You'll wait a long time to hear that on the national talk shows.

And Squier's small exchange with the death-penalty opponent demonstrates exactly why "community" is a useful venture in inefficiency. The modern radio industry is utterly focused on *you*. It's entirely set up around the idea that you are a part of a predictable demographic whose tastes can be reliably commodified as alternative country or classic rock; the whole premise of talk radio is that you can go all day without hearing an opinion you disagree with—Rush Limbaugh's fans, after all, call themselves dittoheads. What could be more efficient than that?

If you listen regularly to WDEV, you'll hear Ann Coulter decrying the treason of the American left, but you'll also hear the American left, or at least the Vermont version of it, decrying plant closings and failing dairy farms, demanding national health insurance, and dissing the president. You hear jazz in the evening, and you hear stock-car racing. You hear *things that other people are interested in*. Which is pretty much the definition of community. If you're a senior citizen, you find out what's going on in the schools, and if you're a jazz fan, you hear some bluegrass, and everyone gets the Norwich ice-hockey scores. Television, of course, is so expensive to produce that it has to chase the largest possible audience, and the Internet, though useful in many ways, by virtue of its design splits people off into narrow avenues of interest. Radio is the ideal broad community vehicle.

Now there are only remnant stations like WDEV hanging on, for who knows how long. Monthly, Squier says, one or another of the big outfits makes him an offer. "The value probably went up another forty percent when the FCC passed the last deregulation." It's hard to see how the station will outlast him.

BUT NOT IMPOSSIBLE. IF CLEAR CHANNEL AND INFINITY ARE THE radio analogues of the big-box stores, there are also at least the beginnings of sonic farmers' markets cropping up around the country.

First and foremost, there is National Public Radio and its network of affiliates. As commercial radio and TV grew less and less interested in education and service, Congress responded not by reining them in but by setting aside a little cash to create public broadcasting. From modest beginnings (I once listened to tapes of the first few weeks of *All Things Considered*, from 1970—incredibly lively, incredibly amateurish), the national network has grown considerably. About twenty million listeners—one American in fifteen—tune in to NPR each week, a number that's grown 66 percent in the last five years, even as the iPod has begun to shrink total radio audiences.[3] Vermont has a considerably better than average public radio station, WVPR. Along with all the NPR shows, it offers a twice-weekly hour-long call-in on local topics, three five-minute commentaries every day by local residents, and a (remarkably good) weather forecast.

True, NPR appeals to a certain market segment, just as the Clear Channel stations do. The NPR listenership skews old and affluent; almost the only time that sports come up is on Saturday mornings between seven and eight, on a (remarkably clever) national show called *Only a Game*. Rock and roll gets a (remarkably lucid) hour on Saturday evenings. You aren't going to hear stock-car racing. Yet public radio stations testify to the instinct for community, if only because they all rely on listeners being willing to pay for something they can get for free. It's not a business model many economists would endorse, but it clearly works.

Many cities across the country also have "community radio stations," most of which picked up their licenses decades ago and have hung on tenaciously ever since. Portland, Oregon, has KBOO, a radio station that played a key role in promoting the city's booming local foods movement and spurring its nation-leading progress in reducing emissions of carbon dioxide. KBOO dates back to the 1960s and, to be frank, sounds like it: "politically correct" doesn't quite do justice to the station's zeitgeist. But it's a rollicking place, too, with funky music (including programs like *Gospel Express, Swing & Country*, and the ever popular *Music People Hate*); programs devoted to bikers, prisoners, and union members; and tons of volunteers running pretty much everything. Similar stations can be found in Los Angeles, the Bay Area, Minneapolis, St. Louis, New York, Little Rock, Denver. Most tilt politically left, in part because commercial radio leans so far to the right. And of course there are scads of college radio stations, busy teaching their listeners what songs they might want to download.

But frequencies are now hard to come by: the spectrum is full. Or at least, that was what people thought until a series of new technologies opened the way for low-power broadcasters to cluster on the dial without overwhelming one another or the commercial stations. If there were already stations at, say, 93.3 and 94.5, the FCC proposed allowing a low-power station in the middle, at 93.9. After truly shameless opposition from, among others, National Public Radio, a compromise version of the law was finally passed allowing at least a smattering of low-power stations, which typically cover an area of a few city blocks or a small rural valley. A group of former radio pirates, led by a fellow with the nom de mike Pete Tridish, have formed Prometheus Radio, which hosts low-power FM "barn-raisings" around the country. Volunteers converge on a given weekend to erect the antenna mast and otherwise work to get a local signal on the air once it wins its FCC license. There's a station in Immokalee, Florida, broadcasting in multiple languages to migrant farmworkers, who used it to organize their battle to win higher wages for tomato pickers. Another in Opelousas, Louisiana, sponsored by the Southern Development Foundation, broadcasts local zydeco music against the "classic rock" and "young country" formats that dominate the region. Just over the spine of the Green Mountains from where I live, Vermont's Mad River Valley launched WMRW in 2005—all volunteer, all-eclectic, with music shows like *Nothing Repeated* ("music spanning genres, eras, rhythms, and media, but guaranteed to rock") and *Green Mountain Global Local* featuring Vermont musicians. There's also *Not Everything Is About You*, where a guest brings in a favorite CD to play and discuss, and *Dinner Hour*, with "fresh, local, and healthy food talk." "We are trying to show the wealth of knowledge that exists within a community," one Prometheus volunteer explains. "The goal of this is not to project one singular message out there but to create radio that can be a locus for the community."[4]

■ ■ ■

"COMMUNITY" IS A WARM AND FUZZY WORD, AND OVERUSED, so that its meaning is slowly disappearing. There's no good working definition of how big a community can be, or how spread out, or how overlapping. Anthropology does provide us a few clues. A generation ago, in his book *Human Scale,* Kirkpatrick Sale noted that indigenous societies from Australian aborigines to Great Plains Indians seemed to cluster in collections of about five hundred individuals—a small enough number for everyone to know everyone else, large enough to provide a sound gene pool. As people began to gather in "cities," the numbers still stayed small: medieval cities often held twenty thousand souls, divided quite literally into four "quarters," each with its own church at the center. Modern architects and planners have hit on roughly similar scales as ideal, pointing out that such densities allow neighborhoods large enough to host schools and shops, but small enough that everything lies within easy walking distance.[5] Are such communities large enough to be stimulating? As Lewis Mumford pointed out, most of the Greek city-states of antiquity averaged ten thousand residents and yet, precisely because they were "cut closer to the human measure . . . the result was not merely a torrential outpouring of ideas and images in drama, poetry, sculpture, painting, logic, mathematics, and philosophy; but a collective life more highly energized, more heightened in its capacity for esthetic expression and rational evaluation, than had ever been achieved before." The Rome of Michelangelo had 55,000 people, Sale notes; "the Florence of Botticelli and Leonardo 40,000." A decade after the American Revolution, at the time of the first U.S. census, New York had 33,131 residents and Boston 18,320; such small communities had produced Washington, Jefferson, Adams, Madison, and Franklin at roughly the same time.[6]

There are other ways to guess at proper human scales: you can distinguish the "general outline, clothes, sex, age, and gait" of an approaching person at about 450 feet, so it's probably no

surprise that that's about the maximum dimension of successful public spaces, such as the Piazza San Marco or the Acropo-
lis, and helps explain why, say, the Mall in Washington (or for
that matter the shopping mall at almost every interstate exit)
seems so outsized. Renaissance architects held that the tallest
buildings should be about a third of the longest dimension of a
plaza, or about fifteen stories, and it's hard to argue with the feel
and the durability of the cities they created on those principles.[7]

But it's not necessary, or probably even very useful, to define the perfect size or shape of a community; it's enough to
say that, for reasons of ecological sustainability and human
satisfaction, our systems and economies have gotten too large,
and that we need to start building them back down. What we
need is a new trajectory, toward the smaller and more local.

Consider Powell, Wyoming, a town about a hundred miles
northeast of the edge of Yellowstone National Park. Powell is
about as red-state as it's possible to be: the county voted four to
one for George W. Bush in the 2004 election. In certain ways,
then, it's the polar opposite of Burlington, Vermont, or Portland,
Maine. And yet, when Wal-Mart opened a Supercenter twenty
miles away in Cody, the residents of Powell decided they didn't
want to see their downtown wither and die. Following the example of a town in Montana, they decided to open their own
clothing store. "We had between five hundred and five hundred
and fifty investors, and they each invested five hundred to a
thousand dollars," said Mike Riley, as we sit in his spare office
behind the Powell Mercantile, which opened in 2002. The Merc
looks pretty much like small-town department stores used to
look, with racks of the inexpensive things people need: cargo
pants, blue jeans, T-shirts, tube socks. (Where I grew up, this
store was called the Bargain Barn; it was where we went for gym
uniforms.) "We sell a lot of the medium price," says Riley, who
has been in the apparel business a long time. "We have four-
dollar shirts, we have ten-dollar shirts. But our best-selling
ladies' pant is fifty-nine ninety-nine."

The Powell Mercantile hasn't solved all the world's problems; it buys from the same sweatshops the big boxes patronize. But it's at least solved some of the *town*'s problems. "Our first-year goal was five hundred thousand dollars, and we took in five hundred twenty-two thousand," says Riley. "This year we did six to eight percent more." Investors—who had been warned to consider their $500 shares "more like a donation to the community"—got a 7 percent return. The Merc has opened a children's-wear annex down the block, and new stores are opening along the main street as more shoppers return to the downtown. Even more to the point, the Merc has inspired co-ops in other far-flung western towns, among them Worland, Wyoming, and Ely, Nevada. "Wal-Mart's biggest game is to kill everyone in town, and they'll do it," says Riley, and with a respectful tone in his voice. "They're awfully good at what they do. But if you want to remember who made this country, it's the little people." And in this case, the little people acting together to build something cooperatively.

SO FAR, THE RENEWED LOCAL ECONOMY EXISTS AS A SERIES OF points: a farmers' market here, a mercantile cooperative there, a radio station over there. If it's going to amount to anything substantial—if it's going to help reduce the atmospheric concentration of carbon dioxide or shift the trajectory of human satisfaction—it will need to sink significant roots.

Besides food, the most important commodity in our lives is energy, and at first blush it seems almost impossible to localize. Our energy lifelines stretch to every corner of the world: years ago, while reporting a story on the New York City utility Consolidated Edison, I found myself in the jungles of Brazil looking at oil wells, in the Gulf of Mexico on gas platforms, in uranium mines deep inside the canyon country of Arizona, and on Hydro Québec's stupendous dams in Hudson Bay. The scale of each operation was almost beyond imagination: the spillway of a single dam in the Quebec project could carry the combined flow of all the rivers of Europe. Americans are the energy-use champions of all time, requiring twice as much fossil fuel to power each of our lives as even the citizens of the affluent countries of western Europe. How could local-scale power generation ever meet this kind of demand?

It probably couldn't. But that's okay, because the first task in any attempt to deal with our energy situation is to radically cut demand, simply by using the best technology we already have available. Consider, for example, the compact fluorescent lightbulb. It provides the same amount of light as an incandescent bulb (I know this is true because almost every bulb in my home uses the technology) while using only 25 percent of the electricity. And it lasts ten times as long. There are plenty of other things that we already know how to do: we can build vehicles out of lightweight composite materials; we can insulate homes with shredded newspaper injected into the walls under high pressure. Some of these things can be done locally, and some can't, but if we do them all we'll save so much energy that local supplies will start to make more sense.

How much energy are we talking about? The chemical company DuPont recently set out to raise its energy productivity by 6 percent a year, in the hope that by 2010 it might cut its carbon dioxide emissions 65 percent below 1990 levels. By 2003, seven years ahead of schedule, it had actually cut those emissions 67 percent, and in the process saved $1.5 billion. "No magic is required," writes Amory Lovins, the longtime energy analyst at the Rocky Mountain Institute in Colorado, "just methodical application of modern techniques." He estimates, in a paper prepared with Department of Defense sponsorship, that if the United States were to spend $180 billion in the next decade, it could cut its oil imports in half, and save $70 billion *annually*.[8] The British government, meanwhile, has estimated that if every household in the United Kingdom double-glazed its windows, insulated its attic, and used the most efficient appliances, total domestic energy use would fall by 40 percent; even if homeowners employed contractors to do the work instead of performing it themselves, they'd get an 8 percent return on their investment.[9]

Still, no matter how thrifty you are, you need to generate some power. For decades, our model for doing that has been highly centralized: we produce electricity in a few huge centralized power plants and then ship it around the country via a network of wires. It's efficient in the same way that huge factory farms are efficient, or that Clear Channel's centralized radio studios are efficient as they feed the same song out across the nation. As long as you don't worry about the side effects, such as carbon emissions, and as long as you have abundant fuel to run it on, then you can provide relatively cheap electricity, and the few people who own the plants can make a great deal of money. And—partly because of the lobbying power of these big players—most attempts to "fix" the energy sector to deal with global warming or peak oil involve marginally improving these giant, centralized plants. For instance, the federal government's single biggest attempt to "deal with" global warming involves subsidizing utilities to explore "clean coal" plants that might someday capture carbon emissions and pump them into old mines for storage. The federal government also underwrites loads of research on nuclear power, because reactors, despite their ruinous expense, fit neatly into the familiar centralized scheme.

We may need some such technologies in the years ahead; the fight to slow carbon emissions is so desperate that it's wrong to rule anything out, especially as a bridge toward some better future. But that future's more exciting possibilities lie elsewhere, in smaller community-scale power systems.

These are hard for us to imagine. We're used to thinking of solar power as a set of panels up on the roof and a set of batteries down in the basement, supporting a grinning, graying hippie happy in his off-the-grid paradise. But there's something too individualistic about this model: it's the hippie's power, for him. The result isn't like a farmers' market; it's like your own vegetable garden, from which you can't even share the extra zucchini with your neighbors. In some places it makes sense, and the people who have pioneered it deserve great credit for leading the way. But for most of America, some intermediate scale— something in between the individual cell powering the individual home, and the one great power station feeding the whole state—seems a better match. Imagine all the south-facing roofs in your suburb sporting solar panels. Imagine a building code that requires all new construction to come with solar roof tiles and solar shutters. Imagine windmills scattered around town in the gustier spots and heat pumps for extracting energy from the earth. Imagine all these pieces linked in a local grid, supplemented with small-scale fuel-burning power plants that produce not just electricity but heat that can be pumped back out to local buildings.

Such a vision makes sense in part because our current way of doing things is extraordinarily wasteful—in fact, it's almost as wasteful to bring energy across a continent as it is to bring a head of lettuce. Those big central plants are usually off by themselves in the hinterlands (if you've seen one, you know why). When they burn coal, an enormous amount of the energy is wasted as heat that simply goes up into the air; one recent British study indicated that 61 percent of the energy value of the coal just disappears. Another 4 percent vanished in the transmission process, because shipping electricity through those long networks is inherently inefficient. And another 13 percent was wasted because people were using inefficient refrigerators and dryers and other appliances in their homes. "Twenty-two percent of primary energy input is eventually used in the home—the rest is lost in the centralized system and wasted through domestic energy inefficiency," the study concluded. Worldwide, three times as much energy is put into the centralized system as is demanded by consumers: that is, three times as much coal is shoveled into the boiler as you'd need if you could eliminate those inefficiencies.[10] Among the biggest problems is reliability. If you depend on a massive central power station to deliver your electricity, you really need another one standing by in case the first one fails.

But if you're relying on dozens of smaller sources, the chances that they'll all go out at once are small to vanishing. So imagine again that, instead of working like a Clear Channel radio station, the energy grid worked more like the Internet—decentralized, and operating in both directions. You get power out, but you can also put power in. "Essentially, you'd have energy producers and users all wound up in one thing," says John Turner, the principal scientist at the National Renewable Energy Laboratory in Golden, Colorado. "It's a whole different look at how we use and make energy."[11]

Some of these ideas are still science fiction, but not all. Plenty of hospitals and universities already have "cogeneration plants," where waste heat from the generation of electricity is captured and used to provide hot water. Some European countries have begun building precisely the sort of local networks I've described. Finland, the Netherlands, and Denmark get between one-third and one-half of their power through such decentralized energy projects. In England, a pilot project in the town of Woking used sixty different local generators—including gas-fired cogeneration boilers and photovoltaic arrays—to power, heat, and cool municipal buildings and the town's housing projects, as well as many of the downtown businesses. Carbon emissions fell 77 percent; in the event of a nationwide blackout, the town could be isolated from the main grid and go on working. (There wasn't even much for potential terrorists to attack.) Woking was able to pay for the pioneering system through energy savings, and pension funds across Europe now invest in such schemes because they like the steady low-risk returns they offer. The pace of such change could pick up considerably if, instead of subsidizing big fossil-fuel plants, governments offered substantial tax breaks for putting in solar panels, changed building codes, and required the large utilities to purchase surplus electricity from such networks at premium prices. You could even offset some of the cost by taxing the waste heat that spews from utility smokestacks.[12]

Twenty years ago, all this would have been impossible. Solar and wind power were still so marginal that only well-heeled enthusiasts could afford to employ them. But that's changing, and quickly. Global wind capacity has shot up at an average annual rate of nearly 30 percent in the last decade, and the power generated by bigger turbines is nearly as cheap as coal. (And the bigger the blade, the less danger to migrating birds.) Solar power seems poised for a similar takeoff. It's still more expensive, but the cost is dropping fairly fast. In Japan, solar power used to be only for pocket calculators, but with strong government promotion, the country now has three times as much photovoltaic capacity as the United States, even though it has far less land, and gets half as much sun as California. With low-interest loans, rebates for homeowners, and laws that force utilities to buy back excess power, Japan has become the world's leader in photovoltaic use—and, not surprisingly, the leader in manufacturing solar panels as well. The program has worked so well that government subsidies are now being eliminated, while the growth in capacity continues.[13]

If the United States were to get serious about doing the same thing, we could match the Japanese achievements. Even after factoring in shade from trees and south-facing exposures and regions that are too cloudy, "residential and commercial rooftop space in the U.S. could accommodate up to 710,000 megawatts of solar electric power," according to a nonprofit consortium called the Energy Foundation. That's three-quarters of all the electricity the United States uses.[14] And around the world? By one estimate, a mere two-thirds of what the rich world spends *in one year* subsidizing fossil fuels would suffice to provide renewable power to all the currently nonelectrified parts of sub-

Saharan Africa. If China set up a decentralized system instead of the massive power plants it's now rushing to build, its eventual carbon emissions would be less than half of what is now predicted.[15]

Perhaps it's thinking about energy in new ways that's hardest. Instead of something that you buy from far away, energy becomes something you help make and distribute to your neighbors. On a sunny day I can walk down to the electric meter under my porch and watch it spin the wrong way. As long as the sun stays out, the solar panels on my roof make me a utility. It's a sweet feeling, knowing that my neighbor's refrigerator is running off the panels above my head. By their very nature, fuels like solar and wind are diffuse and dispersed: instead of a few people digging them from the ground, a great many of us can harvest them from the planet's surface. So to really make localized power generation work you need a community. Ask yourself why Japan leads the world in building a decentralized solar-panel energy economy. Because it has so much sun (it doesn't), or because it has so much fellowship? Because it's equatorial (it's not), or because people feel both an obligation to one another and an ability to trust one another?

In a hyper-individualized world, by contrast, cost is all that matters. I'll get the cheapest possible electricity and not worry about its effects; if you want to tax me to help jump-start other technology, I'll vote for someone else; come back when photovoltaics are cheaper than coal. Randy Udall, who runs a nonprofit organization that builds solar energy systems in Pitkin County, Colorado, expresses his frustration with the hyper-individualized mind-set. "If I heard it once, I heard it a dozen times: 'What's the payback?'" he says. "I heard it from an architect, a rancher, an engineer, an electrical inspector." An average solar system, he notes, costs $10,000. "Americans routinely pay three thousand dollars for a four-pound laptop, and forty thousand dollars for a sport utility vehicle that loses thousands of dollars the moment it leaves the dealer's lot. . . . In no other realm does the 'What's the payback?' mentality prevail." The average cost increase for using solar energy, he adds, works out to $1.44 a day. "Any family that can afford cable television could probably afford to get some power from the sun."[16]

It's true, though, that solar and wind power sources come with big up-front costs. The sun may be free, but for the panels you have to write a check—unless there are enough people in your community willing to make it possible in other ways. In Michigan, a company has begun installing rooftop-mounted wind turbines on customers' buildings for free; it will charge them for electricity, but at a rate guaranteed to be lower than the local utility's. In Hull, Massachusetts, two town-operated turbines take advantage of the winds sweeping across Boston harbor. A few miles away, the city of Lynn is building a turbine to power its wastewater treatment plant; a few miles farther, the Massachusetts Maritime Academy is building one of its own, which will power a third of the campus. A hundred community-scale wind projects are on the boards around the country.[17] In Ontario, a new provincial initiative allows home-owners, farmers, cooperatives, schools, and towns to set up small renewable projects and then sell the power to the grid at a fixed price for twenty years. This is exactly the scheme that en-abled Denmark and Germany to build so many community windmills.[18] "Turbines should be owned by communities, indi-viduals, businesses and cooperatives" instead of giant utilities, says Bill Becker, who builds ten-foot-tall turbines that look "like DNA helixes whirling around a vertical shaft." Distrib-uted power, he says, "builds the model of local self-sufficiency, control, power. People feel they control their lives."[19]

Somewhere there's a sweet spot between too big and too small. Many people have opposed large-scale wind turbine de-velopments in places like the waters off Cape Cod or the ridge-lines of Vermont. Sometimes their arguments are just selfish: Not in View of My Deck. But I've had many earnest people explain to me that they don't think their valley should be overwhelmed just to feed more power down the grid to the rest of the country, because the rest of the country will simply waste it. That's a reasonable point, even if you believe, as I do, that the global warming numbers nonetheless require that we build those big turbines as soon as possible. At any rate, if the power from Cape Cod were staying in Cape Cod there'd be strong incentive to work on energy efficiency, to make sure that your neighbors had enough insulation. You'd understand where your juice came from, and what it really cost, instead of having the current out-of-sight, out-of-mind relationship.

At Middlebury College in Vermont, where I'm on the faculty, planners are trying to figure out how to use biomass—in this case, wood chips—to replace hundreds of thousands of gallons of oil currently heating and cooling the campus. The project was driven by concern over high oil prices and high carbon emissions, but because the wood chips were going to come from close to home, some difficult questions immediately arose. Could the chips be harvested in some ecologically sensible manner, or would we end up deforesting the state? That's the kind of question you ask when all the costs and benefits are local, when you can't simply count on someone removing a mountaintop in West Virginia to get at the coal, or someone else laying down his life to defend an oil pipeline in the Persian Gulf. Such questions lead to creative solutions: could Vermont farmers who are going broke raising milk instead start raising fast-growing willows, which could be harvested for use in the college boilers? If doing that made economic sense, would it also make ecological sense—would the willows soak up decades' worth of nitrogen from the over-fertilizing of corn before it can wash into Lake Champlain? Might the willows provide new cover for nesting birds?

So far the answers all seem to be "Maybe"; there's an eleven-acre test plot of willows in the ground, and the college is inching toward a future in which it spends millions of dollars on local wood rather than on Saudi crude, and does so in a way that strengthens instead of weakens the local community. Prodded by students, Middlebury is converting college vehicles to biodiesel, and now a number of Vermont farms have begun producing that fuel on a small scale. Others are converting their manure piles into methane generators, and selling the resulting "cow power" to the local utilities.

Local economies could also help with the other huge part of our energy problem: the vast amounts of oil we use to transport ourselves and our stuff. As we've sprawled into ever more spread-out suburbs, and allowed big-box stores to replace compact downtowns, we have done more and more driving. In his book *Believing Cassandra*, the ecological economist Alan AtKisson lists a hundred cities by the amount of carbon per capita that their occupants spew into the atmosphere through transportation. The first ten cities on the list are all American, and the first nineteen all in the United States, Canada, and Australia. (Twentieth? That would be Riyadh, Saudi Arabia.) What's really staggering is the size of the gaps between cities. Your average Atlantan releases about eight thousand kilograms of carbon dioxide each year through transportation; your average Londoner or Athenian or Düsseldorfer or Glaswegian, barely an eighth as much. That's partly because the residents of European cities live much closer to their shops, parks, and schools and so can walk or bike five times as often.[20]

These differences build on one another. The Dutch are not biologically different from people in Savannah; both live in relatively flat places with temperate climates. But the Netherlands has built all kinds of bicycle paths, which they use for more than a quarter of all their trips. Of course, the places the Dutch need to go are easily accessible by bike, not moated off by six-lane roads.[21] Meanwhile, Americans have free parking, low vehicle taxes, and heavily subsidized auto roads; no wonder we have the highest rate of car ownership in the world. And no wonder that U.S. bicyclists are twelve times more likely to die per mile traveled than motorists. (It's three times as dangerous to ride a bike here as in the Netherlands.)[22] On the other hand, Portland, Oregon, has seen a rise in pedestrian and bike traffic, but a steady fall in the number of injuries: "If a city increases safety with better intersections and more bike lanes, then more people feel safe to walk and bike." Meanwhile, according to data published in the journal *Injury Prevention*, "the more often drivers encounter walkers or cyclists, the more they expect to encounter them, and the more cautiously they drive."[23] A car is the ultimate expression of individualism; a crosswalk is about community.

And so, of course, is a bus. When your city or town has sprawled wildly, public transportation becomes increasingly difficult; even the finest technology is overwhelmed. Recently, I took a ride on the world's first hydrogen-powered bus, in Reykjavík, Iceland. It was a thing of great beauty as it cruised silently toward downtown. Fuel cells that would have filled the space of several passenger seats five years earlier were now small enough to fit in the roof panels. And out the exhaust pipe: a trickle of water. "You could drink it!" Hördur Gíslason, a bus-system manager, tells me. "You wouldn't want to—but in an emergency!" As I ride, though, the problem becomes obvious: most of the time I have the bus to myself. Not because it's a hydrogen bus; because it's a bus. "The problem is more to have people appreciate it," says Gíslason with a sigh. "The buses are used, but we can't say heavily used. Icelanders can afford a car. . . . And we went pretty much from the individual horse into the private car." Not only that, but as the economy has boomed in recent years, Reykjavík has sprawled. As Gíslason stands at the world's only hydrogen filling station, he points at the horizon: "There's part of Reykjavík here, and part over there, and now a new part over there. . . . We have a European standard of bus service," says Gíslason, "but we have the American syndrome of the private. That's our case."

As interesting as new technologies like hydrogen may someday prove to be, far more important advances will involve what you might call the technologies of community. Years ago I spent some months in the Brazilian city of Curitiba—not particularly wealthy, not particularly advanced, but with a mayor, Jaime Lerner, who was an absolute genius at spreading the idea of cooperation. He built the world's best bus system. It was the best not because the fleet used some exotic fuel, but because the buses ran in dedicated lanes and had doors that slid open like those on a train. Stoplights turned green for the buses whenever they approached, and cars were simply out of luck. As a result, passengers could get on and off quickly, the buses knifed through traffic, and soon everyone was taking them. Lerner had built the equivalent of a subway system at perhaps 10 percent of the cost, and as a result the Curitibanos were using a quarter less energy per capita than other urban Brazilians. The underlying reason was that they had a new idea about their relationship with each other: "In this city, the public is more important than the private," said Lerner. His constituents rejoiced in the pedestrian plazas that replaced many of the old car-filled streets. And many Curitibanos came to enjoy seeing more of each other as they shared the bus. By the end of his term in office, Lerner had an approval rating above 90 percent. The same techniques work elsewhere: When a similar "bus rapid transit" system was built in the southwestern Chinese province of Yunnan, car traffic fell by 20 percent and bus ridership during rush hour jumped 500 percent.[24] But projects like this won't spread fast enough unless we can somehow break the spell of privateness, figure out ways to forge what the mayor of Curitiba called "gregariousness."

The idea that this is somehow foreign to the American character simply isn't true, or at least it wasn't once upon a time. As James Howard Kunstler notes in his account of peak oil, *The Long Emergency*, between 1890 and 1920 American cities and towns built hundreds of local and interurban streetcar lines that together constituted a remarkable network. Save for two twenty-mile gaps in upstate New York, you could ride the trolley lines from Boston to Wisconsin without a break.[25] We could build such a network again—but only if people were willing to get out of their cars and do their errands in the company of others. The hyper-individualistic idea that I need to go exactly where I want to go exactly at this instant, and with the radio station I want playing on the car stereo, is relatively new, but very powerful. To challenge it requires a public commitment to high-quality transit—a bus that comes often enough, say, that riders don't have to stand and wait for half an hour. And it wouldn't hurt, as is the case on the downtown buses in Boulder, Colorado, if you could hand the driver one of your CDs and she'd slap it in the sound system. It makes the experience convivial; it turns other people on the bus into your companions, if only for a little while.

If high-quality mass transit sounds expensive, that's only because of the categories we're used to building in our minds. As Alan AtKisson points out, "It has long been believed that building roads is good for the economy of cities, while public transport is a financial drain." But according to a recent World Bank report, cities that emphasize walking, cycling, and public transport spend a far smaller percentage of their total wealth on moving people around than car-oriented cities do: only 4 or 5 percent of their wealth is expended on transport, compared with up to 17 percent in freeway-dependent cities, like Phoenix. This makes sense, if you think about it. A road used as a busway carries 7,000 people per hour, compared with 2,500 per hour in cars, which adds up to a lot less paving and patching, not to mention more land for other uses. Think of the extra space there'd be if half the parking lots in your town were suddenly free for other purposes. Meanwhile, households can save as much as $750,000 over a lifetime if the bus system works well enough to enable people not to buy a second car.[26] The result might contribute less to GNP growth, but it would surely cut some of the stress that comes with carrying endless debt.

IF THE SPRAWLING NEW SUBDIVISION WITH TWO PEOPLE TO AN acre represents one end of a spectrum, the opposite end might be anchored by the so-called cohousing communities that began to spring up in Denmark in the last few decades and have since spread around the world. They're still relatively few in number in America, but they represent a powerful idea: that the desire for more community might begin to radically alter the ways we imagine our lives. Cohousing communities aren't communes. People have private dwellings, often attached condo style to a block of others. But the houses are small, because the community shares certain facilities: a kitchen and dining hall, playrooms for the kids, guest rooms for visitors, a laundry, tool sheds. Since the duties are shared—maybe you cook dinner once a week for the whole community—residents have more free time. And there's always someone else nearby—which can take some getting used to, but which also offers real pleasures.

I remember visiting one of America's largest cohousing communities, EcoVillage in Ithaca, New York, shortly after it opened in 1996. As the name implies, its residents were good environmentalists, trying to reduce their impact on the planet; they'd superinsulated their clusters of small homes and built them with southern exposures to maximize sunlight. The dining hall composted whatever wasn't eaten; the compost was spread on the community's CSA farm-garden, which took up some of the open space left by the decision to concentrate all the homes in one spot. Residents lobbied successfully for a bus stop by their entrance, and at odd hours they shared cars. As a result, they used about 40 percent less gas and electricity than others in the U.S. Northeast and on average, one engineer-resident had calculated, each member required about fourteen acres of the planet to support him or her, compared with twenty-four acres for the typical American. "Right now our resource use is roughly equivalent to that of someone living in New Zealand or Brazil," the engineer calculated. "To be truly sustainable, we need to match the resource use of someone living in Jordan or Turkey."

But the reason people were attracted to the community had less to do with green zeal than with the possibility for real human contact. In a recent book about the project, EcoVillage's founder, Liz Walker, described the physical decline of one resident who was diagnosed with incurable stomach cancer shortly after she moved to the village. She battled the cancer for three years, with the help of those around her: one of her neighbors, a professional singer, serenaded her during her chemo treatments; when the drugs sickened her, another cooked special meals every day to keep her eating. "Many others visited, helped with transportation or shopping, or just looked in to make sure she was all right," recalled Walker. A few weeks before the woman died, the entire community organized a "living memorial" for her in the dining hall, with music and food and a celebration of her life. Though the dying woman was too sick to attend, someone made a video, which she watched many times in her last days.[27] The knowledge that you matter to others is a kind of security that no money can purchase. No one has systematically surveyed the "life satisfaction" of co-housing occupants, but I'd be willing to place a small wager on what they'd find if they did.

What's interesting, of course, is that these folksinging, hug-giving affluent Westerners are consciously and unconsciously creating the kind of village life that can still be found in most of the developing world, but which melts away daily under the ever-hotter sun of economic modernization. The Ithacans hooked up almost from the start in a sister-city relationship with the Senegalese fishing village of Yoff, home to forty thousand devout Muslims on the outskirts of Dakar. In 1992, a delegation went from upstate New York to the African town, and much of what they found attracted them: "extended families

lived in densely clustered compounds in homes made from local sand mixed with cement. There were almost no cars," just
sand paths; hunger was virtually unknown, because people
lived on the grains and vegetables they grew in their own gardens and the fish they caught in the nearby ocean. "On Fridays, after prayers, local elders mediated conflict under a
baobab tree," notes Walker. Since everyone knew everyone
else, crime was rare. If someone stole, "the thief would not be
allowed back into the village."

But that traditional way of life was under assault. Dakar's
slums grew ever nearer as migration from rural peasant farms
increased—the same migration triggered around the world by
agribusinesses building "more efficient" farms, the same migration that has emptied so much of rural America. Fish were
getting harder to find, mostly because huge foreign trawlers
operating off the coast were efficiently strip-mining the sea.
And young people were leaving. "They watch TV shows like
Dallas and think that's the way all Americans live," one
town leader said. "And then that's the way they want to live,
too." Individualism *is* deeply attractive, all the more so when
it's tied so closely to modernity. When the two villages hosted
a conference, the university-educated Senegalese planners
were all for building more roads and importing more cars,
while the cohousing leaders from upstate New York tried to
steer them toward buses.[28] Doubtless the greatest gift the
Westerners brought was their respect for the value of traditional ways: perhaps, if white experts marveled at what they
were doing, local people would be able to see their lives
through new eyes. Or perhaps not. In a world where everyone
can watch *Dallas*, modernity, hyper-individualism, may be a
phase through which humans need to pass before they can figure out its limitations.

When I first heard about cohousing communities, they
struck me as both enticing and far-fetched, so distant from the
prevailing American ideal of independence that it was hard to

imagine them ever amounting to much. But in the years since, my mother has aged to the point where she's thinking about selling her house and moving, like so many others, into an "assisted living community," one of those retirement complexes where you have a small condo or apartment with its own kitchenette, but where you also take a meal or two every day in common. Where there's always some organized activity under way. Where there's a nursing home attached for the very last years of life. We've visited a few of them now, and they remind me of places like EcoVillage Ithaca, with the unnatural exception that everyone is old. Still, their clear attractiveness to affluent Americans is a sign of both how old community ties have decayed, and how people can decide to reach, albeit often out of a sense of fear, toward more interdependence instead of less.

MOST PROGRESS TOWARD LOCAL ECONOMIES WILL PROBABLY arise not so much from grand visions as from slow modifications. We've talked about food, about radio, about energy, but the same kind of analysis can be done for almost any commodity.

I live in the forested Northeast and have spent most of my life in poor communities where working in the woods is one of the chief ways of making a living. These communities remain poor partly because logging, like farming, has become a globalized and industrialized business aiming at the lowest possible price. Most independent loggers, just like farmers, invest heavily in machinery (a skidder, for instance, which pulls tree trunks from the forest to the road, can easily cost $100,000). Once the note from the bank is hanging over your head, you have to increase your rate of production. As a result, loggers work longer hours than they should and get hurt in all kinds of gruesome ways: you know you're in a logging town when many of the men are missing random fingers. Loggers also take shortcuts that damage the environment: it's "more efficient," for instance, to clear-cut an acre than to carefully select which individual trees should come down in order to open up enough sunlight to release the others to grow faster. Even cutting corners, a logger won't get rich, any more than a farmer will. If he's lucky, he survives and keeps all his limbs, while most of the profit goes to the middlemen at the big mills, who have all the leverage in the system. Meanwhile, the guy buying flooring for his house has no clue about any of this; wood is wood, just like wheat is wheat.

If you start to think a little differently, much can change. In our county, a forester named David Brynn launched a program called Vermont Family Forests. Landowners who sign up have to follow a set of strict ecological guidelines, for instance building good culverts when their skid roads cross a stream. This takes more time, and hence more money, than sloppy logging, and the only way to supply that money is to figure out how to take some of the middlemen out of the picture—to capture more of the price not only for the landowner, but also for the logger and the guy driving the logging truck. One method they've pioneered is to convince buyers that they don't need to use "clear-grain" lumber for building—that knots and mineral stains in the wood, far from being defects, actually show "character." This marketing enables loggers to get a decent price for the lesser trees they thin to improve stands, and makes the forest as a whole more profitable. A Middlebury College professor, John Elder, describes what it's like to walk the halls of the school's big new science building, whose interiors all come from this kind of "inferior" wood from the local forests: "The impact of such variation in the woodwork turns out to be spectacular. Rather than just con-tributing a subliminal element to the overall design, this wood grabs you. I know that I'm often arrested in hurrying down a corridor by the flamed and swirled boards around me, and I've seen any number of faculty members and students pause to study (and touch) these walls in a way that woodwork ordinarily does not inspire." In the end, he adds, though the logging job cost more to do in Vermont than it would have on the industrial Pennsylvania woodlots originally scheduled to supply the wood, because there were fewer middlemen involved and because the wood did not have to be transported as far, the job came in $40,000 under estimate.[29]

Vermont Family Forests has even greater ambitions for the future, including trying to return some of the state's forest land to local people, instead of the second-home owners and big corporations who own it now. In their "community equity forest" model, when acreage comes on the market the local land trust buys the development rights to make sure the land doesn't turn into yet another subdivision. VFF then buys the land itself, and resells it in shares to local people, including many who live below the poverty line. With each share comes the right to cut firewood on the land (and thereby help get rid of the trees that need to be thinned) as well as a share of the profits when, every ten years or so, the land is logged under the program's strict ecological requirements.

To snowshoe on a cold winter day up the Little Hogback in Monkton, the site of VFF's first community forestry project, is to sense this new way of thinking about the woods. As a group of potential owners navigates the snowdrifts, David Brynn points out all the trees, marked with blue paint, that will be cut in the first harvest. "We've got somewhere between forty-nine thousand and fifty thousand board feet set to go," he says, as he demonstrates how to eyeball the amount of usable wood in any given "stem" and then how to multiply it by the amount it will fetch at the mill. But he's just as quick to point out the places on the 116 acres that will never be logged, because "they're too fragile, too shallow to bedrock, too unique." He stops everyone in a clearing, shows them a towering hemlock. "If we do this right," he says, "we'll be able to protect the forest health in perpetuity, and to provide access for community members who might not otherwise be able to afford to own anything around here." No one will make a killing; VFF estimates that the return to shareholders will be about 3 percent annually, which any big corporation would scoff at; it would be far wiser, in a world fixated on economic growth, to chop down every tree, sell the timber to the highest bidder, and then invest the profits in some new scheme earning three times the return on investment. On the other hand, under the VFF plan the forest won't wither away. And sixteen people will be working together toward a new end. It's a different way of looking at the same reality.

Trees don't grow everywhere; in other parts of the country and the world, other raw materials can be incorporated into new economies. A growing number of builders are starting to use cob or straw-bale or adobe—whatever is close to hand in their regions—to build new homes and offices. One upstate New York architect explained to a contractor's journal some of the tradeoffs. "You replace the efficiency of mass production with the efficiency of local gathering of materials," he said. "The balance shifts from material expense to labor expense," just as it does on small farms. The savings aren't enormous, because the walls of a house don't cost as much as the windows and doors and mechanical systems, but such materials lend themselves to teams of friends and neighbors pitching in to build. They also tend to *work* well, holding an even temperature with less energy used for heating or cooling. And, unlike most new houses, they look as if they belong to the landscape. "The fussy, trendy, anachronistic rooflines, cupolas and turrets in contemporary subdivisions," wrote one architect, "are palliative attempts at endowing these spiritless developments with aesthetic substance." To put it another way, new suburban houses all seem to have been built for entry-level monarchs; you almost expect to see moats. By contrast, with traditional building materials, "light catches and plays on hand-plastered walls; subtly imperfect floors offer sensory interest; unusual corners lend variety." They have the same effect as the swirly knotted wood on the walls of the Middlebury science building.[30]

IF YOU REALLY WANTED TO MAKE A LOCAL ECONOMY SOAR, THE most important step might be to create a local currency. Say I lived in Burlington, Vermont, and I had in my wallet, next to my federal greenbacks, a wad of "Burlington Bread," an alternative currency that could be spent only in the metropolitan area. Faced with the choice of buying local food at the farmers' market or food imported from California at the Stop & Shop, I'd be more likely to buy the local product, which I could pay for in Bread, and save my U.S. dollars for something that had to come from a distance—a new car, say. And then the local farmer would have Burlington Bread in her wallet, increasing the likelihood that her next purchase would be local, and so on.

About four thousand "complementary currency" schemes are in operation around the planet; they aim to supplement national money, not to replace it. Few if any of the projects have grown very large; existing mostly in a small ghetto of vegetarian restaurants and politically committed masseuses, they provide a medium of exchange mostly useful for backrubs in college towns. Although Burlington Bread works better than some such systems, most merchants in town aren't willing to take it, much less use it to pay part of their employees' salary. Money is tricky stuff. "Anyone who says they understand money hasn't thought enough about it," the economist Herman Daly once said. (Even the apparently simple question of where money comes from is hard to answer. It's not the government printing press; money really originates when banks make loans. And since they charge interest for those loans, part of the endless-economic-growth model is in place right from the beginning—without the growth, you can't pay off the interest.) Since the

Nixon administration took the United States off the gold standard in the early 1970s, money is no longer backed by anything of intrinsic worth; its value rests merely on the shared confidence of its users in the system that produces it.

Which means, theoretically, that since the value of money is based on trust, there should be room for plenty of currencies to exist side by side. Somehow, though, the various local money systems never seem quite real to most people; that shared confidence doesn't radiate beyond a circle too small to make a real difference in local economies. If the only place I can spend this money is the vegan pizza parlor, do I really want it in my pocket? New ventures are promising—Berk-shares, in western Massachusetts, are issued by three local banks. But there's still no perfect example.

This puzzle has been playing itself out in the mind of Bob Costanza, who now heads the Gund Institute of the University of Vermont and also serves on the board of directors for Burlington Bread. "I got interested in it because it makes so much sense," he said. "Whenever you're transacting things in dollars, you're competing in a global market. With a local currency, you're giving an automatic preference to local manufacturers." The key to making it work on a larger scale is to build the same shared trust that backs a dollar, and the key to *that* is to involve a really big economic player: the city government. "Say the city issues the currency as a small part of employee pay, or welfare payments, or spending on community projects," Costanza says. "And they agree to accept it back for taxes, or licensing fees." Inflation shouldn't be a problem, because the city wouldn't print more of the stuff than it was willing to take back. And once the Bread has begun to circulate, everyone else would be more willing to accept it—as change from the cash register, as part of their wages—because they know they wouldn't be stuck with it. If worse came to worst, they'd use it to pay part of their tax bill. (Or, since Burlington owns its own municipal utility, part of the electricity bill.) "Pretty soon," says Melinda Moulton, one of the city's biggest real estate developers, "I'm able to buy my carrot juice at the deli with it, and then the deli owner goes down to the Intervale to buy some of his carrots from local farmers, and so on." If the city gets involved, then other big players, most notably, the state university, would likely follow.

But the chicken-and-egg problem isn't solved quite yet, because the city government is worried about being stuck with Bread, too, and wants to be sure of a place to spend it. "The onus is on the local-currency people to prove over the next year or two that there are vendors willing to take it from the city," says Ed Antczak, of the city's economic development office. "It's like 'Bring me the broomstick of the Witch of the West.' Because otherwise it's a little 'out there' for the city to get involved."

One of Costanza's colleagues in the university economics department assigned students to survey a random sample of the city's four thousand suppliers of goods and services. Sixty-five percent said they were definitely or possibly willing to take the Bread from the city if the city in turn would accept it for taxes or electricity or both. "That's a pretty substantial number, especially since it was students interviewing them," said the professor, Josh Farley. "If you had the mayor making the case, there'd be a lot more interest still, I imagine." Which is a big if, of course—politicians are quick to avoid anything that might seem a little goofy, like printing your own money. But as more people come to fear the tower of debt atop which the U.S. dollar is precariously balanced, the attractiveness of a fallback plan grows. Perhaps it's the current scheme, with its requirement of endless growth in a finite world, that seems utopian and far-fetched.

YOU CAN MAKE A STRONG ECONOMIC ARGUMENT, EVEN IN CONventional terms, for more localized economies. Think of a

Wal-Mart, taking in a million dollars a day selling you groceries from its network of giant and distant factory farms. When the register finally closes for the night, most of that money is simply sucked back to the corporate headquarters in Arkansas; after the suppliers (those people getting carpal tunnel syndrome cutting the chickens) are paid, and after the company awards its "associates" their poverty-level wages, the profit ends up in the already overstuffed bank accounts of the company heirs or corporate executives (and, of course, with the stockholders, who include average people investing through their pension plans).

If you spent the money with a local farmer instead, it would recirculate in the community at least a couple of times before it leaked away into the larger economy. Even in a small state like Vermont, a recent study found that if local consumers "substituted local production for only 10 percent of the food we import, it would result in $376 million in new economic output, including $69 million in personal earnings from 3,616 new jobs."[31] Other studies around the world find the same kind of ratios: £10 spent at a local British food business is worth £25 to the local economy, but only £14 if spent at a supermarket. "The farmer buys a drink at the local pub; the pub owner gets a car tune-up at the local mechanic; the mechanic brings a shirt to the local tailor; the tailor buys some bread at the local bakery; the baker buys wheat for bread and fruit for muffins from the local farmer. When these businesses are not owned locally, money leaves the community at every transaction." Indeed, writes Brian Halweil, in his study of local food, "this sort of multiplier is perhaps most important in the developing world. . . . In West Africa, for example, each $1 of new income for a farmer yields an average income increase to other local workers in the local economy, ranging from $1.96 in Niger to $2.88 in Burkina Faso. No equivalent local increases occur when people spend money on imported foods."[32]

Tangible commodities such as timber and apples are not

the only ones that might be localized. Take entertainment, for instance. During almost all of human history, people provided it for themselves: music (like food) was something you produced, and the pleasure was as much in the production as the consumption. With the advent of recording, and then of broadcasting, all that changed; the new technologies allowed us to be more efficient and single out the best musicians and let everyone else listen to them simultaneously, much as factory farming allowed 1 percent of Americans to feed the rest of us. We began to take it for granted that music came from somewhere else: Tin Pan Alley, Hollywood, Nashville. Now, of course, new technology is beginning to undermine that century-old system: file sharing allows listeners to, in essence, wander onto the big farmer's fields and glean what they like. The recording industry's short-term solution was to sue file sharers, and the slightly longer-term fix was to sell their music over the Web; if they can't protect their profit margin, they argue, there will be a "reduction in creative activity" because without the possibility of growing rich, fewer people will write songs.

Perhaps. But people wrote songs for millennia before they had any chance of making big money at it. At most, you could make a decent living as a wandering bard—a profession that seems to be coming back into style. The *New York Times* rock critic Jon Pareles wrote recently that while "selling pop music on expensively produced and promoted CD's is a paradigm under siege," "jam bands" in the tradition of the Grateful Dead and Phish "have flourished as concert mainstays and as an alternative to canned music," and in the process bring "music's ancient business model—the roving troubadour—to the interconnected modern world." Imagine, he says, "current pop turned inside out. Playing concerts would be a living rather than a promotional tool, bands would take musical chances nightly, wardrobe would be an afterthought. . . . Music's past would be a foundation rather than a scrap heap."[33] Such changes aren't only taking place in America. In England, government figures showed "a live music renaissance underway across the country," with half of pubs, clubs, and restaurants featuring at least occasional live acts.[34] Bands still sell recordings, but more and more, they sell them to the people who come to the shows, audiences that are interested in a shared community at least as much as virtuosity.

It's as if musicians were suddenly, like the new wave of farmers, able to grow smaller quantities of more interesting crops and find reasonably profitable markets for them. The live shows that provide more of their revenue are the equivalent of farmers' markets, places that customers love not only for the product but for the experience. No one gets superrich, à la Mariah Carey or Archer Daniels Midland or Exxon Mobil; but plenty more people get to do something lovely, whether it's grow berries for their neighbors or write songs for their region. This parallel musical universe may not replace the centralized global one, but it's clearly gaining. How far might it go? Here's a statistic that gives some small indication: in 1900, in the state of Iowa alone, which was then crowded with small farmers, there were also *thirteen hundred* local opera houses, all of them hosting concerts. "Thousands of tenors," writes Robert Frank, "earned adequate, if modest, livings performing before live audiences."[35]

The syndrome of consolidation, and reaction against it, appears in almost every sphere of our life. Consider education. Pursuing economies of scale, we've built ever-larger high schools and universities, saying that they offer "more opportunities." But one of the opportunities they offer is the opportunity for students to disappear into the crowd. Realizing this, many parents have begun looking for much smaller alternatives. Some have taken localism to its extreme and begun homeschooling, the equivalent of growing your own self-sufficient vegetable garden or hoisting your off-the-grid windmill—but most of these parents soon form "homeschool circles" to offer their kids some companionship. More parents and teachers have fought for charter schools, for magnet schools. There are schools that concentrate on computers, or on Spanish, or on theater; they draw supporters from the progressive left and the Christian right; but they all share a vision: smaller size, more attention. More *community*. Such schools are also the equivalent of a farmers' market: you can't get everything in every season, the way you can at the supermarket, but what you do get is good, and it comes from someone you know and trust.

In considering commodities like entertainment and education, we've begun to move away from purely economic goods, such as apples or electrons, and toward more intangible items. The most basic of these, of course, is our democracy itself.

No need here to rehearse the whole tired litany of our political malaise: declining participation, the replacement of debate with combat, our inability to come to terms with the biggest problems we face. Many of these problems stem from scale. Once government reaches a certain size, it becomes hard to imagine that the individual citizen matters—an insight long held by the far left and the far right, but one I'd never paid much attention to. Then, a few years ago, my family moved from New York, America's third-largest state, to Vermont, its second smallest. Our new house was about seventy miles from the old one and, like the old one, stood in the mountains at an elevation of fifteen hundred feet. But the new terrain felt quite different. Vermont really *is* small—spend a year there and you're likely to meet the state's two senators and its lone congressman. You're almost certain to meet the governor, a Republican named Jim Douglas, who attends almost any event that offers a chance to shake hands. While New York's state government was essentially a black box called "Albany," into which money and ideas disappeared, our state representative here in Vermont lives four houses away from us. The state guards that smallness. A few years ago, an out-of-state plutocrat moved into Vermont and announced he was running for the U.S. Senate on the

Republican ticket. This kind of thing happens everywhere, and usually people just shrug; those millions buy enough TV ads to do the trick. In Vermont, the plutocrat found himself with a primary opponent: an octogenarian dairy farmer named Fred Tuttle, the main plank of whose campaign platform was that rich carpetbaggers should live here a little while before trying to run the show. He had two questions for the millionaire in their debate: how many teats on a cow, and how do you pronounce the Vermont town that is spelled "Calais"? The millionaire flubbed both, and Tuttle won the primary easily (though he genially lost in the general election to the equally local incumbent, Patrick Leahy).

Vermont's independence isn't rooted in ideology. For a hundred years after the Civil War, it was the most reliably Republican state in the Union; these days, it elects both a conservative governor and a socialist senator. Its independence comes from its size, and from an institution that takes advantage of that size: the town meeting. Every March, residents of the nine cities and 237 towns in the Green Mountain State assemble in town halls or school gymnasiums for town meetings. The traditional meeting lasts all day—people take it off from work—and features a potluck supper. People sit next to their neighbors on folding chairs and debate the issues the town faces. Should we buy a new road grader? Do we need a library? Should we consolidate our school system or pay the freight to keep our small school open? Town meeting can be dull: the forty-five-minute debate over why *exactly* the roof of the new school is now leaking and what *precisely* should be done to fix it inspires a few thoughts about what might be on television tonight. And this may not be the most efficient way to conduct the town's business—electing a mayor and letting him decide might use fewer person-hours in the course of a year. (Allowing a lobbyist to simply write the legislation he's paid for is simplest of all.) But town meeting is a school for educating residents about public affairs: for making them citizens.

Frank Bryan, a local political scientist who is one of Vermont's iconic figures, has been studying town meetings for decades. Every spring he sends students out to fifty or so of them to record attendance, catalog who speaks about what, describe the tenor of the sessions. In a recent book cowritten with one of those students, Susan Clark, he asserts that the town meeting has inspired Vermont to take a leading role in "thoughtful social innovation" because of "the percentage of its citizens that practice face-to-face democracy as citizen legislators." Town meetings have worked through waves of ethnic immigration that brought people from around the world to Vermont; through waves of economic change that turned the state's residents from farmers into "modern" Americans; through waves of cultural change that in recent decades have seen women emerge as the majority players in many town meetings, "something that has never been true in any (not one!) state legislative session or session of the American Congress in the entire history of the United States of America," note Bryan and Clark. And what are these Vermonters doing? In 2006, five towns voted to ask Vermont's congressman to impeach President Bush, which made the national news. Richmond, reversing a decision it had made a few years back, approved full-day kindergarten; Charlotte voted down a move to cut $150,000 from the road budget; Huntington listened to a local resident demand that the town buy a used sand spreader for $15,000 instead of paying $53,000 for a new one. Alburg voted 315–162 to resume spelling its town's name with a terminal "h."[36]

But there is a threat on the horizon, Bryan and Clark report, and that threat is size. A village with three hundred or four hundred voters can expect 40 percent of them to show up for town meetings; by the time the population reaches four thousand or five thousand voters, the proportion drops below 10 percent. This is both because in the larger town each voter makes less difference, and because there's more social pressure to be a good citizen if you know most of your neighbors.

"There are very few findings in all of political analysis as systematic and as strong as Bryan's size principle," one political scientist reports. This makes it hard to see how to apply the lessons of town meetings across more densely populated places.[37] But it isn't impossible. Clark and Bryan suggest "town" meetings for urban neighborhoods, a tactic pioneered in the Brazilian city of Porto Alegre, where dozens of assemblies are held across the city to set budget priorities (sewers? paved roads?) for each area. Some of the meetings draw more than a thousand people. In twelve years, the number of public schools in Porto Alegre has grown from twenty-nine to eighty-six, and literacy levels have reached 98 percent as adult education classes received extra funding. The experiment has since spread to more than a hundred cities across Latin America.

There is also evidence that those who participate in direct democracy feel better about themselves, more connected to their world. Switzerland provides a useful test case, because some of its cantons, or states, are much more directly democratic than others, holding regular referenda and thereby giving voters far greater involvement. In those cantons, people say they're happier with their lives. That may be partly because they receive better services: democracy works, and as a result their lives are easier. But such practical benefits don't account for the whole effect. Some clever social scientists have studied foreign residents in those areas, who get the benefits of the policies without being able to participate in their making, and have found that "around two-thirds of the well-being effect can be attributed to actual participation itself, and only one-third to the improvement in policy as a result of the participation."[38] We want to be a part of something larger than ourselves, yet still small enough in scale to make sense to us.

Small scale isn't always effective, especially in a world where corporations get ever larger. Imagine that Wal-Mart is planning to build a store in your town. You go out and organize your friends to stop it, mounting a town-wide campaign, and the town meeting passes a bylaw prohibiting stores over thirty-five thousand square feet. So Wal-Mart builds its store just across the town line, and your local merchants are still devastated. If you're taking on targets the size of Wal-Mart, you need to be bigger. The question is How big?

Smaller and more local units of government may actually be nimble enough to address some of the world's toughest problems. It's not the U.S. federal government, for instance, that's done anything about global warming. Instead cities and states have been active: San Francisco adopting a commitment to solar power, California cutting auto emissions, seven eastern states banding together to control power plant emissions. States have taken the lead on everything from stem cell research to medical marijuana to the right to die. Figuring out the right level on which to work often means figuring out the economics. What economies of scale will support a standard of living most of us can be happy with, yet not overwhelm the earth's physical systems? And part of that process will be psychological. Where will we find the sweet spot between individuality and community? This transition will be guided by many forces. The pace of global warming and of the rise in energy prices will create new opportunities and close off old ones, and good old-fashioned greed will play its role: every time a barrel of oil rises another dollar, someone else figures out how to make a buck with small hydro plants or community-scale windmills. Some of the impetus for change will come from the mix of hope and fear that is already driving "post-carbon" planning in hundreds of cities and towns, where people gather weekly to plot how their suburbs might survive and even flourish without cheap fossil fuel.

Some states and towns are requiring schools and hospitals to buy more of their food from local farmers. The board of supervisors in Woodbury County, Iowa, passed a law in 2005 requiring that government agencies serving food give priority to nearby farmers. They trod carefully: "This is not a subsidy of local farmers," said a spokesman. "It is expected that with the savings from reduced transportation costs, and bulk sales of local food, the price will remain competitive with historic costs for these food items." But as food activists across the country pointed out, the new rule represented real innovation, especially coming from a heartland county in a big agricultural state. Similar laws are now before legislatures across the country. They draw less on any well-worked-out theory of the future economy than on the simple, growing desire for connection with place and for community.

Consider how a newfound interest in salmon is helping make the northern Pacific coast a smaller, more integrated place—"Salmon Nation," some have begun to call it. In a book of that name, the activist Seth Zuckerman writes: "The dream of living with the salmon and healing the relations between our species has motivated hundreds of initiatives by citizens groups and entrepreneurs throughout the fish's range. . . . It has spawned watershed councils, fish-rearing projects, and bronze sculptures, and led otherwise sedentary individuals to spend Saturdays pulling brush and planting trees," all in the hope of working out "mutually beneficial terms for sharing the North Pacific basin. By doing so, we have begun to redevelop the principles for cooperation with one another."[39] Instead of treating salmon as our industrial food system currently does, as a kind of "McFish" to be reared as cheaply as possible despite the effects on the ocean, the residents of the upper Northwest are treating the fish as an organizing principle, an excuse for reintroducing themselves to each other and to the possibility that we need to think about something other than More. Salmon's *reality* helps set some standards for our shared life: if you want the fish to thrive, you can't build vacation houses on every riverbank.

It's easy—indeed, it's useful—to say that only our growth-driven affluence lets us even contemplate the salmon, imagine a salmon festival, wax poetic about a Salmon Nation. This is true (though it's also true that the Native Americans, when they ruled the coast, did much the same). It should remind us what an economic margin we possess, as a society if not as individuals. We've piled up three times as much stuff as people had fifty years ago; we should be able to figure out how to gradually refashion our lives without crashing and burning. Take Sundays off to go to church and/or clean out the salmon stream? We should be able to handle that.

Once it gets rolling, the building of connections can accelerate quickly. We learn once again what skills and gifts our neighbors possess, and they become valuable to us again, literally valuable, people we can start to depend on for some of our food, our fuel, our capital, our entertainment. In a sense, this process is already under way on the Web. Internet scale is neither big nor small; it's *distributed,* as energy and food supplies may someday be. The small nodes hook together into something much larger, but not so monolithic it can't easily hive off into new sites and communities and forums. Despite every effort to turn it into one more television set controlled by the largest info-conglomerates, the Internet continues to operate more like—to use my favorite metaphor—a farmers' market, where a million people bring their produce to sell. Or, really, to give away.

The Internet can also make us more solitary and disconnected, of course, just as television has done. But this constant, cleansing flow of information offers at least the possibility that local communities and economies might settle into place without becoming completely hidebound or parochial—that good ideas (about how to control the pests on your apple trees, or cant the blades on your wind turbine, or write the budget for your urban precinct) would keep circulating even in a world where regions produced more of their own commodities. We'd trade fewer ingredients but more recipes. If someone in upstate New York invented a way to provide cheap, low-cost medical insurance (the Ithaca Health Alliance), word would get around.

In the googling glow of the infosphere, you could really be a resident of downtown Burlington, with some Burlington Bread in your pocket; and of Vermont; and of the United States; and of the larger world.

In recent years, users of the Internet have helped organize Fair Trade campaigns to change the way that certain products (coffee, tea, chocolate, bananas) that can't be produced everywhere are sold around the globe. These campaigns exemplify what I mean about putting grit into the system: it's clearly more efficient to grow coffee on huge sun-baked plantations soaked in chemicals and tended by semi-slave labor, worrying neither about human rights nor bird populations nor soil erosion. But it's also clearly possible to pay a little more, in time and in money, to seek out coffee or cocoa that comes from people paid a living wage and working land that is more or less intact. Such coffee leaves (in every way) a better taste going down, even if you can't afford quite as much of it. The beans don't come from a single Fair Trade plantation, but from thousands upon thousands of small farms and villages, able to use the new technologies of information to export both their story and their product. These are still small and tenuous efforts, barely begun, but they are growing quickly.

In a sense, all discussion of local economies is about Fair Trade—about raising wheat and lettuce in a way that honors both farmer and soil; about growing timber in a way that allows loggers to work at a reasonable pace and in a living forest; about saving and producing energy in quantities that don't require military adventure or climatic upheaval. About giving up some measure of efficiency for other values. Some of this trade must take place at a distance; as much as possible should take place closer to home, where it saves more energy and builds tighter bonds. As this effort spreads, our politics will eventually start to change as well. In a world where more people paid attention to the lives of farmers here and abroad—met them at the market or on the Net—it would be hard to maintain the current system of corporate subsidies and ruinous "free trade" agreements. If fairness demands a slightly higher price, and if that means we need to get along with somewhat smaller quantities, I am confident we will eventually find the tradeoff worth making.

Confident for the rich parts of the world, anyway, where our affluence allows us a cushion for experimentation. The unanswered question is whether a smaller and more local economy also makes sense for the rest of the world, or whether only endless economic expansion can provide dignified lives for the poorer half of humanity.

5 | THE DURABLE FUTURE

If you want to see the spiritual center of the cult of More—its Vatican, its Mecca, its Potala Palace—you should probably visit the Chinese city of Yiwu, four hours by crowded train from Shanghai. Yiwu didn't even appear in my nine-hundred-page tourist guide to China, but it boasts sights every bit as awesome as the terra-cotta warriors of Xian, or even the Great Wall disappearing over the toothy hills. Consider the "Suitcases and Bags, Including School Bags" section of the International Trade City. It comprises about eight hundred ten-foot-by-twelve-foot stalls, each representing a different factory, each displaying its wares to buyers in the hope they'll order lots of ten thousand or twenty thousand or thirty thousand. There are stalls with duffel bags, change purses, wallets of every kind. Fanny packs, metal lunchboxes, jewelry cases. The International Trade City is also a headquarters of dubious English: "I dream of being the best basketballer in the town"; "Durable Performance Based on the 58's 123-45 Vintage Spirit"; "My grandfather has white hairlike snow." (I stared for a long time at a backpack emblazoned "All Things Grow with Love," before I figured out that it sounded weird because it was actually English.)

"Suitcases and Bags, Including School Bags," took up only half a floor of this giant building, the biggest I've ever been in.

The story above was entirely devoted to "Hardware Tools and Fittings," which is another way of saying pretty much everything on earth: knife blocks, car jacks, chaise lounges, surge protectors, lint rollers, jumper cables, carabiners, bike pumps, rubber bands, cheese graters. One stall had thousands of "Livestrong" bracelets in a rainbow of colors. Lucky rabbits' feet, singing birthday cards, nail clippers, safety pins, ratchet sets, thigh trainers, bathroom scales, toilet bowl deodorizers, plaid wheelchairs, feather dusters, meat-pounding mallets. Dozens of models of magnetic patriotic ribbons for the backs of American cars ("Freedom Is Not Free"). Pruning shears, putty knives, carafes, egg cups, cake-decorating nozzles, depilatory machines, giant martini glasses, immersion heating coils, disposable cameras, hip flasks, sake sets, mortars and pestles, cereal dispensers of the kind you see on the buffet table at the Motel 6, rolling pins, exit signs, sander belts, key rings, rubber gloves.

The International Trade City ("A Sea of Commodities, A Paradise for Purchasers") is only two-fifths built and there are still whole sectors of the manufacturing economy you have to go elsewhere to see. (China has a sock town that produces billions of pairs a year, while cigarette lighters are down the coast in Wenzhou.) But the two huge buildings already standing—they each look like the Empire State Building laid on its side and mated with a fleet of aircraft carriers—demonstrate the almost unavoidable truth that anything that can be easily made by human beings can be easily and cheaply made in China. In the "Regular Toys" section of Building 1, there are hundreds of stalls offering variations on those weird squishy rubber balls: skull-shaped balls whose eyes pop out when you squeeze; "yucky maggot balls." Not to mention boogie boards, plastic hand grenades, squeaky mallets, bow-and-arrow sets, toy pianos, "small chef" ovens. After twenty minutes of walking you emerge into the "Electric Toys" section ("Does thinking the son and daughter become the scientist? Then start growing from the electronic toy bricks! Train pilot! Look for the

Bill Gates!") and then the "Inflatable Toys Section" and then, biggest of all, "Fabric Plush Toys." The next floor is divided between artificial flowers and hair ornaments; touring this, you suddenly realize that there are 3 billion women on this planet, many of whom would probably be happy to have a ribbon in their hair. And on the floor above that, miles of kitsch: the "Tourism Crafts" section that could stock every gift shop on earth, with light-up Virgin Marys, "African" carvings, novelty bottle openers, refrigerator magnets by the millions. On the top floor, you find the stalls that bring the world Christmas. Groves of artificial trees blinking with lights, squads of illuminated Santas playing electric guitars and riding exercycles and spinning hula hoops. Tinsel tinsel tinsel. And all very ecumenical— some of the same stalls stocked red paper lanterns for the Chinese New Year. And, for Halloween, lifelike rubber masks of Osama bin Laden and Saddam Hussein.

THIS FLOOD OF STUFF REPRESENTS THE FUTURE OF POOR NA- tions, at least according to prevailing economic wisdom. Nor is this a hard or cruel wisdom, but a tender one—wrongheaded, in my view, but tender nonetheless. The argument, advanced most eloquently in recent years by journalists like Thomas Friedman in his book *The World Is Flat* and by economists like Jeffrey Sachs in his book *The End of Poverty*, goes like this. First, you industrialize agriculture. As farms grow more productive, they need fewer farmers. Those displaced move to the city, says Sachs, "drawn by higher wages that in turn reflect the higher productivity of work in densely settled urban areas." Meanwhile, the division of labor increases. It's true, Sachs points out, that the average poor rural African farmer has many talents—he can grow and cook his own food, build his own house, tend animals, make clothes. But such people "are also deeply inefficient. Adam Smith pointed out that specialization, where each of us learns just one of those skills, leads to a general improvement." Output increases if you're concentrating on just one thing, and soon you have a surplus to sell.[1] What follows, Sachs argues, is "a progression of development that moves from subsistence agriculture toward light manufacturing and urbanization and on to high-tech services."[2]

It is a reassuring gospel. Everyone emulates us, and everyone turns out like us. The *New York Times* articulated it in capsule form in an editorial that appeared in the spring of 2006: "The better off China is, the better off the rest of the world is—poor countries because they will get a shot at the jobs that leave China; rich countries because many more people all over China will finally be able to afford the expensive goods that are made in America."[3] All sorts of good-hearted people have rallied to this banner. The economist Deirdre McCloskey wrote recently in the liberal *Christian Century* magazine, "If India can restrain its Gandhian impulse to throttle the market, it can adopt American ways of retailing, Japanese ways of manufacturing, and German ways of chemical-making and enter the modern world of a wider human scope. There is no racial or cultural reason why India cannot in five or ten decades have an American standard of living. The 21st century can be a grand alternative to the Century of Protection (and Slaughter) just concluded."[4]

To this way of thinking, a future of more local economies, shorter supply lines, and reduced growth is both economically unsound and, at least with respect to the developing world, morally suspect. These economists argue instead that the only way to relieve the planet's grim poverty is to speed up the cycle of economic expansion. For proof, they point to the "tiger economies" of Asia, such as South Korea and Taiwan, which have emerged from the developing world to create economies with per capita incomes approaching those of Europe and North America. Most of all, they point to China itself, which in the last decade has seen growth like no nation in history—annual rates of 10 percent, year after year, meaning that the average income per person is doubling every seven years and that the percentage of people existing on a dollar a day has dropped from two-thirds of the population to less than a fifth.[5]

In China, you can see this change at every turn, not just in the booming skylines of the cities, but in the stories of so many people. In chapter 1, I described the shower-curtain factory north of Beijing: multiply that example by a hundred thousand. One sweaty July night, I drove out past the fifth and final (for now) ring road around Beijing. My translator and I steered through a huge new condo development with its own McDonald's, and then turned onto a road that in two hundred yards carried me into a totally different world—a once rural village now surrounded by city, soon to be swallowed up itself for yet more new condos, but for the moment home to tens of thousands of migrant families. At the north end of town, down a dark alley, we came to the home of Cao Zhong-Long, fifty-seven years old, who came to the city from Jiangxi province in 1987. "Our village didn't have enough food. *There was not any meat, not any alcohol,*" he recalled. They weren't poor, they were *poor*, the kind of poor that doesn't have enough to eat and that works so hard you just wear out.

Cao's cousin had started a construction team, so Cao went to work pedaling a tricycle-wagon to ferry materials to the job site. Before long, he'd learned how to lay ceramic tiling, then how to plaster and paint, and then he had gone into business on his own. He, his wife, and their three daughters share a room perhaps ten by twenty-five feet, one third of which is occupied by a tiny store (all evening long, people popped in to buy beer from the cooler). They sleep in one bed. And yet Cao is a poor man no longer. He's saved enough to build two houses back in his village, one two stories tall and the other three. (Every village I drove through boasts these tiled McMansions, constructed with wealth sent home from the city.) Cao's mother lives in one, and he rents out the other. In Beijing, he made only enough money to live in this slum; on the other hand, if he were home in the countryside, living in his three-story building, he'd have no way to make money. And he had things still to accomplish in the city. His second daughter had just graduated from university and was now working for a joint-venture pharmaceutical company, at a starting salary of 2,400 yuan—$240—a month. I asked him if, when she had been born out in the countryside, he had imagined she might someday go to university. He just looked at me and started to laugh.

Drawn by such successes, Chinese in staggering numbers pour out of the countryside and toward the city. It's the biggest migration in earth's history: perhaps 30 million people a year join it, although in the city they are treated as hicks and worse. They come from a hopelessly crowded countryside, where in many places the average farmer tends a plot no larger than a sixth of an acre.

It is easy to understand the motivation behind this migration. One hot night in Shanghai, I strolled along the Bund, the strip of old European banking houses that faces the river. On the other side, in the Pudong district that China has made its great urban showpiece, huge towers rose in neon splendor—the Jin Mao Tower, with the highest hotel on earth taking up its top forty floors; the Oriental Pearl TV tower, its enormous kitschy globes glowing pink against the sky; the Aurora building, with its thirty-story-high-TV screen showing ad after ad. It was enough to draw tens of thousands of spectators, content just to stand there in the dark and look. Many, perhaps most, were new arrivals from the countryside, in shabbier clothes and with darker faces than the city folk; they posed for pictures along the railing with the promise of China glowing behind them. The only neon spectacle I've ever seen that compares is Las Vegas, with its pyramids and dancing waters. But what is Las Vegas? It's the search for new stimuli for the jaded, offering thicker meat and pricier alcohol to people who've been packing away meat and alcohol for decades. It's an attempt to figure out what More might mean when you've already had too much. Whatever else it is, China's not like that at all.

BUT CAN THE CHINESE MODEL, HOWEVER ADMIRABLE, REALLY work, for the Chinese, or for anyone else?

Let's concede, for the sake of discussion, that the good-hearted economist was right when she said that there's no reason that the Indians or Chinese couldn't be as rich as Americans in a few decades, if they follow our economic model. What would that mean? Well, if China alone were to match America in the extent of car ownership, there would be 1.1 billion more vehicles on the road. Those vehicles might be "clean," in the sense that the Chinese would be able to afford catalytic converters for their tailpipes. But they would also produce more carbon dioxide annually than the whole of the rest of the world's transportation systems. A 2002 report by the UN pointed out that if China consumed as much seafood per capita as Japan now does, it would require 100 million tons of fish all by itself. This exceeds the total of the current world catch, which is already so large that many fisheries are being pushed to extinction.[6]

Changes in this direction are happening right now. If you stand in any Chinese city, look at the horizon, and rotate 360 degrees, you will see a dozen construction cranes; in some places, you'll see a hundred, even if the smog cuts visibility to half a mile. China has more than a hundred cities with populations topping a million; by some estimates, it needs to add an urban infrastructure equivalent to Houston's every four weeks just to keep pace. Global production of crude steel grew 8.8 percent in 2004, passing the billion-ton mark for the first time—almost entirely because of Chinese demand.[7] China already uses more steel than the United States, and it has surpassed us in grain and coal consumption as well.

As prices for commodities rise because of American over-consumption and Chinese growth, the first to pay the price have been poor people elsewhere in the world. African countries, for example, spend an estimated 80 percent of their export earnings importing oil.[8] Remember those numbers from chapter 1: if the Chinese ate meat the way we do, they'd use two-thirds of the world's grain harvest; if they drove as many cars as we do, they'd use all the oil the world currently produces plus 15 million extra barrels a day. "The western economic model," the eco-statistician Lester Brown says simply, "the fossil-fuel based, auto-centered throwaway economy is not going to work for China. And if it does not work for China, it will not work for India, which has an economy growing at 7 percent a year and a population projected to surpass China's in 2030. Nor will it work for the other three billion people in the developing world who are also dreaming the American dream."[9]

The planet is already buckling under the weight of one America—we've seen the rising temperatures, the erratic and extreme weather, the melting ice caps. Each of us uses 6 times as much energy as the average Mexican, 38 times as much as the average Indian, 531 times as much as the man in the Ethiopian street.[10] That gives you some rough idea of what it would mean if most of the rest of the world even approached our level of consumption. We'd need extra planets, several of them.

You can sense the approach of some of these limits just wandering around China. One day in Beijing I piled into a Chinese-made SUV with a telecom programmer, Zhang Jun-Feng, who volunteers with a local environmental group monitoring the capital's water supply. Our goal was to follow the Chao River, the main supplier of Beijing's chief reservoir. It was a trip neither of us had taken before, and it was revealing in all too many ways.

Though the lowlands were covered in corn (and when you

walked the rows you discovered they were carefully inter-planted with potatoes, something that doesn't happen on a tractor-planted Iowa industrial farm), the hills were essentially bare. Treeless, they were eroding, a reminder that as China tries to cope with its environmental troubles, it does so in a landscape that's been used hard for two thousand years. They've seen especially hard wear in the last fifty, having had to cope with Chairman Mao. In 1958, for instance, the Great Helmsman declared the Great Leap Forward, which required most of the peasantry to stop raising crops and start making iron in their backyards. Making iron requires heat, which required wood, which required deforestation, and since not making iron would have been a bad idea, the hills were soon bare.

Grasslands have disappeared under capitalism the way forests did under Mao. With newly prosperous urban markets demanding meat, the number of livestock swelled. Lester Brown estimates that there are 280 million goats and sheep in the country, compared with 8 million in the United States. "I've been in areas where the farmers have to put human clothes on their mohair goats to keep them from grazing each other," he reports. "There's nothing to eat." Without roots to hold the soil, much of the countryside has simply turned to sand. Deserts advance hundreds of kilometers annually, and the dust storms of April and May are now a recognized Beijing season, just like spring and fall. Think Dust Bowl circa 1934, except in Pennsylvania and New Jersey instead of Oklahoma, and without a nice empty California to send the refugees to. To produce eight ounces of beef takes twenty-five thousand liters of water, on average.[11] And yet, of course, people *want* meat. And alcohol. "To raise beer consumption for each Chinese adult by just 1 bottle per year takes an additional 370,000 tons of grain," says Brown. "Three additional bottles per person would take the equivalent of Norway's annual grain harvest." And even, say, pet food. "All over the world, ownership of companion animals and pet food sales rise with incomes," notes Alex Avery of the Hudson Institute. "Already, China's small-family policy is stimulating increased pet ownership. It is reasonable to project that China in 2050 will have more than 500 million cats and dogs, translating into significantly increased demand for pet food, including more meat, fishmeal and protein meal."[12] The point, of course, is not that we should have it and they shouldn't; it's that extending Western-style consumption to the developing world is not going to work.

Water may be China's single greatest challenge. The south of the country floods chronically; the north is parched. As flows along the Chao and other rivers have declined, Beijing has been drawing more and more of its water from an underground aquifer, and as a result the water table is sinking by meters every year. "Some northern cities will simply be out of water in eight or ten years," says Ma Jun, the author of *China's Water Crisis*, the one great environmental book China has so far produced. The earth subsides into sinkholes in dozens of places every year now, and fissures yards wide suddenly appear like earthquake faults. *National Geographic* came for a look recently and decided the country was committing "ecological suicide." To deal with the water crisis, China's leaders have dusted off a plan Mao dreamed up in 1952: a pair of thousand-mile-long canals designed to carry water from the south to the north. That's an almost insane idea, roughly comparable to putting Lake Superior in an aqueduct in order to let Phoenix keep watering its lawns. But the situation is so grave that even environmentalists like Ma cross their fingers and hope for the best. "People in the north have been using water in a crazy way for the last fifty years because they knew it would someday flow from the Yangtze," he says. "Now the time has come for the promise to be realized."

The problem, he quickly adds, is that the extra water will probably just be used to fuel a new round of rapid economic growth and frivolous consumption. For instance, Beijing has thirteen ski slopes in the surrounding mountains, all of them relying on man-made snow. And the city has just opened a fourteenth—indoors. This is the point at which the challenges of China's past intersect with the challenges of its future. Which is to say, how on earth do you grow at the rate the Chinese are growing, and not collapse?

As my translator and I drove back to Beijing along the bone-dry White River, another of the city's main water sources, we passed one new high-tension line after another, their massive, still shiny steel towers stretching over the hills in the same rippling waves as the Great Wall. In each of the past two years, China has added 65 gigawatts of generating capacity to its grid. You can picture this any number of ways: they're adding California to their electric system annually, or half of India, or Brazil. No power grid on earth has ever grown anywhere near that fast. Despite utterly unprecedented growth in supply, the grid is stretched to the breaking point; twenty-four of China's thirty-one provinces had rolling blackouts last year. "In some provinces plants only operate three or four days a week," says Yang Fuqiang, the Beijing-based director of the Energy Foundation. "You get five or six or seven percent loss in GDP." In late July, the Beijing authorities announced that the 4,689 local factories "will arrange week-long summer vacations for their employees in the coming four weeks" to save power, and then offset the holidays by "adopting a temporary six-day-week schedule in the coming fall."

The explanation for this surge is relatively simple, and it has everything to do with those farmers streaming into the city: Yang, hunched over his computer in a Beijing office where the thermostat is turned to 82 degrees in summertime to save energy, says the best guess is that as many as 30 million people come to the cities every year. There, they make enough money to start consuming power. The average rural Chinese peasant uses the equivalent of about one 100-watt bulb annually, but in the city people buy small refrigerators and take jobs making shower curtains and spatulas and suitcases.

And building even cement huts for them requires all sorts of resources—10 percent of China's fuel may go to producing cement alone. That's what growth *means*.

Again, it's not as if the Chinese haven't noticed that big problems come with this kind of growth. By some estimates, 8 or 10 percent of the country's GDP goes to deal with pollution and its effects on health. In an interview of rare candor, Pan Yue, the country's deputy environment minister, told *Der Spiegel* in 2005 that the country's economic "miracle will end soon because the environment can no longer keep pace." That's the word from the front. Do the math.

THERE ARE A COUPLE OF OTHER PROBLEMS WITH THE IDEA THAT the poor nations of the world are going to grow their way out of poverty by draining their countrysides, moving into shantytowns, working in factories, and exporting stuff to the rest of the world. One struck me as I wandered the endless aisles of the Yiwu trade city. It's pretty clear that China alone, even with 60 percent of its people still back on the farm, can produce most of the stuff that the world would ever need. Even a world of 6 billion people can use only so many shower curtains.

This is not a theoretical point. Lobbyists like Jack Abramoff worked hard to make sure that factories on Saipan, in the northern Mariana Islands, would have low-tariff, low-wage access to the American market. This worked—until world quotas on Chinese clothing fell, and Chinese exports surged. Then the Saipan factories started to close fast; the Saipan Garment Manufacturers Association predicted that sales would drop by 50 percent in 2005. For many of the female workers who once ran the looms, a *New York Times* reporter found, "the most lucrative option is a furtive life of hunting male tourists who will pay $50 for a 'special massage.' "[13] The effects of the Chinese export boom are being felt everywhere. By May 2005, calculated one watchdog group, "46 factories had closed in Sri Lanka, with

26,000 jobs lost, and 20 factories had closed in Cambodia, with another 26,000 jobs gone—one tenth of jobs in the [garment manufacture] industry. According to some reports, 1,900 factories had closed in Bangladesh by April 2005."[14] As Thomas Friedman put it recently, "You have to feel sorry for the Mexicans; they are hearing the giant sucking sound in stereo these days—from China in one ear and India in the other." Mexico has lost 500,000 manufacturing jobs; even plastic Virgins of Guadalupe come from China.[15]

The Chinese have made a strategic decision to emphasize industry and the export earnings it brings. Thanks to water shortages, soil erosion, the replacement of fields with factories, and some bouts of hot weather, Chinese grain harvests have fallen sharply in recent years. Their gamble is that all that stuff at the Yiwu International Trade City—the Virgins of Guadalupe and the school bags and the disposable lighters and the Livestrong bracelets—will earn enough that they can buy their grain (and their oil) on the world market. It's a pretty good bet, too; the Chinese trade surplus with the United States is enormous, and America produces most of the world's surplus wheat and corn. *But the Chinese strategy is not a strategy that can work for everyone.* World grain yields, after rising faster than the rate of population growth for the three decades after World War II, started to plateau in the mid-1980s. In per capita terms, the earth produces considerably less rice, wheat, and corn than it did a generation ago. And if China becomes a big buyer instead of a big producer (2005 was its first year as a net importer), food will be scarcer and more expensive for everyone else. China's is not, as I said, a strategy anyone else can emulate—not Bangladesh, not India, not Africa, not anyone. The world can't produce enough grain.

Meanwhile, the growth that has taken place in China and in other developing countries is in many ways suspect. Much of it has come from onetime mining of resources: Indonesia saw a decade and a half of 7 percent annual growth in the latter part of the twentieth century, but when the World Resources Institute recalculated the figures to subtract the value of the extracted oil and logged trees from the country's stock of assets, that growth rate was halved.[16] The Cambridge economist Partha Dasgupta says such scenarios are common: "GNP misleads because it does not acknowledge that capital assets depreciate. This happens if increases in GNP are brought about by mining capital assets—for example, degrading ecosystems and depleting oil and mineral deposits—without investing appropriate amounts of output in the accumulation of other forms of capital such as knowledge and skills." In fact, that's a perfectly typical scenario: if someone with political connections manages to gain control of, say, a mangrove swamp that serves as the basis of a community fishery, he can cut down the mangroves, put in a shrimp farm, and export the prawns to Japan. He gets rich, and the GNP goes up, but most people get steadily poorer. After four or five years, he abandons the shrimp farm because the waters have grown diseased, eliminating even the few jobs he originally provided. In studying the three decades between 1965 and 1993, Dasgupta found that the "inclusive" or actual wealth of every country save China declined, even as their GNPs shot up. Bangladesh appears by the official tally to be growing steadily more prosperous, but by Dasgupta's more useful measure, "at the end of the period the average Bangladeshi was only about half as wealthy as he or she was at the beginning."[17]

You can see this phenomenon most easily when you look at farming, far and away the most important part of the developing world's economy. When I was last in Bangladesh, I came across a fascinating report prepared by the World Bank called "Vision 2020." It urged that the country make use of its best asset, cheap labor, by pushing to the city many of the 80 percent of Bangladeshis who still live on the farm. In the city, they could make T-shirts or shower curtains. Meanwhile, the land could be turned into larger plantations perfect for growing export crops; two the report mentioned were giant prawns and cut flowers for the Japanese wedding trade. Which would be nice for the Japanese, and for Bengali prawn exporters, but would also mean the end of the small-scale peasant landholding system that still supplies four-fifths of the country's people with their livelihood.

The agricultural analyst Brian Tokar observes that in virtually every corner of the developing world, Western economic planners have "underwritten policies that diverted once independent farmers toward the chemical-intensive production of cash crops. . . . For marginalized farmers throughout the world, this has brought an increasing dependence on unstable world crop prices, rising indebtedness for costly equipment and chemical inputs, and, often, the forced removal of people from traditional lands that have sustained their communities for countless generations." The effect, in the words of the Japanese economist Ichiyo Muto, has been to transform "traditional poverty into modernized poverty designed to function smoothly in the world economic system."[18] In practice, that means moving people off farms and into slums. A few places, like China, are actually seeing real cities arise; in most places, though, as Mike Davis points out in his book *Planet of Slums*, what's growing are empires of corrugated tin and cardboard, miles of hovels filled with people who have nothing to do. Ninety-five percent of the population growth this century will occur in the cities of the developing world, "overwhelmingly in poor cities, and the majority of it in slums."[19]

In Central America, the U.S. Agency for International Development has promoted export-oriented farming, complete with the need for farmers to go into debt for American-made pesticides and seed. "Many of the new crops, such as melons and pineapples, reaped greater profits," writes the journalist Christopher Cook, "but not for the farmers—rather for U.S. agribusiness firms such as Dole and Del Monte. Meanwhile, production of staple foods such as corn and beans plummeted."[20] In Mexico,

the North American Free Trade Agreement (NAFTA) was supposed to "rationalize" agriculture, as, in a sense, it has. Great
floods of subsidized corn grown in factory farms across the Midwest have "washed away 1.3 million small farmers in Mexico,"
according to Michael Pollan.[21] Mexican farmers can grow corn
for 4 cents a pound, compared with the 6 cents a pound it costs
to grow on American farms, but government subsidies bring our
price down to 3 cents a pound, thereby setting the world price,
wrecking the Mexican countryside, and enriching firms like
Archer Daniels Midland.[22] "Unable to compete, they have left
their land to join the swelling pools of Mexico's urban unemployed," reports Pollan. "Others migrate to the U.S. to pick our
crops—former farmers become day laborers." The small farmers
forced off their land sell out to larger farmers, who, adopting the
industrial agricultural practices of the north, use far more water
and chemicals. "Mexico's scarce water resources are leaching
north, one tomato at a time," Pollan says. "It's absurd for a
country like Mexico—whose people are often hungry—to use its
best land to grow produce for a country where food is so abundant that its people are obese—but under free trade, it makes
economic sense."[23]

Name a crop. Coffee? Ten years ago, 30 percent of its retail
value stayed in the country where it was grown. Then countries like Vietnam were urged by the World Bank to stop growing rice for domestic production and start growing coffee, and
"by 2000, with the heavy use of fertilizers," the British journalist Felicity Lawrence reports, "Vietnam had turned itself
into the second coffee-producing country in the world, after
Brazil." This accomplishment required "severe deforestation"
and "negative ecological effects caused by over-fertilization
and widespread irrigation." As Vietnam and other export producers came on line, the bottom dropped out of coffee's world
price. Now the countries that grow the beans keep only 10 percent of their retail value. Lawrence describes a recent trip to an
impoverished corner of Uganda, where she sat with a coffee-

growing family that could no longer afford school fees for their children. Her translator tried to explain to the farmer how much a cup of coffee sold for in a Starbucks: one cup cost the equivalent of 5,000 Ugandan shillings. "A confused smile flickered across his face," Lawrence reports, "registering disbelief, but then his eyes filled with tears. 'No, you mean one kilo, no, no, this is painful to hear. I only got two hundred shillings a kilo for my coffee this year.' "[24] What about bananas, up there at the front of the store, one of the "known value items" that supermarkets compete on in order to draw customers? As a result of pressure from the big chains to drive down costs—one of the world's biggest supermarkets dropped the price it would pay by 40 percent between 2001 and 2003—worker pay in the world's banana zones fell below a living wage, benefits were slashed, and workers' unions were crushed.[25]

In Iraq, one of the first laws adopted by the U.S.-led transition government in 2003 protected the patenting of plants and seeds, even though 97 percent of Iraqi farmers used seeds saved from their own crops or from local markets to grow their food. "The new law is presented as being necessary to ensure the supply of good quality seeds in Iraq, and to facilitate Iraq's membership in the World Trade Organization," reported the GRAIN, an international organization promoting sustainable agriculture. "What it will actually do is facilitate the penetration of Iraqi agriculture by the likes of Monsanto, Syngenta, Bayer, and Dow Chemical."[26] Does this sound overly suspicious? Daniel Amstutz, the man named by the U.S. government to oversee agriculture reconstruction in Iraq, was a former Cargill executive. "It's like putting Saddam Hussein in the chair of a human rights commission," one observer said. "This guy is uniquely well-placed to . . . bust open the Iraqi market, but singularly ill-equipped to lead a reconstruction effort in a developing country."[27]

■ ■ ■

ECONOMISTS CAN ARGUE ENDLESSLY ABOUT THE MEANING OF such decisions. Is GNP growth worth the sacrifice of individual families? Are we just in some long transition, waiting for a blessed payoff at the end? Increasingly, the people who live in the developing world are making their own on-the-ground perceptions pretty clear. Across Latin America, the governments that followed the neoliberal, export-led, growth-at-all-costs model have been voted out of office one after another, by citizens disgusted with precisely the kind of inequalities and injustices that economists like Partha Dasgupta describe. In India, where Jeffrey Sachs had been advising the government of Prime Minister Atal Behari Vajpayee to aim for even higher annual growth rates, voters turned Vajpayee's party out of office in 2004, mostly because they saw all the benefits of the expansion accruing to the relatively few Indians who live in big cities.

The Chinese, of course, can't vote. But even in China, where growth has been most spectacular, it's far from clear how the benefits really tally up. Dasgupta says that if soil erosion and urban air pollution are factored into the statistics, even the Chinese may not really be growing wealthier. By many estimates, seventy-five thousand or more riots and demonstrations take place every year against factories that seize peasant land or pollute common waters: a decade ago, there were about ten thousand such demonstrations a year. When my guide and I were following the Chao River out of Beijing, we drove through one small town where farmers had hung a straightforward banner across the road: "For our children, give us back our clean water. Stop the gold mine!" In the next small town we came to the mine itself, where the day before farmers had clearly rioted—all the paving stones had been pulled up and piled in a barricade across the paint-splattered entrance of the now empty facility. And that was tame. That same week, the *New York Times* correspondent Howard French reported on a larger conflict in the village of Xinchang, 180 miles south of Shanghai:

"As many as 15,000 people massed here Sunday night and waged a pitched battle with the authorities, overturning police cars and throwing stones for hours, undeterred by thick clouds of tear gas." They were protesting a chemical plant whose owners had seized local land and made farming all but impossible. " 'Our fields won't produce grain anymore,' said a 46-year-old woman who lives near the plant. 'We don't dare to eat food grown from anywhere near here.' "[28]

A large part of the problem, of course, is that growth is producing wild inequities around the developing world. *Nations* don't get richer; people in them do, and often not very many of them. In chapter 1, I talked about the Gini coefficient, a tool economists use to measure inequality. The American index has soared to .40 in recent decades, but the Chinese, for all their economic success, are doing even worse, at .45. (In Japan, by contrast, the number was .25.) Even within the closed world of high-level Chinese politics, numbers like that are causing a stir. The government shelved plans for more privatization in 2006 after critics said the new laws amounted to offering "equal protection for a rich man's car and a beggar man's walking stick." The party started a campaign to emphasize "social equity" alongside rapid growth.[29]

It's also worth remembering, though for now the matter is largely theoretical, that even should economic growth enrich *many* people, at a certain point that will turn into a mixed blessing for them. Most people in the developing world still have so little that more money means more satisfaction and the sacrifices of community for stuff are worth making. But those who have begun to "make it" have also begun to resemble Westerners in less-than-happy ways. Trading traditional diets for more processed food, for instance, makes people start to look like us: the proportion of Chinese men classified as overweight rose from 4 percent to 15 percent between 1997 and 2005, and the percentage of overweight women has doubled to 20 percent of the population. "Mexicans now drink more Coca-Cola than milk," said one nutritionist.[30] And even as the Chinese emulate our notions of success (when I was there, a new reality show debuted: *Wise Man Takes All*, modeled on Donald Trump's *The Apprentice* and judging contestants on "audacity, professionalism, leadership, negotiation skills, and ability to withstand pressure"), they also begin to feel the effects. A recent survey by the *China Youth Daily* found that 66 percent of young people "considered themselves under heavy pressure" to do well. Mark Magnier, a reporter for the *Los Angeles Times*, quoted one typical man in his thirties, with an $11,000-a-year job and a degree from the country's finest university: "Life is so stressful, I feel enormous pressure on my shoulders all the time. If I could only do better somehow, I might become rich and happy."[31]

GROWTH IN THE DEVELOPING WORLD IS OFTEN INEFFECTIVE; when it does work it can lead to the same cul-de-sacs we in the rich world have already entered; and, in any event, there's not enough stuff for our model to spread around the globe. But what else is on offer?

Begin with this: if the rich countries of the world can't change course, then the poor countries won't. America's biggest exports are television programs and movies—modeling our idea of the good life, which is wildly out of scale with what the rest of the world uses and what the planet can deliver. (By one calculation, an American family will use more fossil fuel between the stroke of midnight on New Year's Eve and dinnertime on January 2 than a Tanzanian family will use in an entire year.)[32] If we continue to idolize Donald Trump, then the Chinese will create their own versions of him. If we can't move away from the ideal of the hyper-individual, then much of the world will keep running in the same direction. So first-world economies must become less interested in growth and more locally rooted. But, assuming such a change actually begins here at home, what might that deep economy eventually look like in the poor world?

Most obviously, if the rich world began making less extreme demands on the planet, poor countries would have more physical margin to work with—a little slack. This is desirable, of course, because the poor world *is* too poor. As the agronomist Jules Pretty has put it, "A connectedness to place is no kind of desirable life if it brings only a single meal a day, or children are unable to attend school for lack of food and books, or options for wage earning are degrading and soul-destroying."[33] If home is a hut and there's no chair for anyone to sit on, that's wrong. The planet should be able to produce enough chairs, enough basic educations, enough refrigerators to keep vaccines cool. These things will require the burning of fossil fuel and will thus send more carbon into the atmosphere. If we Americans can use less coal and gas and oil, we'll in effect free some of the atmosphere to absorb the carbon that the poor world must emit to meet basic needs. And, we should do more than that: having become rich by filling the air with our effluents, we should share some of that wealth with the developing world in the form of aid and technology. You can even put a number on how much money we're talking about. If you value carbon at current rates, each American owes the rest of the world between $273 and $1,086 a year for the privilege of polluting more than our fair share. At the lower end, that's about $73 billion annually, which would accomplish an awful lot of "development."[34]

But the next question is: what should that development look like? It should look to the local far more than to the global. It should concentrate on creating and sustaining strong communities, not creating a culture of economic individualism. It should worry less about what's ideal from a classical economist's view of markets, and far more about what's ecologically possible. It should aim not at growth but at durability. It should avoid the romantic fantasies offered by the prophets of endless wealth in favor of the blunter realism of people looking out for each other, much as they have over the millennia of human existence. In other words, it won't be all that different from what we need to achieve in the rich world, though we begin so unimaginably far apart that for a very long time North and South will continue to look very different.

CONSIDER, AS BEFORE, AGRICULTURE FIRST. IF WE WANT TO MAX-imize the amount of food grown per dollar of investment, then industrialization—prawn farms, cut flowers, endless seas of corn—is the way to go. It's possible to grow more food per farmer that way; one guy in a giant combine can take care of a thousand acres, as long as he's got enough oil and chemicals. A couple of guys can handle one hundred thousand chickens in a barracks.

But in most of the world, there's no shortage of farmers. In India, 60 percent of the population works on the land. If you "modernized" their agriculture to the Western ideal, 600 million people would need to find new jobs, not to mention new places to live, new cultures, new identities.[35] So remember the good news from chapter 2: the abundant evidence that if it's *food* you're worried about, not dollars, the most productive farms are often much smaller. Peasant farms, not Cargill farms.

Those farms are more productive still if they can rely on commonly held resources—pastures and woodlots and the like. "For as long as people have managed natural resources, we have engaged in forms of collective action," writes Jules Pretty. "Farming households have collaborated on water management, labor sharing, and marketing; pastoralists have co-managed grasslands; fishing families and their communities have jointly managed aquatic resources. Such collaboration has been institutionalized in many local associations, through clan or kin groups, water users' groups, grazing management societies, women's self-help groups."

Governments and aid agencies rarely pay much attention to these local institutions, in part because they get in the way of industrialized "efficient-scale" production, and in part because environmentalists allowed themselves to become preoccupied with the idea of the "tragedy of the commons."[36] In the late 1960s, the ecologist Garrett Hardin argued that if a community held a piece of land where everyone could graze, the arrangement would inevitably deteriorate because someone would take advantage and put too many of his own cows on the pasture, who would eat its grass down to the roots, leaving desert behind. The "tragedy of the commons" really reflected what happened when hyper-individualism came into contact with older, more community-oriented ideas about the land. In fact, all around the world, as long as communities remained intact so did the commons; there exist forests, pastures, and fisheries that have been collectively managed for millennia. Even in the United States, such systems are still at work. The garlic farmer Stanley Crawford, for instance, has written with moving authority about the *acequias*, the commonly managed irrigation ditches of New Mexico, which are still maintained by shared labor and an ancient code of conduct.[37]

But even in the poor world, such systems fall into disrepair when all the funding and attention are sucked up by big, privatized operations. In India, where the poorest part of the population may derive 40 percent of their income from common pastures, forests, and ponds, the number of villages that enforce these old laws "has declined steadily over the last fifty years," according to Pretty. We can hear an echo of the enclosures that fenced off the fields and forests of Britain two hundred years ago, and for that matter, of the American decision to turn the commons of the broadcast frequency over to big conglomerates. But commons that have been weakened can be strengthened again; indeed, there are signs of life in many places. In India, for example, the Navdanya ("Nine Seeds") movement protects local varieties of rice and other staples by cataloguing them, declaring them common property, and setting up locally owned seed banks.[38]

Let me tell a similar story that I think of often, this one from neighboring Bangladesh. I spent some time in the countryside there a few years ago with the leaders of the Nayakrishi Andolon (or New Farming) movement, and one village sticks most powerfully in my mind. Gorasin, on the edge of the Louhajang River, had no stores that we would recognize as such, no car, no electric lines, no television, no telephones. There were just small fields, a cow, some chickens, barefoot children, banana palms swaying in the breeze. The call to prayer from a nearby muezzin drifted over the croplands. Gorasin was about as far from the center of the world as you can possibly get. Our guides that day were the people who lived there. Their dwellings were small huts, smaller than trailer homes. They were showing us sesame seed plants, loofah sponge gourds, eggplants, sugarcane, bamboo. Onions, pulses, all manner of local leafy greens. All grown without pesticides, without fertilizer, and without seed imported from the laboratories of the West. Gorasin sits in a large self-declared pesticide-free zone, one of several organic oases established around the country by adherents of the Nayakrishi Andolon.

The movement arose in response to numerous environmental hazards that the villagers traced to pesticides. "When we women went to collect water, we would be affected," one villager was saying. She was in her twenties, beautiful, gregarious. "Our skin would absorb the poisons. We would get itchiness, get gastric trouble. Now we've adopted our own solution. The water is pure again."

"The cows used to eat the grass and drop dead," one man added. "And then the villagers would fight each other."

"We grew up with a saying: 'We Bengalis are made of rice and fish,'" said another man. "Then the fish started catching diseases. We are not scientists, but we made the connection between pesticide and fish death. Since we've started organic farming, the fish are now healthier and more plentiful."

"A fertilized plant jumps up fast and falls right over," said a third. "Our plants are strong and healthy. Theirs, you eat it and you get sick. The minute you say 'Nayakrishi' in the market, though, people will pay more, because they know they're saving on health care."

The people of Gorasin are not "primitive," "traditional" farmers. A few miles away, at the Nayakrishi training school for the Tangail district, 25 varieties of papaya were growing, along with 112 varieties of jackfruit, all catalogued by the farmers by taste, size, color, season, habitat. Wicker baskets and clay pots in a darkened shed contained 300 varieties of local rice, 20 kinds of bitter gourd, 84 varieties of local beans. "Do you know how much it costs to build a gene bank like the ones where botanists store plant varieties?" asks Farhad Mazhar. Mazhar is a founder of the Center for Development Alternatives (known by its Bengali acronym, UBINIG), a Dhaka-based organization that helped launch the Nayakrishi movement. "No scientist can afford to catalogue hundreds of varieties of rice. But farmers are doing it as part of household activity. Our little seed station has more vegetables than the national gene bank, which spends millions. But we can do it for free."

In the process, activists insist, they can rejuvenate village life. Farida Akhter, Mazhar's partner in running UBINIG, is one of Bangladesh's leading feminists. She set up the nation's only women's bookstore and led a long fight against forced sterilization by international agencies. If you ask her what single step would most improve the lot of Bengali women, she does not hesitate: "I'd want rural women to have control over seeds again. That's women's power, or was before the multinationals started selling their new varieties in the last few decades. Traditionally, the woman is the one who knows what a good seed is, what will germinate, how to store it. Maybe they like the sound of the seed when they flick it, the weight of it on the winnowers, how it looks. They'll cut a seed with their teeth and listen to the sound it makes. They know how to dry it, how many times to put it under the sun, and whether to use the morning sun or the afternoon sun. Men used to discuss with their wives what kind of crop to raise for next year. But now they listen to the seed seller. The woman has become redundant, a burden."

Our last night in Gorasin, we sat in the courtyard by everyone's small huts. The whole village of thirty-five or forty people was on hand. Two babies were using a grapefruit as a ball, which every person in the village would roll back to them with great smiles. It takes a village to raise a child, indeed, and to raise a crop. And to raise a song: one of the men, Akkas Ali, mentioned that he had written a hundred songs praising organic agriculture, tunes he and the other men had sung at local markets in an effort to convert other farmers. We ate fat bananas and listened as the sun set. "Nayakrishi has corrected my mistakes," he sang in a reedy Bengali, as the rest of the village clapped rhythmically. "Food from Nayakrishi is so much better. No longer do I eat the poisons. Why should I eat that life-destroying stuff? Bangladesh will come to an end, unless you turn to Nayakrishi. If you use organic fertilizer, the Almighty will be behind you, and you'll be having no more gastric problems."[39]

It's easy to romanticize happy village life. (Just as it's easy to romanticize "modern agriculture," especially if you're Archer Daniels Midland, with the money to hire ad agencies and churn out commercials populated by smiling farm families.) What's important is simply to realize that places like Gorasin represent another data point, one well outside a conventional view of the world. There are many other data points. Those farms springing up on the abandoned lots of Detroit; the 220 acres of former dump now providing about a tenth of the fresh food in Burlington, Vermont. I've already described the buses in the Brazilian city of Curitiba; the city administrators were agricultural innovators, too. There, as across Latin America, the shantytowns swelled with new arrivals pushed off their land by the expansion of factory farming. But in every poor favela the city government had set up small farm plots, where some of the older men would teach the kids how to plant and grow. Soon the shantytown inhabitants were supplying themselves with a good deal of food, and supplying the city with all the trees and flowers for its extensive parks. In the years since, the city's mayor became the governor of the state and established a series of villages meant to constitute a new farm belt, to push back against encroaching agribusiness. By even more recent Brazilian standards, he is far from radical; in other parts of the country, the movement of landless peasants continues to occupy giant plantation lands, trying to wrest control back from absentee owners.

The new forms of local farming often rely on technologies that are subtler and in many ways more powerful than the oil-and-poison brew of industrialized agriculture. Around the developing world, for instance, people are making more use of biogas digesters. If you have a cow, you can shovel its manure into a cement tank, where it ferments, giving off enough gas to heat your shower and fire your wok. (In China I even saw rice cookers that had been converted to biogas.) The residue from the fermentation is ideally suited for fertilizer, so the process is a closed loop, which contributes to dignified lives without contributing much to the GNP. It's clever, like the hundreds of clever ideas the Cubans came up with once they could no longer rely on the standard chemical armory.

Often, clever ideas can even begin to repair some of the damage caused by industrialized agriculture. In West and Central Africa, according to a report in the *Ecologist*, the invasive lilylike water hyacinth poses a huge problem. Water hyacinth has spread wildly, clogging waterways across the continent, as subsistence farms gave way to big export-oriented monocultures that used vast amounts of synthetic fertilizer, much of which inevitably washed into the rivers. Those rivers were already soaked with nutrients because industrial logging, and forest clearing for those factory farms, had dramatically increased the erosion of topsoil. Once all those nutrients were in the rivers, they just sat there, because a series of big dams had not only displaced millions of farmers but also turned fast-flowing streams into stagnant lakes. As the water hyacinths therefore bloomed out of control, experts tried to check them in any number of modern ways. They used herbicides, for instance, but the hyacinths have a fifteen-year germination period, meaning you need to get at the roots and seeds, so the main effect of the chemicals was to "destroy entire aquatic ecosystems and the livelihoods that depend on them," without solving the hyacinth problem.

Then a few people tried cleverness instead of force. Dried water hyacinth makes a superb bed for growing mushrooms. The mushrooms, sold across the region, "are particularly rich in potassium, magnesium, iodine, and calcium," and the system is small and cheap, perfect for microfinance schemes that give peasants small loans. Meanwhile, the cultivation of mushrooms breaks up the cellulose in the water hyacinth, leaving a medium perfect for raising earthworms, who in turn produce a high-quality humus that can be used instead of synthetic fertilizer. Chickens feed on the worms, providing eggs, and chicken droppings supply the biogas digester, which in turn reduces the need to cut trees for firewood. Any hyacinth left over can be fed to cattle, whose manure goes right back on the fields.[40]

Not all of this activity shows up as "growth." Indeed, if you're able to use water hyacinth instead of buying fertilizer in sacks, the process probably *reduces* growth. But to see such systems in operation is to understand how many kinds of wealth there are. In Bangladesh one afternoon I ate lunch on the porch of a small farmstead. In the space of an acre or so I could see guava, lemon, pomegranate, coconut, betel nut, mango, jackfruit, apple, lichee, chestnut, date, fig, and bamboo trees, as well as squash, okra, eggplant, zucchini, blackberry, bay leaf, cardamom, cinnamon, and sugarcane plants, not to mention dozens of herbs, far more flowers, and a flock of ducklings. A chicken coop produced eggs and meat, and, since the coop was built over a pond, the chicken waste fell into the water, nourishing schools of fish that produced thousands of pounds of protein annually as well as a healthy crop of water hyacinths that were harvested to feed a small herd of cows, whose dung in turn fired one of those biogas cooking systems. "Food is everywhere, and in twelve hours it will double," said Sajed Kamal, my host. "People say that it's a miracle Bangladesh can survive its food and energy crises, that it somehow perseveres," he added. "The real miracle, though, is that you could contrive a way to have a food crisis. If you stick something in the ground here, it grows."

Not only that, but the diverse crops raised in villages like Gorasin ward off the micronutrient deficiencies that sprang up everywhere in the developing world in the wake of the green revolution. When people converted to monoculture grain crops, they needed to make money to pay off the seed merchants, so they planted nothing but, say, rice, just as the big-time grain farmers of Kansas rarely have time or space for a vegetable patch. Regions of monoculture thus become "food deserts." Rice monocultures attracted pests, so the farmers had to spray lots of pesticide, meaning that even the leafy greens that grew wild on the edges of the field could no longer be eaten. The "modern" answer to this problem is to genetically engineer rice so it carries surplus Vitamin A. I was actually in Gorasin the day an international expert arrived to explain about this so-called golden rice. The villagers listened for a few minutes, and then they started muttering. Unlike most of us in the West who worried about eating genetically modified organisms, they weren't much concerned about "frankenfood." Instead, they instantly realized that the new rice would require fertilizer and pesticide, meaning both illness and debt. More to the point, they kept saying, they had no need of golden rice because the leafy vegetables they could now grow in their organic fields provided all the nutrition they needed. "When we cook the green vegetables, we are aware not to throw out the water," said one woman. "Yes," said another. "And we don't like to eat rice only. It tastes better with green vegetables."

These new/old technologies look different in every corner of the world, because—unlike industrialized agriculture—they acknowledge that the world is a diverse place, with different climates and altitudes and nutrients and customs. Elsewhere in Asia and in Africa, farmers have started raising fish in their rice paddies; the fish need almost no extra feed, and their waste fertilizes the rice crop. In a recent issue of *Orion* magazine, Conrad Fox told the story of a Guatemalan cooperative that has begun to manufacture farm machinery from old bicycles; instead of spending a week beating cobs with a stick to loosen the grains, then grinding them for meal in a hand-cranked mill, the average small farmer can now do the job in a day and a half, thanks to a machine that "resembles a primitive exercise bicycle" and is called a *bicimolino*, or bike mill. The company also has bike-driven irrigation pumps, a pedal-powered machine that produces cheap, strong roofing tiles, and bicycle trailers for taking crops to market.

If you're not buying oil or electricity to accomplish such tasks, you may not show up in the national economic statistics—but you don't show up in the carbon dioxide statistics, either. And now you have extra time, and extra human energy. You're not worn out. Such technologies "expose a flaw of conventional planning: most people in developing countries do not need sophisticated, capital-intensive technology. They need an improvement on traditional technology, something intermediate," says Andrew Scott, a British pioneer of low-cost development solutions. "It's something that people will use, and then further develop themselves." Indeed, before long, users of the *bicimolino* had developed a way to shell macadamia nuts with mountain bike tires, and a method for using a "bike-blender" to craft shampoo. The Guatemalan cooperative that makes the machines sells them at full price to individuals, but at cost to groups and cooperatives. Since it uses abandoned, rusting bikes as its raw material, the firm is now self-supporting.[41]

It's not that every village in the world will end up grinding macadamia nuts or using bikes to make shampoo. It's that there are ways to make workable economies out of almost anything, if you think small and work through communities. Here's another story, this one from Sichuan province in China. The capital city, Chengdu, is one of those showpieces of urban growth. Giant factories line the road to the airport; the new Intel plant looks as big as the Boeing factory outside Seattle. But the most interesting person I met in the whole region was a man named Ren Xuping.

To find him, I drove about an hour from the center of Chengdu to the edge of a town called Dayi, where I parked by a long concrete wall painted with giant murals of rabbits: a German Giant, a Japanese Big Ear, and so on. Behind the wall, a six-story apartment block loomed. This was Ren Xuping's palace, built with the money he'd made raising rabbits. He'd begun as a teenager, but in a very limited fashion. Then, in 1984, the American aid group Heifer International gave him forty-eight California and New Zealand rabbits as breeding stock, along with lots of technical advice. "At first I didn't really believe it was something free," he said. "It was like some pie dropping from heaven." Anyway, rabbits did that for which they are most famous, and Ren prospered. Within four years he was a millionaire, "the rabbit king of China," with his big building. But, inspired by Heifer, he then became a kind of philanthropist, spending most of his wealth and time training others; by latest count, three hundred thousand Chinese have passed through his rabbit-raising academy. The poorest leave with rabbits of their own to embark on their new livelihood;

as many as 40 percent of the rural households in the surrounding area now raise rabbits. Rabbit farming doesn't supply a huge income, but it is a steady living. "Raise one rabbit and the income buys your salt, oil, and vinegar," says a sign in Ren's courtyard. "Raise ten rabbits and it will help you find a wife. With fifty rabbits, a better home." Not only a better home but a better homeland: the great advantage of rabbits is that they'll thrive on grass alone. All those eroded Chinese hillsides can be planted to grass instead of corn, to stabilize the soil, yet still provide a sustained income.

"One family had a case of bad kidney exhaustion, and no hope, because it takes big money to change a kidney," Ren explained as we ate a lunch of stewed rabbit, fried rabbit, rabbit in rabbit sauce. "But now he has twenty rabbits from Heifer, and eighteen are pregnant. Soon there will be eighty rabbits!" For others, he says, "This can resolve the problem of supporting the old people and educating the children. In two or three years you solve the main problems you face, the past and the future." After lunch we climbed into his VW Passat and drove off to the brand new rabbit-raising academy Ren has built on the outskirts of town. (He's turning his old building into a factory to make rabbit-fur clothes, offering jobs for some of the local unemployed.) A dissected rabbit lay in state in the first classroom we entered, where an instructor was showing peasants, many of them displaced when China built the massive Three Gorges Dam, how to count the teeth. We wandered through the rows of cages, as the rabbit king kissed many of his subjects: Belgian crosses with circles around the eyes, great flop-eared lumps. The cages were, inevitably, connected to a biogas digester that powered the showers and the kitchen. We stopped in another classroom, and another. "Most of the trainees are women. When they leave, they know how to check if the rabbit is pregnant. How to breed them, how to see if they're diseased. We teach everyone from a village in a group so they'll be able to help each other."

And with that we sped off for a nearby village called Chun Ming, just up the road from the mountain where Taoism was born. It's as typical, and as sad, as many Chinese villages. It's here that the girl I described in the first pages of this book lives—the girl whose mother had abandoned her to work in a factory, whose father beat her because she wasn't a boy, who was facing the end of her schooling because she couldn't afford the fees. She wasn't the only unhappy person in the rundown compound: her cousins were married, but their husbands went to work each day in one of the thousands of outlaw coal mines that dot the countryside, where a couple of hundred miners are killed each week.

There are many possible futures for all these people but, at least for now, they've chosen rabbits. A few weeks earlier, Ren had brought them their starter bunnies, and now he was here to see how they were doing. The house was dark and fetid, because a huge pig lived in one room. But the rabbit cages were clean and the grass fresh. Ren lifted one after another out for a quick inspection. "Put your hand on the rabbit's back," he said. "If it's straight, he's good. If his ass is very round, that's good. If his hair is very white, that's good. This one is losing hair. It's okay, though, she's very good; she'll grow it back soon. This one is fifteen days pregnant. Very good!"

In certain ways, Ren is turning people into capitalists, which is a useful thing to do. The process could be speeded up, in China and around the world; as the Peruvian economist Hernando de Soto has pointed out, for instance, hundreds of millions of squatters and black-market business owners could get an immediate boost of capital if their governments simply deeded them the land they already occupy and granted them licenses to operate without making them navigate labyrinths of corrupt bureaucracy. The whole point of his work, says Ren, is "to make a family become positive instead of passive. They say, 'Oh, I live in a remote area; I'm illiterate; I'm poor.' That's a passive attitude, and it can be changed. You want to make them become a bigger farmer, an enterpriser. The key is they have to have a dream for the future, develop a mission."

But if that enterprise stays rooted in the community—which is Ren's goal, and the Heifer Project's as well—it will sacrifice some growth for other goals; it will be more like a farmers' market than a supermarket. Somewhere there's a sweet spot, that produces enough without tipping over into the hyper-individualism that drives our careening, unsatisfying economy. The mix of regulation and values that might make such self-restraint more common is, of course, as hard to create in China as in the United States; far simpler just to bless an every-man-for-himself economy and step aside. *But creating those values, and the laws and customs that will slowly evolve from them, may be the key task of our time, here and around the world.*

As it happens, Ren has a competitor for the title of Rabbit King (or Queen), this one a twenty-eight-year-old woman in Shandong province named Wang Yumei. She's more in the mold of the new Chinese businessperson, with big breeding farms in 140 counties, fixed assets of 80 million yuan, and a plan to go public in order to avoid the "clogged fund-raising channel" of bank loans. Her goal, she says, is to become "the *world's* rabbit king," the Frank Perdue of bunnies, using the proceeds of her stock sale to "expand its production scale further." Two different models, one based on spreading modest-scale farming technology to hundreds of thousands of homes, emphasizing always that people must advance within communities, not only as individuals; the other based on consolidating a network of giant farms to "meet the requirements of a modern market economy" and in the process making everyone's lives, rabbits included, as efficiently miserable as possible.[42] I have no doubt which of these two monarchs will make more money, and which will be celebrated in a Harvard Business School case study—but I also have very little doubt about which one represents a useful future.

It's that emphasis on community, on people working together, that really counts. The most interesting development expert I've ever met is a West Virginian named Daniel Taylor, whose small nonprofit organization, Future Generations, is involved in projects in Tibet, Afghanistan, Peru, India—all across the poor world. His mantra, based on a series of principles he calls Seed-Scale, goes like this: Forget big plans. Development is not a product, not a target, not some happy future state—it doesn't consist of a set of "millennium goals" to be ticked off as they're reached. Instead, it's a process, measured not in budgets but in energy. "Change doesn't happen because of how we invest our money," says Taylor. "Change happens because of how we invest our human energy, and it always has since we came down from the trees. Everyone's got a margin of discretionary energy—ten percent, twenty percent—that isn't used up making their way in the world. That's the energy that's available for social change. If you can get a whole community to start focusing their energy together, building on success just as a business builds on successful products, then you get social change." The key document in any development program, then, is not a budget, but what Future Generations calls a work plan, which details the next project the community has decided on and describes the steps necessary to make it happen.

In such a scheme it barely matters where people begin, and in a certain sense it doesn't matter what they accomplish at any given time. What's crucial is the process, the momentum. One day in a community remote even for Tibet (it lay under the snout of a rapidly melting glacier), I spent a while looking at the small hydroelectric system that the villagers, with minimal training from Future Generations, had installed. The water flowed through a series of split-bamboo pipes, and then through a turbine that used the dynamo from a junked car. A hydrology expert could have helped them build a more efficient system, but all the locals knew how to repair this setup.

"And it doesn't matter that the system's capacity is small, because if we come back next year they'll have two or three of these ganged together—plenty of power," said Taylor. (Also, the hydrology expert might not have thought to use the water pouring out of the turbine to spin a prayer wheel.) "Development is typically viewed as a snapshot, but you have to understand it's a process," says Taylor. "It began at the beginning of time, and it's going to go to the end of the future. Your job is to go with the flow."

The best thing about such an approach may be that you can scale it up pretty fast. Consider what happened in Afghanistan. The Future Generations representative was a man named Abdullah, who used to manage fourteen Pizza Pizza franchises in Toronto. Once back in his home country, says Taylor, "He decided the real problem was the ex-combatants, the Taliban guys, coming home with poppy seeds to plant and not much else to do. So one day he cooked up some kebabs and some naan and got a bunch of these guys sitting around talking. 'Let's start the Pagal party'—'pagal' being the world for 'mad,' as in 'crazy.' As in, 'If you're so crazy to believe a better world is possible, let's get a movement going.' They decided the entry fee would be two hundred sun-dried bricks. Now, anyone can make that many bricks. But it's not enough for anyone to build anything with. So you have to talk with four or five of your buddies if you want to, say, rebuild the entrance to an irrigation ditch. Which teaches you how to work together as a team, instead of following a warlord, a boss. And you have to pick a project, so you have to agree on a social purpose, so there's momentum for community-centered behavior. Then more people pile on—maybe you rebuild the mosque, and everyone gets together and has some more naan and some more kebabs and they're feeling pretty good about themselves. So then you say to them, 'Hey, there's this process called Seed-Scale, and it can really change things.'" And it did: before long, the UN had certified the province where they were working as the only gun-free and poppy-free district in the country.

Sometimes there's almost no success to build on. Whenever Abdullah went to headquarters for staff meetings, he bunked with his relatives, who lived in one of the big slums around Kabul. They'd ask him what he was doing, and he'd describe the Seed-Scale process he was using out in the provinces. "Can we try that?" they asked him. "The very first job they did was to give a street name to every alleyway and to paint a number on every place someone was living," says Taylor. "When they'd finished that, they found that they had sixty-five thousand people living there in this particular slum. It just happened that elections were coming up, so in their work plan they made their first objective registering everyone to vote. And then, because Abdullah had been in Canada, they invited all the candidates to come and have a debate. They decided who to vote for, and on election day one guy got ninety-five percent of the votes. Now they have an electric line into the slum. Their next work plan had called for starting a school, and soon they had five—they were teaching photography, art, how to grow gardens in window boxes. They came up with the idea of starting a library, and they said to everyone, 'If you have a book you're not using, give it to us.' Soon they had several hundred volumes. Someone had heard about microcredit when they were in a refugee camp in Pakistan. So they started a savings fund, and they used the money to buy a bus and create a transit service to downtown Kabul, so that people from the slum could now get jobs in the central part of the city." And on and on. The work plans are painted on the walls of the buildings the community is using for schools, so everyone can keep track. "At one point, they decided they needed a logo," Taylor says. "They picked an eagle with its wings outstretched and talons bared and grasping—the women made a great tapestry. Because they were a community taking off, and because they were grasping for knowledge."

Community engagement—an unwillingness to embrace the individualism that often comes with modernity and a desire, instead, to build from solidarity with your neighbors—can work in the oddest of places. I spent a few days with Taylor in the tribal hills of Himalayan India, at a village called Shimong. As we hiked the steep path to get there, our guide said, "You will think we are very poor. But we are wealthy in our natural setting and in our self-sufficiency." Indeed they were. The tribespeople had lived on this hillside for a very long time; they had fields scattered in the woods for many miles around; their leading men, whom we met when we finally got to the longhouse, wore tiger skulls around their necks, proof of the good hunting.

We were here because the land the tribe controlled should be preserved. It's a key wildlife habitat, and full of tourist potential; the mythical Buddhist kingdom of Pemako, a kind of portal to heaven, has its physical incarnation at the mountain at the top of their land. (Being animists, the tribespeople celebrate the mountain and make a certain amount of fun of the Buddhist pilgrims who they think worship a rock beneath it.) Future Generations had sent a biological survey team there seven or eight years before, and found that the jungle, while largely intact, was also largely empty, having been hunted out.

The standard conservation-development approach to this problem would be to construct a "biosphere reserve," with some core areas where nothing could go on, and some buffer zones with hunting or agriculture or whatever. But the Shimong tribesmen were not keen on giving up control over their land (indeed, the literature is full of accounts of what can happen on such reserves once the government takes control: "conservation refugees" forced from their homes, and angry locals busy poaching). Future Generations and government officials had therefore been talking about something new, a "community biosphere reserve," where the locals would keep their title to the land but also work out a conservation scheme, one that might lead to some significant tourism. We were warmly greeted, but it wasn't completely clear the meetings would run smoothly. I mean, we were fairly far back in time: one morning I followed an old man headed out to collect sago palm, and he showed me the graveyard, where a fresh grave was adorned with the skulls of the animals the deceased had killed. This was, the old man explained, the graveyard for people who had died natural deaths. There was another, lesser graveyard for people who had died by mischance.

"I have no idea how this is going to go," said Taylor the night before. "They've gotten it together enough to have a committee to feed us and house us; that's a good sign, a success to build on. But God only knows what happens now. You've just got to keep reminding yourself that control is failure."

The next morning, in the longhouse, we began with speeches from the elders. If you wanted to talk, you needed to hold the spear (and if you wanted to make a point, you needed to plunge it into the ground with some force; I was reminded of earnest Americans passing the talking stick around their discussion circles, and would have giggled except that I was pretty near the spear). One man, Onyok Sitang, who'd been the best hunter in town, talked about how he'd given up the gun; instead, he used a video camera that the Future Generations team had left behind on their last visit. "If the animals are killed, no one will come and visit," he pointed out. Others weren't so sure. "The best meat in all the world is takin meat," pointed out one old-timer. "Out of this deal, are we going to get a good meat supply?" The next fellow added that since time immemorial they'd gone to the woods in what would be the core area to gather aconite, a plant that they had used for poison to tip their arrows. But each of the speakers added that if it meant development for their young people, well, takin meat be damned. "If in some way that I don't quite understand this can advance the young people, then perhaps it is good. I'm an old man and will soon die," said one fellow in a loincloth. "I'm older than he is," said the next speaker. "I think we should save the mountain."

After lunch, and after Daniel Taylor sang a medley of John Denver tunes as an entertainment, we got down to what for any American conference-goer is the utterly familiar part of the day: the break-out session, with the big pieces of paper and the magic markers. What do you know, it translates pretty easily across cultures. Before an hour had gone by, groups were presenting their plans for developing an eco-friendly trekking route (which would originate at their village, all porters to be members of the tribe), and for a wildlife survey, and for an awareness campaign (this called for writing songs with lyrics about the sacred mountain). Also, people were talking about building a new water supply with bamboo pipe. Before long the first work plan was posted on the wall of the longhouse, right above one of the fire pits. Taylor had ponied up $1,000 for airline tickets to Nepal so the villagers could see some trekking routes—and, more important, some examples of local success—firsthand. The young tourism guy from the state government was promising a Web site before the month was out. The guy with the poison arrows was showing them off. Everyone was passing around the local moonshine.

It cannot be said with any confidence that the Shimong Community Biosphere Reserve will be a success. Maybe it won't; at the very least, it will take some nurturing. But by day's end something was under way in that community that hadn't been under way before, not ever in its history. There was some new sense of what was possible, and how it might be reached. The people had some sense that the future wouldn't simply wash over them, that they would play a role in choosing it. As the sun went down over the Brahmaputra far below, things seemed to be . . . developing.

■ ■ ■

IF ALL THIS SEEMS ANECDOTAL, THAT'S BECAUSE IT IS. THE MOD-
ern economic model has spread so far and wide that there are
relatively few large-scale experiments testing whether an alternative might actually work. But, it's worth recalling the data
in chapter 2 about the amazing spread of sustainable farming
in the last ten years: the hundreds of thousands of Indonesian
rice farmers, the Central American corn growers, all the rest.
Entire nations are at least thinking a little differently. In recent years, for instance, a few journalists have trekked to the
Himalayan mountain kingdom of Bhutan, intrigued by the
news that it has stopped calculating GNP and replaced it with
a "happiness index." The journalists usually describe Bhutan
as "tiny" and "insular." It's also poor, with household incomes
among the world's lowest. But the kingdom has managed to
increase life expectancy by nineteen years since the mid-1980s,
and it spends what money it has on education, health care,
and the environment. "The goal of life should not be limited
to production, consumption, more production and more
consumption," Thakur S. Powdyel, a senior official in the
Bhutanese Ministry of Education, told Andrew Revkin of the
New York Times. "There is no necessary relationship between
the level of possession and the level of well-being." This isn't
mere words. Sixty percent of Bhutan has been set aside to remain in forest. "We have to think of human well-being in
broader terms," the country's former prime minister told
Revkin. "Material well-being is only one component. That
doesn't ensure that you're at peace with your environment
and in harmony with one another."[43]

The point is not "Old ways good, new ways bad." Rather,
each locality, instead of relying solely on Adam Smith as fil-
tered through the World Trade Organization and the World
Bank, needs to figure out what its mix of tradition and resources
and hopes allows. Rarely will a community do so in isolation;
there aren't that many hidden Himalayan kingdoms. But those
of us watching from the outside would do well to remember

that there are many kinds of paternalism, *including the assumption that for poor people only material things matter.* Meat and alcohol and stuffed animals and health care are useful goals, but they're not the only things. Just like us, people in the developing world need dignity, security, identity. Some of these can be achieved through economic growth, and some of them can be undermined by it. Negotiating modernity requires creativity.

For instance, people everywhere (anyway, men everywhere) think cars are cool. But they may be completely willing to settle for mobility, whether it's supplied by bus or bike. Curitiba, in Brazil, built the world's best bus system and thereby managed to reduce its per capita energy use by a *quarter*. Bogotá followed its lead, and so have Jakarta and Guayaquil. The development of excellent transportation would be easier still, of course, if the rich world offered some leadership—which is also possible. Rome, which used to be renowned for the planet's worst traffic, has cut auto use in the center city by 25 percent. Want to drive into central London? That will cost you £10—a tariff that's been greeted as a great success. Holland, where 30 percent of urban trips are made via bike, now partners with cities like Pune in India, Dakar in Senegal, and Dar es Salaam in Tanzania to build bikeways. According to the journalist Jay Walljasper, "Leaders in poor countries are impressed at hearing about all the bicycles in the Netherlands, a wealthy country where families can easily afford a car." The manufacturer Trek is making a special $70 "California bike" for poor markets, its name and bright yellow frame chosen to add glamour. "In Africa, bike riding is stigmatized as a rural backward thing," explains Aimee Gauthier of the Institute for Transportation and Development Policy. "If people start to associate bicycles with status, it will make a big difference."[44]

If developing countries are looking for an example closer to home, for some proof that China is not the only path to success, the best evidence I know of can be found in the south of

India, in the state of Kerala. Kerala is neither tiny nor insular; its population of 30 million is roughly equal to California's, squeezed into an area not much larger than Vancouver Island. Kerala is poor, one of the poorer states of India. When I went there many years ago while writing a book called *Hope, Human and Wild*, it was my first real experience of Asian village life, of huts where beds were rare. The per capita income is at most a few dollars a day, less than a fiftieth of the American average. The population is roughly evenly divided among Christians, Muslims, and Hindus, which in many places would be a recipe for chronic low-grade warfare.

But Kerala is statistically the oddest place on earth. Despite its poverty—and despite its low rate of economic growth in comparison with the dynamic "software cities" in the rest of India—its life expectancy is now seventy-three years for males. As Amartya Sen, the Nobel Prize–winning economist, points out, that means the average resident lives longer than the average black person in the United States, and not much less than the general American average.[45] The literacy rate, after a five-year campaign conducted by volunteers who organized classes under coconut trees and by riverbanks, approaches 100 percent; the United Nations has recognized Kerala as the world's first fully literate place, and the rate of newspaper readership is the highest on earth. The percentage of Keralites with postgraduate degrees is higher than the percentage of Americans. Kerala's birthrate is lower than ours and falling faster, a decline accomplished not by edict, as in China, but through the voluntary decisions of women and men. (Kerala's birthrate, in fact, is 40 percent below that in the rest of India.) More striking yet, Kerala is virtually the only place in Asia where baby girls outnumber baby boys. Simply its avoidance of that holocaust of baby girls says something lovely about Kerala.

The story of how all this happened is long, complicated, and fiercely debated by development experts, but it makes it clear that "doing things the old way" is not the main answer. Kerala was the most caste-ridden corner of Hinduism in the nine-teenth century: Brahmins there strolled the streets preceded by criers to make sure that they wouldn't have to even see "Untouchables." But a wave of religious reform prepared the ground for Gandhi's ideas to strike deeper than elsewhere; after Indian independence, elected left-wing governments managed to enact the world's most sweeping land reforms, breaking up the industrialized plantations of the British and giving almost everyone some land of his or her own. The spirit of volun-teerism stayed strong; even today, groups such as the Kerala People's Science Movement carry out huge projects such as the detailed mapping of individual villages, enabling residents to see where the soil and water will allow for improved farming. Such work is always in the context of community: in one re-gion, for instance, owners of paddy fields were asked to allow their land to be used, free of charge, as community gardens be-tween rice crops. This allowed the vegetables to be sold at mar-ket for less than agribusiness imports. In a rough-and-tumble way, Kerala comes closer to an experiment in sharing than any place on earth. Not surprisingly, then, it feels different from much of the rest of the developing world. On the streets of Trivandrum and in the fields of the broad central plateau, Ker-alites greet visitors straightforwardly, as equals, with none of the combined servility and resentment that often marks the di-vide between the First World and the Third. Keralites are proud of what they've accomplished.

Kerala is far from perfect. Because unemployment is high, many of its educated youth go abroad to work, helping support the economy with their remittances home. And the economy is stagnant, because it's hard to attract big factories to a place so concerned with economic justice. Even some of its fans have said it's perennially in danger of becoming a "populist welfare state." An Indian economist, Joseph Tharamangalam, recently called the lack of economic growth a "debacle"; as budget deficits escalate, services are harder to maintain.

But viewed in a different way, Kerala's lack of economic growth is precisely what makes it so interesting. We "know" that getting rich is what leads to longer lives, higher literacy, more equality, more political participation. Benjamin Friedman, in his recent book, has even argued that economic growth is precisely what allows us to act generously toward each other. Kerala simply shows that we're wrong; growth may accomplish those goals, but there are other means to them as well. Kerala does little to raise the world's temperature or to drain its oil fields; any American suburb has more cars than the whole crowded Indian state. By that measure alone, you could call Kerala's society profoundly more successful than ours. Keralites may still suffer materially, but they conclusively prove it's possible to thrive on considerably less than we consume.

IMAGINING *LESS* IS A PROBLEM, OF COURSE. AS WE TURN OUR gaze back from the Third World to the First, from the developing world to the overdeveloped, there's always the danger of freaking out, of clinging to our present approach lest we end up living in caves. So instead of *less*, let's imagine Europe.

When we want to visit elegance and sophistication and grace, where do we head? France, Italy, Spain, Sweden. Western Europe is in many ways the most cosmopolitan part of the world, in its food, its wine, its art, its class.

It's also the most generous part of the world; Europeans now provide more than 50 percent of all the civilian development assistance in the world, and 47 percent of all the humanitarian assistance. Our government provides about a third as much assistance, gives much of that aid to corrupt regimes, and ties nearly 80 percent of it to agreements to purchase U.S. goods and services. In fact, as Jeremy Rifkin points out in his important book *The European Dream*, when the Center for Global Development and *Foreign Policy* magazine ranked the world's richest countries according to how much their development assistance helps or hinders the economic and social development of poor countries, sixteen of the nineteen top countries were European, while the United States came in near the bottom of the list.[46] In their own countries, as well, Europeans have managed to make sure that most people have enough: while the poverty rate is 17 percent in the United States, it's 5 percent in Finland, 6.6 percent in Sweden, 7.5 percent in Germany, 8 percent in France.[47] Crime rates are far lower in these nations, too, even though Europe has abolished the death penalty and still embraces the idea of rehabilitation. Europeans also live longer and healthier lives.

And here is the important point. The Europeans have achieved all this while consuming less—much less—than we do. The average new European home is less than half the size of one of ours. Europeans drive smaller cars shorter distances, taking public transit or walking or biking far more often. (Partly that's because they live in closer quarters—but even in the similarly crowded U.S. Northeast, we live more like Texans than like Italians.) When all is said and done, Europeans use about half as much energy per capita as Americans: the British, for instance, consumed about 166 million BTUs apiece in 2003, compared with 350 million for the average American.[48] They produce far less carbon than we do; they drain far fewer oil wells. And they're making determined efforts to cut their use still further: all the EU nations have announced targets of at least 50 percent reductions in carbon dioxide emissions over the next few decades, while the official U.S. energy plan foresees this nation spewing 25 percent *more*. (This is especially embarrassing because the Europeans have so much less low-hanging fruit to pick. They already use efficient appliances and drive small cars. They're going to have to work harder than we will to make progress.) Again: *Europeans use half as much energy as we do*. Half is a big chunk. It doesn't solve global warming, but it sure helps.

The point is not that Europe is perfect. Anyone who has

watched Muslims rioting in France in recent years knows the continent has plenty of unresolved problems. European unemployment rates are higher than ours (though some economists have pointed out that we simply don't bother counting "discouraged workers" and that having 2 percent of the potential male adult workforce behind bars further reduces our total).[49] On the other hand, European workers are every bit as productive as ours; both German and French workers, for instance, produce more per hour than American workers. So why do Americans make 29 percent more money than Europeans? Because we work longer hours. *Much* longer hours—Americans average 25.1 working hours per person per week, but the Germans average 18.6; the average American works 46 weeks a year, while the French average is 40.[50] Europeans work to live, not the reverse; they spend more time with their families, which may have something to do with why their divorce rates are much lower. And of the money Europeans make, more goes toward taxes, to support health care and university education and the other things that they have to worry less about than we do.

For Americans caught up in the orthodoxy of getting and spending, that may not seem like such a bargain. A writer based in Oslo, for instance, recently wrote a piece for the *New York Times* with the lovely title "We're Rich, You're Not. End of Story." He pointed out that while Americans had $32,900 per person to devote to "private consumption," the European averages ranged between $13,850 and $23,500. That is indeed a big difference; the Europeans were definitely "poorer" than we, and the writer delighted in listing the ways. "They hang on to old appliances and furniture that we would throw out," for instance. And this: "One image in particular sticks in my mind. In a Norwegian language class, my teacher illustrated the meaning of the word *matpakke*—'packed lunch'—by reaching into her backpack and pulling out a hero sandwich wrapped in wax paper. It was her lunch. She held it up for all to see. Yes, teachers are underpaid everywhere. But in Norway the *matpakke* is ubiquitous, from classroom to boardroom. In New York, an office worker might pop out at lunchtime to a deli. . . . In Norway she will sit at her desk with a sandwich from home."[51]

What does all that add up to? Once you've taken the home-made sandwiches and the smaller houses and the guaranteed health care and the extra weeks of vacation and added them all together, what do you get? In 2005, the *Economist* developed a new system to rank not GNP but "quality of life." Using indexes of everything from divorce rates to community life, material well-being to political freedom, the magazine's researchers found that the ten highest-ranking countries were all in western Europe. The United States, despite having the highest income per capita of any place but Luxembourg, nonetheless came in thirteenth, well behind, say, Spain, where people earned barely 60 percent as much.[52] Does "quality of life" mean anything? Here's perhaps the most important statistic: in recent years, while, as we have seen, Americans grew steadily less satisfied with their lives, the percentage of Europeans predominantly satisfied with their lives "increased . . . from 79 to 83 percent." As the economist Richard Layard concludes, "The decline in happiness is largely an American phenomenon."[53]

In the world as we know it at the moment—the world of a race to the bottom, in search of ever greater "economic efficiency"—Europe may be hard pressed to retain its distinctiveness. German automakers, for instance, are cutting back on vacation time and increasing working hours, insisting that they'll move to China unless workers agree. Siemens told its German staff that the firm would start making cordless phones in Hungary unless they worked five hours more a week and gave up vacation pay. "Of course the family will come off worst," one worker told a reporter.[54]

But despite such strains, the European difference runs deep.

It can be summed up like this: Europeans have a higher regard for community, a more measured sense of the individual. As Rifkin puts it, they emphasize "community relationships over individual autonomy, cultural diversity over assimilation, quality of life over the accumulation of wealth, sustainable development over unlimited material growth, deep play over unrelenting toil, and universal human rights." Americans define freedom as "autonomy and mobility, which require amassing wealth. Europeans define freedom in community—in belonging, not belongings."[55] What does that mean in practice? Sixty-nine percent of Europeans believe that environmental protection is an immediate and urgent problem, and more than half agree that "it is necessary to fundamentally change our way of life and development if we want to halt the deterioration of the environment." In contrast, only one American in four is "anxious about the environment." Asked to rank their priorities, 95 percent of Europeans put helping others at the top of their list; 84 percent said they "put a high value on being involved in creating a better society." Financial success came in dead last, perhaps because you're allowed to go to the doctor, or to college, or to retire even if you don't make a lot of money.[56]

IN THE TWENTIETH CENTURY, TWO COMPLETELY DIFFERENT models of how to run an economy battled for supremacy. Ours won, and not only because it produced more goods. It also produced far more freedom, far less horror.

In the twenty-first century, the choices are a little less stark. No one wants to do away with markets, or to centrally plan economies; outside of China, most people are committed to some form of democracy. But the choices are no less crucial, and the stakes may be even higher. The ecological upheaval promised by global warming is more disruptive than any military threat humans have yet faced.

Meeting somewhere in the middle may be our only hope. The poor nations of the world need to develop. But if they develop according to our model, the planet will break under the strain. We in the rich nations need to change, not just for environmental reasons but because our way has stopped producing as much human happiness as it should. That middle ground is hard to define, and we will take generations to reach it, because we start so far apart. But it is more local than the world we know now, and less individualistic. It measures not More but Better.

We've gone too far down the road we're traveling. The time has come to search the map for better possibilities, to strike out in new directions. Inertia is a powerful force; marriages and corporations and nations continue in motion until something big diverts them. This book has been about those big somethings: our dawning understanding of our ecological peril and our psychological malaise. We have much to fear, and also much to desire, and together our fear and our desire can set us on a new, more promising course.

AFTERWORD

I've done my best to make this book properly hopeful—tried to suggest ways of running our economy that would waste less energy, spew less carbon, and produce more satisfaction. I've tried, too, to show that such a future is not just important and desirable, but possible—that models of these new economies can be found in embryo, in adolescence, and occasionally even in something resembling maturity here and around the world. They're exciting possibilities, experiments to try out, ways to imagine humans thriving more fully and more durably than at present.

I can't close this book, however, without adding that they may also be necessary for human survival, and that change must come sooner rather than later.

Even in the year that I've been sitting at my desk and writing, the strain on the planet has grown more palpable. We've found some new oil—a big field in the Gulf of Mexico may be holding enough crude to supply us for two years. But there's also been plenty of evidence that the biggest oil fields in the world are playing out more quickly than we'd imagined. Bank analysts, for instance, concluded that the Saudis were simply lying about the state of the Ghawar field, the world's largest, which outside experts have concluded is in "irreversible decline."[1] Early in 2006, Kuwait reported what one official called "an incredible revelation": the world's second-largest field, at Burgan, was yielding less oil than expected—1.7 million barrels a day, not the 2 million barrels per day previously forecast for the next forty years.[2] The Mexican state-run oil company announced that the world's third-biggest field, the Cantarell deposit, had peaked at 2.2 million barrels a day and would decline to 1.4 million barrels a day by 2010.[3] Supplies are so tight that those who still hold reserves have unusual leverage; Russia, for instance, temporarily cut off gas supplies to Ukraine early in 2006, punishing its new America-friendly government; Iran has tried to turn down the international heat over its nuclear ambitions by threatening to turn off the oil spigot. Even President George W. Bush, in his 2006 State of the Union address, announced that we were "addicted to oil," a recognition slow in coming (akin, say, to Abraham Lincoln using his Second Inaugural Address to note the existence of slavery down south) and therefore all the more ominous in its implications. As the political analyst Michael Klare points out, if even senior administration officials "have come to believe that the U.S. and the rest of the world face a . . . permanent energy crisis that imperils the health and well-being of every society on earth," then you know there must be something going on. That something, adds Klare, will be very different from the oil shocks of the 1970s or the California blackouts of the 1990s. "It is likely to last for decades, not just months or a handful of years; it will engulf the entire planet, not just a few countries."[4]

Consider global warming, the other predicament I discussed in chapter 1 and one that in the end is far more dangerous even than peak oil. I've been reporting about climate change since the late 1980s, when it was still a hypothesis and the idea that humans were burning enough coal and oil and gas to alter the climate seemed far-fetched and counterintuitive to many. By 1995, after scientific investigation more intense than on any comparable topic in history, the hypothesis had become consensus. Human beings, the world's climatologists agreed, were heating the planet. The decade after 1995 was a time of confirmation: nine of the ten warmest years on record, and a slew of physical changes to show what that damage would mean.

But the eighteen months that began in the summer of 2005—that's been really scary. If you read *Science* or *Nature*, the two main peer-reviewed scientific journals, you see almost weekly some new study about the pace of climate change, and virtually every one finds the speed and magnitude of global warming is going off the top end of the old ranges of prediction. For instance:

The old record for Atlantic hurricanes and tropical storms in a year was twenty-one, set in 1933. The summer and fall of 2005 saw twenty-seven named storms, including one with the lowest barometric pressure ever recorded in the hemisphere; a tropical storm was still spinning in the Gulf of Mexico in January 2006. A series of landmark papers clearly linked the storminess to increases in sea surface temperature.

A British team demonstrated that as the planet warms, its soils are becoming more microbially active, giving off much of the carbon stored there. This kind of giant positive feedback can also be seen elsewhere—in the Arctic, for instance, where white ice is giving way to blue water. The ice had reflected the sun's rays back to space, but the water absorbs them, accelerating warming. When Arctic sea ice failed to fully reform in 2006 for the second straight winter, one researcher called the changes "irreversible."[5] Meanwhile, the British soil scientists explained the implications of their findings in stark terms: "All the consequences of global warming will occur more rapidly."[6]

Perhaps most disturbing, new measurements announced in the winter of 2006 showed that the Greenland and Antarctic ice sheets were melting much more quickly than previously estimated, largely because thawing ice was letting water sink to the bottom of glaciers, where it lubricated their speedy passage into the oceans and threatened to raise sea levels much more quickly than had been anticipated.[7]

Driven by such new data, NASA's James Hansen, the world's premier climate modeler, decided to speak out in the course of the winter about the dangers such phenomena posed. The federal government attempted to prevent him from talking to journalists, but Hansen—a calm and personally almost bland man—went ahead anyway. The earth had ten years to start producing less carbon dioxide instead of more, he warned; if it failed, we would have a "different planet."[8] Hansen's warning was by no means the starkest. A few weeks later, James Lovelock, the British scientist who built the equipment that allowed us to measure deterioration of the ozone layer, said he believed the "tipping point" had already passed, and that world and human society face disaster to a worse extent, and on a faster time scale, than almost anybody realizes. "Before this century is over, billions of us will die" from the effects, he predicted.[9]

These problems, as I've said, are intimately tied to growth. One study tries to quantify the effect: a Scottish economist, Malcom Slesser, has calculated that *about 55 percent of the energy we consume is required by the economic growth process itself*. This seems extraordinarily high, but consider: the key components of growth, such as putting up new buildings and buying new machines and building new roads, require lots of steel and aluminum and cement, all of which are wildly energy intensive.[10] (China, for instance, currently uses 40 percent of the planet's cement.)[11] To once more quote from Benjamin Friedman's long and otherwise glowing defense of economic growth, carbon dioxide "is the one major environmental contaminant for which no study has ever found any indication of improvement as living standards rise."

■ ■ ■

LOCAL ECONOMIES CAN PLAY AN IMPORTANT ROLE IN REDUCING these problems. If we grew most of our food close to home, we'd use far less energy in the process, helping alleviate both oil shortages and climate change. But even so, it's becoming increasingly clear that it's too late to ward these crises off altogether. They're coming at us very fast.

So here's the punch line: the movement toward more local economies is the same direction we will have to travel to cope with the *effects* of these predicaments, not just to fend them off. The logic is fairly clear: in a world threatened by everhigher energy prices and ever-scarcer fossil fuel, you're better off in a relatively self-sufficient county or state or region. In a world increasingly rocked by wild and threatening weather, durable economies will be more useful than dynamic ones. And in both cases, the increased sense of community and heightened skill at democratic decision making that a more local economy implies will not simply increase our levels of satisfaction with our lives, but will also increase our chances of survival in a more dangerous world. Hyper-individualism is not just lonely; it's also, in the world we are starting to see emerge around us, insecure and foolhardy.

This sounds scary. It *is* scary. But one of the reasons I spent so much time showing that local economies equal community, which in turn equals a better shot at deep satisfaction, was to demonstrate that it's not *just* scary. It's also appealing.

No one knows precisely how fast the coming changes will engulf us. If they come rapidly, they may spur us to action; if they come more slowly, we may dally. National and international action would certainly make everything much easier, but cheap energy and cheap food are dear to the most powerful interests in our society, not to mention a broad majority of citizens, and waiting until those interests are moved to take action seems a recipe for disastrous delay. As well, by their very nature, local economies need to grow up . . . locally. So I'm all for political efforts on every level—but also for building farmers' markets and radio stations and neighborhood windmills. At the very least, we need as many models in place as possible for the day when it all hits the proverbial turbine blade.

As much as we need those working instances of new economies, we also need a new mental model of the possible. I would be content if this book helped shake our ingrained belief that growth is still an obvious necessary goal of our economy—content if the reader wondered a little the next time he or she heard some newscaster happily declare that the economy had gotten 3 percent larger. And content, as well, if my work helped shake the idea that there was no alternative to growth save miserable recession. If economists can shed their inclination to serve as priests of the current cult, they will play a crucial role in helping us understand what options we have, what scales of enterprise may work to serve all our needs, which kinds of efficiency help and which harm. For them—for all of us—this is a far more interesting intellectual adventure than merely trying to keep the present system accelerating a little longer.

It's extremely hard to imagine a world substantially different from the one we know. But our current economies are changing the physical world in horrifying ways. It's our greatest challenge—the only real question of our time—to see whether we can transform those economies enough to prevent some damage and to help us cope with what we can't prevent. To see if we can manage to mobilize the wealth of our communities to make the transition tolerable, even sweet, instead of tragic.

NOTES

1 AFTER GROWTH

1. John Maynard Keynes, "Economic Possibilities for Our Grand-children" (London: 1987 [1930]), p. 1.

2. Gordon John Steele, "What Has Watt Wrought?" *Forbes*, July 1997, p. 144.

3. Benjamin Friedman, *The Moral Consequences of Economic Growth* (New York: 2005), p. 47.

4. Ibid., p. 72.

5. Jeremy Rifkin, *The European Dream* (New York: 2004), p. 115.

6. Robert M. Collins, *The Politics of Economic Growth in Postwar America* (Oxford: 2000).

7. Margaret Legum, *It Doesn't Have to Be Like This* (London: 2002), p. viii.

8. Collins, *Politics of Economic Growth*, p. 227.

9. Brian Czech, *Shoveling Fuel on a Runaway Train* (Berkeley, Calif.: 2000), p. 1.

10. Douglas Heingartner, "Now Hear This, Quickly," *New York Times*, October 2, 2003.

11. Friedman, *Moral Consequences*, p. 12.

12. Ibid., p. 5.

13. Derek Rasmussen, "The Prices vs. the Priceless," *Interculture*, no. 147 (October 2004), p. 5.

14. John McMillan, *Reinventing the Bazaar* (New York: 2002), pp. 7–8.

15. Collins, *Politics of Economic Growth*, p. 240.

16. New Economics Foundation, *Real World Economic Outlook 2003* (London: 2003), p. 36.

17. Heather Boushey and Christian E. Weller, "What the Numbers Tell Us," in James Lardner and David A. Smith, eds., *Inequality Matters* (New York: 2005), p. 36; David Cay Johnston, "The Great Tax Shift," in Lardner and Smith, *Inequality Matters*, p. 167.

18. Molly Hennessy-Fiske, "That Raise Might Take 4 Years," *Los Angeles Times*, July 24, 2006.

19. New Economics Foundation, *Real World Economic Outlook 2003*, p. 36.

20. Dinesh D'Souza, *The Virtue of Prosperity* (New York: 2001), p. 43.

21. Clive Crook, "The Height of Inequality," *Atlantic*, September 2006, p. 36.

22. Molly Ivins, "Connect the Dots," *Boulder Daily Camera*, January 15, 2003.

23. Jenny Anderson, "That Line at the Ferrari Dealer? It's Bonus Season on Wall Street," *New York Times*, December 28, 2004.

24. Celia Dugger, "The Food Chain's Survival of the Biggest: Supermarket Giants Crush Central American Farmers," *New York Times*, December 28, 2004.

25. Juliet Schor, "The New Politics of Consumption," *Boston Review* (Summer 1999), http://bostonreview.net/BR24.3/schor.html.

26. Jeffrey Sachs, *The End of Poverty* (New York: 2005), p. 32.

27. K. Enshayan, *Living Within Our Means: Beyond the Fossil Fuel Credit Card* (Cedar Rapids, Iowa: 2005), p. 35.

28. Sachs, *End of Poverty*, p. 41.

29. Shankar Vedantam, "Report on Global Ecosystems Calls for Radical Changes," *Washington Post*, March 30, 2005.

30. Union of Concerned Scientists, "World Scientists Warning to Humanity" (1992), http://www.ucsusa.org.

31. Lester Brown, *Plan B2.0* (Washington, D.C., 2006).

32. "Climate Change a Deadly Threat," BBC News, May 15, 2006.

33. Friedman, *Moral Consequences*, p. 384.

34. Ibid., p. 385.

35. Worldwatch Institute, *Vital Signs 2003* (New York: 2003), p. 57.

36. Marvin Fertel, testimony before House Committee on International Relations, October 7, 1997.

37. Richard Douthwaite, *The Growth Illusion* (London: 1999), p. 211.

38. Andrew C. Revkin, "British Government Report Calls for Broad Effort on Climate Issues," *New York Times*, October 30, 2006, p. 1.

39. Douthwaite, *Growth Illusion*, pp. 36, 210. In addition, it should be noted in Nordhaus's defense that we've never spent anything even approaching 2 percent of our income on dealing with climate change.

40. Kenneth E. Boulding, "The Economics of the Coming Spaceship Earth," in Henry Jarrett, ed., *Environmental Quality in a Growing Economy* (Baltimore: 1966), p. 14.

41. Robert Costanza, "Embedded Energy and Economic Valuation," *Science*, vol. 210, December 12, 1980.

42. Clifford Cobb and John Cobb, *The Green National Product* (Tucson: 1994), p. 6.

43. Andrew Revkin, "A New Measure of Happiness," *New York Times*, October 4, 2001; Alan AtKisson, *Believing Cassandra* (White River Junction, Vt.: 1999), p. 50.

44. Kenneth Arrow et al., "Are We Consuming Too Much?" *Journal of Economic Perspectives*, vol. 18, no. 3 (September 2003), pp. 147–72.

45. Gordon Bigelow, "Let There Be Markets," *Harper's*, May 2005, p. 44.

46. Craig Lambert, "The Marketplace of Perceptions," *Harvard Magazine*, March–April 2006, p. 50.

47. Daniel Kahneman, Ed Diener, and Norbert Schwartz, *Well-being: The Foundation of Hedonic Psychology* (New York: 1999).

48. Ibid., p. 5.

49. Richard Layard, *Happiness: Lessons from a New Science* (New York: 2005), pp. 10–11.

50. Robert Frank, *Luxury Fever* (New York: 2000), pp. 70–71.

51. Eben Goodstein, *Economics and the Environment*, 3rd ed. (New York: 2002), pp. 202–3.

52. Alan Durning, *How Much Is Enough?* (New York, 1992), p. 1.

53. D'Souza, *Virtue*, p. 16.

54. Layard, *Happiness*, p. 10.

55. Ibid., p. 22.

56. Sharon Jayson, "Unhappiness Quotient Rises in the Past Decade," *Burlington Free Press* (Vt.), p. 1.

57. New Economics Foundation, *Real World Economic Outlook 2003*, p. 135.

58. Frank, *Luxury Fever*, p. 73.

59. Layard, *Happiness*, p. 22.

60. Ed Diener and Martin Seligman, "Beyond Money: Toward an Economy of Well-Being," *Psychological Science in the Public Interest*, vol. 5, no. 1 (July 2004), p. 30.

61. Douthwaite, *Growth Illusion*, pp. 4–5.

62. New Economics Foundation, *Real World Economic Outlook 2003*, p. 5.

63. Douthwaite, *Growth Illusion*, p. 10.

64. Ibid., p. 13.

65. Layard, *Happiness*, pp. 176–77.

66. Diener and Seligman, "Beyond Money," figure 2, p. 5.

67. Layard, *Happiness*, p. 33.

68. New Economics Foundation, *Real World Economic Outlook 2003*, p. 7.

69. Sharon Begley, "Wealth and Happiness Don't Necessarily Go Hand in Hand," *Wall Street Journal*, August 13, 2004.

70. Diener and Seligman, "Beyond Money," p. 2.

71. Deirdre McCloskey, "Capital Gains: How Economic Growth Benefits the World," *Christian Century*, May 4, 2004.

72. McMillan, *Reinventing the Bazaar*, p. 212.

73. Layard, *Happiness*, p. 60.

74. Frank, *Luxury Fever*, p. 5.

2 THE YEAR OF EATING LOCALLY

1. Craig Lambert, "The Way We Eat Now," *Harvard Magazine*, May–June 2004, p. 44.

2. Brian Halweil, *Eat Here: Reclaiming Homegrown Pleasures in a Global Supermarket* (New York: 2004), p. 68.

3. Jim Scharplaz, "Weeding Out the Skilled Farmer," *Prairie Writers Circle*, November 26, 2003.

4. Felicity Lawrence, *Not on the Label* (New York: 2004), p. 162.

5. R. W. Apple Jr., "For Baking, for Mashing, Forever," *New York Times*, November 25, 2003.

6. Vern Grubinger, *With an Ear to the Ground* (Burlington, Vt.: 2004), p. 61; Robert Hadad, "Livestock on the Farm," *Natural Farmer*, Winter 2004–2005; Ron Schmid, *The Untold Story of Milk* (Washington, D.C.: 2003), p. 211; Mark Lapping, "Toward the Recovery of the Local," *Ethics, Place, and Environment*, vol. 7, no. 3 (2004), p. 9.

7. Halweil, *Eat Here*, p. 47.

8. Aziz Choudry, in Brian Tokar, *Gene Traders* (Burlington, Vt.: 2004), p. 124.

9. Clint Peck, "Beef Chat: The Wal-Mart Way" (June 1, 2003), http://beef-mag.com/mag/beef_walmart/.

10. Joanna Blythman, *Shopped: The Shocking Power of British Supermarkets* (London: 2004), p. 180.

11. Ibid., p. 210.

12. Ross Parsons, "Survival and Success," *Los Angeles Times*, May 5, 2005.

13. Bruce Gardner, "The Little Guys Are O.K.," *New York Times*, March 7, 2003.

14. Christopher Cook, *Diet for a Dead Planet* (New York: 2004).

15. Halweil, *Eat Here*, pp. 63–64.

16. Ibid., p. 60.

17. Cook, *Diet*, p. 123.

18. Candace Page, "Dairy Decline Continues," *Burlington Free Press* (Vt.), February 23, 2005.

19. Russell Libby, "Building New Solutions for Rural Maine Agriculture," in Lisa Pohlmann and David Vail, eds., *Spreading Prosperity to the "Other Maines"* (Portland, Me.: 2005).

20. Zac Goldsmith, "Down on the Farm," *Ecologist*, October 2003, p. 6.

21. Lawrence, *Not on the Label*, p. 141.

22. Halweil, *Eat Here*, pp. 60–61.

23. Steven Blank, *The End of Agriculture in the American Portfolio* (Westport, Conn.: 1998), pp. 3, 17, 126.

24. John Nichols, "Needed: A Rural Strategy," *Nation*, October 21, 2003.

25. Halweil, *Eat Here*, p. 87.

26. "Rural, Old Churches Losing Congregations," Associated Press, May 27, 2004.

27. Jamie Daniel, "Injuries to All," *In These Times*, June 20, 2005.

28. Cook, *Diet*, pp. 212–13.

29. Mark Jacobson, "The Hunt for Red Gold," *OnEarth*, Fall 2005, p. 26.

30. Kevin G. Hall, "Modern-day Slavery," Knight Ridder news service, September 19, 2004.

31. Halweil, *Eat Here*, p. 54.

32. Daniel Imhoff, *Farming with the Wild* (Healdsburg, Calif.: 2003), p. 10.

33. Andrew Martin, "Factory Farm Foes Fed Up," *Chicago Tribune*, March 24, 2004.

34. Lawrence M. Wein, "Got Toxic Milk?" *New York Times*, May 30, 2005.

35. Paula Zahn, "America's Food Supply Vulnerable?" CNN, December 6, 2004.

36. "How to Stop the Next Killer Flu," *Seed*, February/March 2006.

37. Jules Pretty, *Agri-Culture* (London: 2002), pp. 64–65.

38. Lawrence, *Not on the Label*, pp. 1, 3, 12.

39. "Threats of Peak Oil to the Global Food Supply," *Museletter*, no. 159 (July 2005).

40. Daniel Imhoff, *Paper or Plastic* (San Francisco: 2005), p. 112; Danielle Murry, "Oil and Food, a Rising Security Challenge," Earth Policy Institute, May 9, 2005.

41. Tom Philpott, "Archer Daniels Midland: The Exxon of Corn?" *Grist*, February 2, 2006.

42. Michelle Nijhuis, "Beyond the Pale Green," *Grist*, November 17, 2003; Lapping, "Recovery," p. 141.

43. Halweil, *Eat Here*, p. 29.

44. Douthwaite, *Growth Illusion*, p. 252.

45. Halweil, *Eat Here*, p. 36.

46. David Reay, "Climate Change Begins at Home," *Northern Sky News*, September 2005.

47. Halweil, *Eat Here*, p. 36.

48. "Threats of Peak Oil," p. 3.

49. Imhoff, *Paper or Plastic*, p. 30.

50. Halweil, *Eat Here*, pp. 6–7.

51. Ibid., pp. 39–40.

52. Lawrence, *Not on the Label*, p. 78.

53. Rich Pirog et al., "Food, Fuel, and Freeways" (June 2001), http://www.leopold.iastate.edu/pubs/staff/ppp/.

54. "The Local Solution," *Adbusters*, March–April 2006.

55. "Father of Modern Agriculture: Activists Threaten World Food Supply" (October 18, 2005), http://www.consumerfreedom.com/ news_detail.cfm/headline.2902.

56. Nathan Weaver, "Walk Your Pastures," *Farming*, Fall 2003, p. 18.

57. Halweil, *Eat Here*, p. 54.

58. James Morrison, Rachel Hine, and Jules Pretty, "Survey and Analysis of Labour on Organic Farmers in the UK and Republic of Ireland," *International Journal of Agricultural Sustainability*, vol. 3, no. 1 (2005).

59. Lawrence Woodward, "Can Organic Farming Feed the World?" http://www.population-growth-migration.info/essays/woodwardorganic.

60. Pretty, *Agri-Culture*, p. 84.

61. Pretty, author interview, July 29, 2005.

62. Pretty, *Agri-Culture*, pp. 79–80.

63. Ibid., p. 89.

64. Randy Brummet of the International Center for Aquatic Resource Management, quoted in ibid., p. 95.

65. Pretty, *Agri-Culture*, p. 84.

66. R. W. Apple Jr., "A Peach . . . No, a Honey of a Farmer's Market," *New York Times*, September 26, 2004.

67. Pretty, *Agri-Culture*, p. 121; Cook, *Diet*, p. 256; Lapping, "Recovery," p. 4.

68. Grubinger, *With an Ear to the Ground*, p. 57.

69. Halweil, *Eat Here*, p. 92.

70. Kate Stohr, "In the Capital of the Car, Nature Stakes a Claim," *New York Times*, December 4, 2003.

71. Lisa M. Collins and Curt Guyette, "Outside the Box," *Detroit Metro-Times*, January 26, 2005.

72. Zach Dundas, "Attack of the $3 Tomato," *Willamette Week*, August 17, 2005.

73. Halweil, *Eat Here*, p. 93.

74. Margot Roosevelt, "What's Cooking on Campus," *Time*, November 9, 2005.

75. Joe Yonan, "Food for Thought," *Boston Globe*, October 7, 2004.

76. Halweil, *Eat Here*, p. 156.

77. "River's Future Inspires a 'Meating' of the Minds," *Missoulian* (Missoula, Mont.), May 24, 2005.

78. Pesticides Action Network, "Subsidies Increase for Industrial Agriculture," November 11, 2004; Elizabeth Becker, "You Can Go Home Again," *New York Times*, December 1, 2003.

79. Cook, *Diet*, p. 224.

80. Becker, "You Can Go Home."

81. Felicity Lawrence, "This Food Racket Just Can't Go On," *Independent* (UK), December 2, 2004.

82. Halweil, *Eat Here*, p. 138.

83. Jason Mark, "Food Fight," *Earth Island Journal*, Spring 2006, p. 44.

84. Diane Brady, "The Organic Myth," *BusinessWeek*, October 16, 2006, p. 51.

85. Burkhard Bilger, "Salad Days," *New Yorker*, September 6, 2004, p. 44.

86. Julia Moskin, "Supermarkets Take the Artisan Out of Artisanal Bread," *New York Times*, March 10, 2004.

87. Carlos Petrini, "Slow Food," *New York Times*, July 26, 2003.

88. Kirkpatrick Sale, *Human Scale* (New York: 1980), p. 237.

89. Halweil, *Eat Here*, p. 161.

90. "Surprising Truths About Organic Consumers," *Organic Processing*, October–December 2004, p. 6.

91. Halweil, *Eat Here*, p. 45.

92. Cook, *Diet*, p. 18.

3 ALL FOR ONE, OR ONE FOR ALL

1. Quoted in Rifkin, *European Dream*, p. 120.

2. Frederick Engels and Karl Marx, *The Communist Manifesto* (New York: 2002 [1848]).

3. James Howard Kunstler, *The Long Emergency* (New York: 2005), p. 22.

4. Rifkin, *European Dream*, p. 155.

5. June Fletcher, "The Dysfunctional Family Home," *Wall Street Journal*, March 26, 2004.

6. Peter Preston, "There Is No Such Thing as Community," *Guardian* (UK), July 18, 2005.

7. Ralph Blumenthal, "Eliminate the Negative, Accentuate the Prosperity," *New York Times*, March 30, 2006.

8. Douthwaite, *Growth Illusion*, p. 334.

9. Deborah Campbell, "Post-Autistic Economics," http://www.adbusters.org/metas/eco/truecosteconomics/post-autistic.html.

10. Layard, *Happiness*, p. 180.

11. Kahneman et al., *Well-being*, p. 385; Samantha Bennett, "Dumped Mates in Red States," *Pittsburgh Post-Gazette*, February 9, 2005.

12. Layard, *Happiness*, p. 180.

13. Kahneman et al., *Well-being*, p. 383.

14. Quoted in Rifkin, *European Dream*, p. 35.

15. Pete Engardio, "Nice Dream If You Can Live It," *BusinessWeek*, September 13, 2004.

16. Laza Kekic, "The World's Best Country," *Economist*, http:// www.economist.com/theworldin/international/displayStory.cfm?story _id=3372495&d=2005; "Quality of Life in the U.S. and Progressive Politics" (August 7, 2005), http://www.dailykos.com.

17. Frank, *Luxury Fever*, p. 33.

18. James Lardner, "What's the Problem?" in Lardner and Smith, *Inequality Matters*, p. 15.

19. William Blum, "Letter from America," *Ecologist*, October 2003.

20. Halweil, *Eat Here*, pp. 11–12.

21. Stephan J. Goetz and Hema Swaminathan, "Wal-Mart and Countywide Poverty," AERS Staff Paper no. 371 (October 2004), http://cecd .aers.psu.edu/pubs/PovertyResearchWM.pdf.

22. Tracie Rohzon, "Teaching Wal-Mart New Tricks," *New York Times*, May 8, 2005.

23. Art Woolf, "Green Mountain Shoppers, Unite," *New York Times*, June 6, 2004.

24. Layard, *Happiness*, p. 275.

25. Ibid., p. 83.

26. Barry Schwartz, "Tyranny of Choice," *Chronicle of Higher Education*, January 23, 2004.

27. Layard, *Happiness*, pp. 88–89.

28. Ibid., pp. 8, 104–95.

29. New Economics Foundation, *Well-Being Manifesto* (London: 2005), p. 16.

30. Erin Middlewood, "Social Medicine," *Orion*, September–October 2005, p. 26.

31. Kahneman et al., *Well-being*, p. 364.

32. Diener and Seligman, "Beyond Money," p. 16.

33. Layard, *Happiness*, p. 234.

34. Ibid., p. 226.

35. James Twitchell, *Branded Nation* (New York: 2004), p. 2.

36. Sut Jhally, "Advertising at the Edge of the Apocalypse," http:// www.sutjhally.com/onlinepubs/apocalypse.html.

37. Juliet Schor, "The (Even More) Overworked American," in John DeGraaf, *Take Back Your Time* (New York: 2003), pp. 4, 10.

38. Steven Greenhouse, "Forced to Work Off the Clock, Some Employees Fight Back," *New York Times*, September 19, 2004.

39. Schor, "Overworked American," p. 10.

40. Jonathan Rowe, "Out of Time," *Yes!*, Winter 2006, p. 17.

41. Camilla Fox, "What About Fluffy and Fido?" in DeGraaf, *Take Back Your Time*, p. 52.

42. Layard, *Happiness*, p. 54.

43. Hara Estroff Marano, "Suburban Blues" (March 22, 2005), http://www.psychologytoday.com/articles/pto-20050322-000002.html.

44. Tim Kasser and Kirk Brown, "Time, Happiness, and Ecological Footprints," in DeGraaf, *Take Back Your Time*, pp. 110–11.

45. Schor, "Overworked American," p. 10.

46. Benjamin Hunnicutt, "When We Had Time," in DeGraaf, *Take Back Your Time*, p. 118.

47. Jonathan Rowe, "Wasted Work, Wasted Time," in DeGraaf, *Take Back Your Time*, p. 65.

48. Douglas Harper, *Changing Works* (Chicago: 2001), p. 176.

49. Victor Canto, "Two Americas," *National Review Online*, September 4, 2004.

50. Eduardo Porter and Mary Williams Walsh, "Retirement Turns into a Rest Stop as Benefits Dwindle," *New York Times*, February 9, 2005.

51. Layard, *Happiness*, p. 168.

52. Bob Lewis, "Judge Approves Injunction of Sunday-Off Law," Associated Press, September 3, 2004.

53. Douthwaite, *Growth Illusion*, p. 125.

54. Connie P. Ozawa, *Portland Edge* (Portland, Ore.: 2004), p. 3.

55. Peter Whybrow, *American Mania* (New York: 2005), p. 10.

56. Ibid., pp. 7–8, 36.

57. Ibid., p. 253.

58. Alynda Lynch, "Company Town," *Fortune*, April 24, 2003.

59. David Cay Johnston, "Study Shows the Superrich Are Not the Most Generous," *New York Times*, December 19, 2005.

60. Robert Sapolsky, "A Natural History of Peace," *Harper's*, April 2006.

61. Schor, "New Politics of Consumption."

62. Friedman, *Moral Consequences*, p. 178.

63. Jon Gertner, "What Is a Living Wage?" *New York Times*, January 15, 2006.

64. Jacob Hale Russell and Jess McCuan, "The Global Climate Change Island Guide," *Wall Street Journal*, October 29, 2005.

4 THE WEALTH OF COMMUNITIES

1. Citizen's Feedback Forums and Communications Law, http://www.ourmediavoice.org/feedback_law.html.

2. Eric Magnuson, "Anyone Listening?" *Nation*, May 23, 2005.

3. http://en.wikipedia.org/wiki/National_Public_Radio.

4. Alyson Zureick, "Local Radio," *American Prospect*, August 17, 2005.

5. Sale, *Human Scale*, p. 182.

6. Ibid., pp. 77–78.

7. Ibid., p. 175.

8. Amory Lovins, "Winning the Oil Endgame," Rocky Mountain Institute, Executive Summary (2004), http://www.oilendgame.com.

9. Douthwaite, *Growth Illusion*, p. 245.

10. Greenpeace, "Decentralising Power: An Energy Revolution for the 21st Century" (July 2005), http://www.greenpeace.org.uk/Multimedia Files/ Live/FullReport/7759.pdf.

11. Frank Guteri and Andrew Roman, "Power People," *Newsweek*, September 20, 2004.

12. Greenpeace, "Decentralising Power."

13. Janet Sawin, "Mainstreaming Renewable Energy in the Twenty-first Century," Worldwatch Institute (Washington, D.C.: 2004), p. 32.

14. Energy Foundation, "An Assessment of Solar Power on Rooftops" (May 2, 2005), http://www.newrules.org/de/archives/000057.html.

15. Greenpeace, "Decentralising Power."

16. Randy Udall, "Grid-Connected PV . . . What's It Worth?" http://aspencare.org/images/pdf/whatsitworth.pdf.

17. Stephanie Ebbet, "Wind Turbines Gaining Power," *Boston Globe*, February 24, 2006.

18. Wind-Works.org, "Ontario Takes Historic Step Towards Energy Future" (March 21, 2006), http://www.wind-works.org/FeedLaws/Canada/OSEAHistoricStep.html.

19. Josh Weil, "A New Spin on Wind," *Orion*, November 12, 2005, p. 44.

20. AtKisson, *Believing Cassandra*, pp. 377–78.

21. Ibid., p. 381.

22. Worldwatch Institute, *Vital Signs 2005* (Washington, D.C.: 2005), p. 58.

23. "Pedestrian Safety in Numbers," *Cascadia Scorecard Weblog*, October 5, 2005.

24. Worldwatch Institute, *State of the World 2006* (New York: 2005).

25. Kunstler, *The Long Emergency*, p. 269.

26. AtKisson, *Believing Cassandra*, p. 28.

27. Liz Walker, *EcoVillage at Ithaca, New York* (New York: 2005), p. 108.

28. Ibid., p. 170.

29. John Elder, "Into the Wood," *Middlebury Magazine*, Winter 2006, p. 28.

30. Aby Wilson, "Natural Building, Green Building," *Environmental Building News*, May 2005, p. 6.

31. The Vermont Job Gap Study, Phase 6, "The Leaky Bucket: An Analysis of Vermont's Dependence on Imports" (July 2000), http://www.vtlivablewage.org/JOBGAP6a.pdf.

32. Halweil, *Eat Here*, pp. 54–55.

33. Jon Pareles, "A Night to Honor Jam Bands," *New York Times*, March 28, 2004.

34. "Live Music on the Rise," *Guardian Unlimited*, August 25, 2004.

35. Frank, *Luxury Fever*, p. 38.

36. Special Town Meeting Section, *Burlington Free Press*, March 8, 2006.

37. "Spring Rite," *Burlington Free Press*, September 21, 2003.

38. New Economics Foundation, *Well-Being Manifesto*, p. 16.

39. Seth Zuckerman, "Towards a New Salmon Economy," *Salmon Nation* (Portland: 2004), p. 76.

5 THE DURABLE FUTURE

1. Sachs, *End of Poverty*, pp. 34–37.

2. Ibid., pp. 18–19.

3. David Barboza, "Trading Up In China," *New York Times*, April 8, 2006.

4. McCloskey, "Capital Gains," p. 40.

5. Sachs, *End of Poverty*, p. 155.

6. AtKisson, *Believing Cassandra*, p. 372.

7. Worldwatch Institute, *Vital Signs 2005*, p. 52.

8. Sawin, "Mainstreaming Renewable Energy," p. 13.

9. Lester Brown, "China Forcing World to Rethink Its Economic Future," *Earth Policy News*, January 5, 2006.

10. D. Murali, "Yes, yes, yes...no," *The Hindu Business Line*, Internet Edition (June 9, 2003), http://www.blonnet.com/mentor/2003/06/09/stories/2003060900421000.htm.

11. Worldwatch Institute, *Vital Signs 2005*, p. 14.

12. Alex Avery, "Meeting the Needs of a Hungry World," http://www.cgfi.org/materials/speeches/pork_congress.htm.

13. James Brooke, "Made Elsewhere: An Island's Quandary," *New York Times*, April 9, 2005.

14. Corporatewatch, "Off the Peg: Tesco and the Garment Industry in Asia" (June 2005), http://www.corporatewatch.org/?lid-1825.

15. Thomas Friedman, "What's That Sound?" *New York Times*, April 1, 2004.

16. Cobb and Cobb, *Green National Product* p. 3.

17. Partha Dasgupta, "Economic Growth Often Accompanies a Decline in a Poor Country's Wealth," *New Statesman*, November 3, 2003, p. 29.

18. Brian Tokar, "The World Bank," in Tokar, *Gene Traders*, p. 52.

19. Tom Engelhardt, "Tom Dispatch Interview: Mike Davis" (May 2006), http://www.tomdispatch.com.

20. Cook, *Diet*, p. 240.

21. Michael Pollan, "Exporting Cheap Corn and Ruin," The Land Institute (April 27, 2004), http://www.landinstitute.org/vnews/display.v/ART/2004/04/27/408ec4c975493.

22. Craig Sams, "Subsidized Theft," *Resurgence*, May/June 2006, p. 14.

23. Pollan, "Exporting Cheap Corn."

24. Lawrence, *Not on the Label*, pp. 171–72.

25. Blythman, *Shopped*, pp. 258–59.

26. Focus on the Global South and GRAIN, "Iraq's New Patent Law: A Declaration of War Against Farmers" (October 2004), http://www.grain.org/bio-pr/?id=419.

27. A. V. Krebs, "Building the Agribusiness Empire," *Rural Vermont Report*, July–August 2003.

28. Howard French, "Riots in a Village in China as Pollution Protests Heat Up," *New York Times*, June 29, 2005.

29. Joseph Kahn, "A Sharp Debate Erupts in China over Ideologies," *New York Times*, March 12, 2006.

30. "As America Gets Bigger, So Does the World," *New York Times,* April 19, 2005.

31. Mark Magnier, "Driven to Be Made in China," *Los Angeles Times,* July 11, 2005.

32. New Economic Foundation, *Real World Economic Outlook 2003,* p. 61.

33. Pretty, *Agri-Culture,* p. 6.

34. New Economics Foundation, *Real World Economic Outlook 2003,* p. 66.

35. Colin Tudge, "Time for a Peasant Revolution," *Resurgence,* May–June 2005, p. 14.

36. Pretty, *Agri-culture,* p. 6.

37. Stanley Crawford, *Mayordomo: Chronicle of an Acequia in Northern New Mexico* (Albuquerque: 1993).

38. Halweil, *Eat Here,* p. 54.

39. Bill McKibben, "An Alternative to Progress," *Mother Jones,* May–June 2001, p. 34.

40. "Clumsy Attacks on the Hyacinth," *Ecologist,* October 2003.

41. Conrad Fox, "Pedal Power," *Orion,* September–October 2005, p. 24.

42. "'My Goal Is to Become World's Rabbit King,' Says NPC Deputy," *People's Daily,* March 12, 2001.

43. Andrew Revkin, "A New Measure of Well-being from a Happy Little Kingdom," *New York Times,* October 4, 2005.

44. Jay Walljasper, "Car Trouble," *Ode* (January 2006), http://www.alternet.org/envirohealth/30057/.

45. Douthwaite, *Growth Illusion,* pp. 310–11.

46. Rifkin, *European Dream,* p. 286.

47. Ibid., p. 40.

48. "All Consuming," *Wall Street Journal,* October 20, 2005.

49. Rifkin, *European Dream,* p. 53.

50. Alberto Alesina, Edward Glaeser, and Bruce Sacerdote, "Work and Leisure in the U.S. and Europe; Why So Different?" Harvard Institute of Economic Research, Discussion Paper no. 2068, April 2005.

51. Bruce Bawer, "We're Rich, You're Not. End of Story," *New York Times Magazine,* April 17, 2005.

52. "The Economist Intelligence Unit's Quality of Life Index," *The World in 2005,* p. 4, http://www.economist.com/theworldin/international/displaystory.cfm?story_id=3372495&d=2005.

53. Layard, *Happiness*, p. 20.

54. Mark Landler, "Europe Reluctantly Deciding It Has Less Time for Time Off," *New York Times*, July 7, 2004.

55. Andrew Moravcsik, "Europe Is the New Role Model for the World," *Financial Times*, October 16, 2004.

56. Rifkin, *European Dream*, p. 383.

AFTERWORD

1. "Bank Says Saudi's Top Field in Decline," Al-Jazeera, April 12, 2005.

2. Peter J. Cooper, "Kuwait's Biggest Field Starts to Run Out of Oil," *Kuwaiti Times*, January 26, 2006.

3. Javier Blas, "World's Thirst for Oil," *Financial Times*, March 15, 2005.

4. Michael Klare, "The Permanent Energy Crisis" (February 8, 2006), http://www.tomdispatch.com.

5. Steve Connor, "Climate change 'Irreversible' as Arctic Sea Ice Fails to Re-form," *Independent* (UK), March 14, 2006.

6. Tim Radford, "Loss of Soil Carbon Will Speed Global Warming," *Guardian* (UK), September 8, 2005.

7. Miguel Llanos, "NASA Puts Its Weight Behind Warming Signs," MSNBC (March 13, 2006), http://www.msnbc.com/id/11745704/.

8. Derrick Z. Jackson, "Muffled Warnings on Global Warming" (February 4, 2006), http://www.boston.com/news/globe/editorial_opinion/oped/articles/2006/02/04/muffled_warnings_on_global_warming.

9. Michael McCarthy, "Environment in Crisis: We Are Past the Point of No Return, *Independent* (UK), January 16, 2006.

10. Douthwaite, *Growth Illusion*, p. 226.

11. Li Yong Yan, "China's Way Forward Paved in Cement," *Asia Times Online* (January 7, 2004), http://www.aitimes.com/aitimes/china fe04ad02.html.

ACKNOWLEDGMENTS

For a book about the local, this one has required lots of traveling; I'm grateful to *Harper's* and Luke Mitchell for supporting several trips as well as supplying editorial guidance; ditto *National Geographic* and Oliver Payne. I'm also grateful to *Gourmet* and Jane Daniels Lear for letting me write about staying, and eating, close to home. Daniel Taylor, Frances Fremont-Smith, Nick Mitsos, Zheng Baiyan, and Future Generations played an invaluable role in one journey; Randy Kritkausky, Zhao Ang, and Wen Jie in another; Ken Squier and Tod Murphy in a third.

I have several intellectual debts to repay. Robert M. Collins's book on the politics of economic growth helped me understand the newness of what sometimes seems like a part of nature; Bob Costanza and his colleagues at the University of Vermont's Gund Institute were essential in helping me understand the possible economic future. Brian Halweil's book on local food pointed me in myriad useful directions, and the English agronomist Jules Pretty helped me figure out how those directions fit together—as, of course, did the delightful and informative journalism of Michael Pollan. Richard Layard's wonderful treatise on the new science of happiness underpins much of my thinking in these pages, as did Jeremy Rifkin's powerful book on the differences between Europe and America. Other happiness researchers, especially Ed and Carol Diener and Martin Seligman, also helped educate me with their writings. And some of my debts are anonymous—for instance, someone in the audience at a talk one day suggested "durable" as a substitute for the vague and clinical "sustainable," a felicitous proposal I immediately borrowed. In addition, I have one preeminent source who's not cited in the endnotes, but whose ideas permeate this book: Wendell Berry, to whom it's dedicated.

My colleagues at Middlebury College were, as always, very helpful. They include Nan Jenks Jay, Ron Liebowitz, John Elder, Chris Klyza, Jon Isham, Helen Young, Steve Trombulak, Kathy Morse, Becky Gould, Alison Byerly, Rich Wolfson, Helen Young, Chris Shaw, Janet Wiseman, Pete Ryan, Jay Leshinsky, Sarah Ray, Adrienne Tucker, Mike McKenna, Maria Stadtmueller, and Sue Kavanagh. There are many, many students who have taught me much; they include Bennett Konesni, Jean Hamilton, Will Bates, May Boeve, Jen Warnow, Phil Aroneau, Jamie Henn, Jeremy Osborn, Michael Silberman, Andrew Savage, and all the participants in the college's Sunday Night Group and in Middlebury's college garden project. (The Nordic ski team and Patty Ross, Terry Aldrich, Andrew Gardner, John Rubright, Tim Reilly, and Jim Benson have played a large role by keeping me sane.)

This is a story about home. I'm blessed with exceptional neighbors and friends on both sides of Lake Champlain, a list much too long to even hope to make comprehensive, but let me thank Jackie and Nick Avignon, Gary and Kathy Wilson, Russell Puschak and Kate Gardner, Peter Bauer and Kathleen Collins, Jack and Mary Jean Burke, Barb Lemmel and Mitch Hay, Warren and Barry King, Jim and Sheila Hutt, everyone connected with the North Branch School (especially Tal Birdsey, Eric Warren, and Rose Messner), Dick and Missy Foote, Win and Joanna Colwell, Connie Leach, Johanna Miller, Mike and Carrie Hussey, Willem Jewett and Jean Cherouny, Ian Pounds and Suzi McKinley, Steve Maier, Rita Elder, Roger Beaudet, and Don Stratton. Sam and Lisa Verhovek and Shawn and Michael Considine were, as always, essential.

My colleagues at Times Books—especially Paul Golob, who pushed and prodded this book into shape—and John Sterling, David Wallace-Wells, Tara Kennedy, Maggie Richards, and Lisa Fyfe were all magnificent. As were, of course, Gloria Loomis and her colleagues Jacqueline Hackett, Katherine Fausset, and Justin Allen.

And, closest to home, Sue Halpern and Sophie Crane McKibben put up not only with the usual travails of living with a book in progress, but also with eating inordinate quantities of root vegetables. If it weren't for those two, I wouldn't bother with any of this!

INDEX

ABOUT THE AUTHOR

BILL MCKIBBEN is the author of ten books, including *The End of Nature*, *The Age of Missing Information*, and *Enough: Staying Human in an Engineered Age*. A former staff writer for *The New Yorker*, he writes regularly for *Harper's*, *The Atlantic Monthly*, and *The New York Review of Books*, among other publications. He is a scholar in residence at Middlebury College and lives in Vermont with his wife, the writer Sue Halpern, and their daughter.